Dialect and Dichotomy

Dialect and Dichotomy
Literary Representations of African American Speech

Lisa Cohen Minnick

THE UNIVERSITY OF ALABAMA PRESS
Tuscaloosa

Copyright © 2004
The University of Alabama Press
Tuscaloosa, Alabama 35487-0380
All rights reserved
Manufactured in the United States of America

Typeface: Adobe Garamond

∞

The paper on which this book is printed meets the minimum requirements of American
National Standard for Information Science–Permanence of Paper for Printed Library
Materials, ANSI Z39.48–1984.

Library of Congress Cataloging-in-Publication Data

Minnick, Lisa Cohen.
    Dialect and dichotomy : literary representations of African American speech /
Lisa Cohen Minnick.
        p. cm.
    Includes bibliographical references (p.) and index.
    ISBN 0-8173-1399-0 (cloth : alk. paper)
    1. American literature—African American authors—History and criticism. 2. American
literature—Southern States—History and criticism. 3. American literature—White
authors—History and criticism. 4. American literature—20th century—History and
criticism. 5. Dialect literature, American—History and criticism. 6. English language—
Spoken English—United States. 7. English language—Dialects—United States. 8. African
Americans in literature. 9. African Americans—Language. 10. Black English in literature.
11. Americanisms in literature. 12. Speech in literature. I. Title.
    PS153.N5M56 2004
    810.9'975—dc22

                                                                                    2004000606

Contents

Tables

Acknowledgments

A preliminary version of chapter 4 was originally published in *Language and Literature* in May 2001 under the title "Jim's Language and the Issue of Race in *Huckleberry Finn*" and is included here by permission of SAGE Publications. Also, an earlier version of chapter 6, "Representations of Speech and Attitudes about Race in *The Sound and the Fury*," first appeared in the *Southern Journal of Linguistics,* Spring/Fall 2001, and appears here by permission of the publisher, the Southeastern Conference on Linguistics (SECOL). My thanks to SAGE and SECOL.

It is hard to imagine this book having come to fruition without the wisdom and insights generously shared with me by many colleagues and friends. Many thanks to Bill Kretzschmar not only for introducing me to literary dialect analysis and directing the dissertation that evolved into this book but also for many years of first-rate mentoring and friendship. I am grateful also to the Graduate School at the University of Georgia for the Finishing Doctoral Research Assistantship I was awarded for the 2001–2002 academic year, which funded most of the research and drafting of the dissertation that was the basis for this book. Nelson Hilton deserves profuse thanks for his support of my candidacy for that award.

Marlyse Baptista and Lee Pederson have been and continue to be invaluable mentors, teachers, and friends. Bill Provost and James Nagel provided challenging and useful comments in response to my manuscript at the dissertation stage. Susan Tamasi, Lamont Antieau, Ellen Johnson, and Allison Burkette have generously offered their feedback in response to conference papers related to the research herein and have also been all-around excellent friends.

Maria Carreira offered her observations and also some very kind words in response to the manuscript, even though we have yet to meet in person. Walt Wolfram helped me find answers to questions about real-life North Carolina speakers like those portrayed in the writing of Charles W. Chesnutt. My students at Georgia Tech have taught me by example to try out new ways of thinking, as have the great friends I've made there. The staff at the University of Alabama Press has been a pleasure to work with. They and the external reviewers they selected have given the manuscript the kind of close and intelligent consideration for which every writer hopes. Thanks to all.

Many thanks to my family, all of whom have been great sources of support and kindness, especially my husband, Greg Minnick. His generosity, thoughtfulness, sense of humor, and belief in me have made many things possible. For these reasons and many more, I dedicate this book to him.

Introduction

Analysis of authorial representation of spoken language variation in literary works constitutes an important linguistic application to literature as well as a literary approach to language study. The studies of literary dialect in general, and literary representations of African American English in particular, offer opportunities to go beyond traditional areas of English language studies and still apply the important theories and methods of empirical and computational linguistics, particularly those of language variation. Additionally, qualitative literary methods allow for linguistic approaches to literature that do not disregard artistic elements in literary works, elements that have sometimes been overlooked in linguistic analyses of literature. Empirical exploration of how authors use literary dialect offers useful opportunities for insight into how authors, audiences, and even characters perceive social and ethnic variation as influencing speech behavior. Employing empirical methods thus offers not only new approaches to the analysis of literary texts using linguistic tools, but these methods also make it possible to use the rich resources of literary texts as data for helping to understand variation and change in, as well as attitudes toward, spoken varieties of American English. Such applications challenge the widely held belief that literary representations of dialect have little or nothing to offer to a study of language variation.

Traditionally, critiques of literary dialect have often been impressionistic reactions to how the representations of speech look on the page. These reactions are understandable in light of Dennis Preston's findings about negative reactions to the attempts of linguists, folklorists, and other researchers to represent nonstandard linguistic features, especially phonological features, in print. In his analysis, Preston does not address authors of literary dialect, but there is no reason to believe that the "affective response" he describes would not also apply to the reactions to those same kinds of speech representations as constructed by literary authors ("Syndrome" 328).

But such impressionistic reactions have in the past cost writers such as Paul Laurence Dunbar and Zora Neale Hurston their reputations. Paul Laurence Dunbar's dialect poetry and much of the literary writing of Zora Neale Hurston were widely maligned for their use of dialect and for, critics claimed, representing falsely imagined versions of black life. It is difficult to extricate entirely the issues of dialect from the nonlinguistic concerns about literary portrayals of African American life, but for our purposes the focus will be on the dialect questions. In Dunbar's case, the criticism was both for the ways he used dialect, as outlined in his friend James Weldon Johnson's position that Dunbar used stereotyped conventions of black speech, as well as for the inauthenticity some critics felt that his use of dialect represented about African American experiences. For Dunbar, the most intense criticism came some years after his death in 1906, beginning with the sympathetic but still strongly critical analysis of black dialect poetry, including Dunbar's, and the representations of speech therein, in James Weldon Johnson's preface to his 1922 *Book of American Negro Poetry*. However, Dunbar himself had agonized over the popularity of his dialect poetry at the expense of his other work. He was also disturbed by his public image as a contributor to the plantation tradition, which mythologized and celebrated antebellum plantation life and downplayed the atrocities of slavery. At times, he even questioned his own talent. "I have not grown," Dunbar said to Johnson during his last illness, not long before his death at age thirty-three. "I am writing the same things I wrote ten years ago, and am writing them no better" (qtd. in Johnson 878).

In Hurston's case, the conflict is not only over the quality of her dialectal representations but also over her decision to represent dialect at all. African American dialect continued to be associated well into the twentieth century with the plantation tradition, especially as defined by the works of Thomas Nelson Page, Thomas Dixon, and, some critics argue, Joel Chandler Harris. Similarly, black dialect had long been a staple of the minstrel tradition and therefore in Hurston's time was still inextricably linked to negative, stereotypical portrayals of African Americans. Michael North has observed more recently that Hurston's use of dialect was an attempt to reclaim and destigmatize black vernacular, which many of her contemporaries continued to avoid in their perception of it as "a language obscured by travesty and stereotype" (North 176). However, Hurston's attempts at reclamation were often misinterpreted by her literary contemporaries. She stood accused, most famously by Richard Wright in his condemning review in *New Masses,* from the moment her second and most important novel, *Their Eyes Were Watching God,* appeared in 1937. The novel—and its author—spent the next several decades in obscurity. It is thanks in large part to Alice Walker's work in the 1970s that Hurston has been restored to her rightful place among American literary masters.

While Hurston's literary resurrection occurred only years after her death in 1960, Dunbar's dialect poetry faced a different kind of peril, open scorn rather than obscurity, but that kind of treatment was also enough to disqualify his dialect poems from serious scholarly and readerly consideration for many years. Fortunately, though, as with Hurston, new views of Dunbar's writing, and particularly his use of dialect, have begun to challenge the long-standing assumptions about the functions of that dialect in his work.

Reactions to dialectal representations without analysis of the specific strategies incorporated into those representations is not far removed from dismissing individuals without knowing anything about them, simply on the basis of their speech characteristics. Certainly many linguists today are hard at work to try to reduce stigmatization of linguistic features, and thus here is another interesting and unexpected link between linguistics and literature. A closer look at previously neglected work, such as that of Dunbar and Hurston, shows that controversy is not a good enough reason to dismiss the value of a work of literature nor to forego studying the strategies of speech representation. In fact, if the goal of art is to engender an emotional response, as the old adage goes, then perhaps some of the most intense reactions are the smoke that points to the fire of superior artistic creation. While certainly controversy does not herald excellence in all cases, the work of writers such as Hurston, Dunbar, and also Mark Twain—all three taken to task (for different reasons) for their attempts to reproduce in writing African American dialectal speech—stands in direct contradiction both artistically and linguistically to the view that unsparingly dialectal writing is necessarily poorly executed and inartistic, and worse, that the literature it appears in is therefore itself altogether without merit. Another author whose work still faces this type of disapproval is Joel Chandler Harris, whose heavily dialectal Uncle Remus stories are dismissed on that basis by Roger W. Cole as "artistic failures . . . regardless of their other merits" (6). Such a view unfortunately overlooks the research possibilities that a particularly striking dialectal representation can raise as well as the artistic complexities that are bound up within the dialectal representations.

The rejection of the work of writers solely in response to their use of dialect is perhaps considerably more serious than dismissing literary dialect as irrelevant to a study of language, but the latter position is certainly no more scientifically or critically valid. How authors represent speech is an artistic matter, but it is also a linguistic issue. While there is an abundance of skepticism about the linguistic value of literary dialect—which is defined here as written attempts at representing social, regional, or other types of spoken linguistic variation—still the analysis of literary dialect can be as important to linguistic study as it is to literary study. Much of the argument over whether literary dialect is an appropriate subject of analysis for linguists has long been framed by the perception that because writing is not speech, and because written attempts at representing speech can never really reproduce speech, then for many linguists, written representations of orality cannot be worth studying. Cynthia Goldin Bernstein attributes this view to the long-accepted Saussurean emphasis on the sounds of language, which she contends has led to a privileging of spoken language not only over written language but especially over written attempts to replicate speech ("Contextualization" 3–4). But as the current discussion intends to show, literary dialect can be an important source of linguistic data, not only in the form of attestations, for which it has traditionally been used by those linguists open to using literary data at all, but also in terms of other linguistic functions. These functions include insights into how and why authors represent dialect in the ways that they do, which has much to do with the social determinants and consequences of variation, as well as with perceptions and attitudes about variation.

But the central question addressed in this study, in addition to considering the conflicts between literary and linguistic goals related to literary dialect analysis, has to do with specific literary representations of speech. "Does dialect literature limit or liberate?" is an important question posed by John R. Rickford and Russell J. Rickford in their book *Spoken Soul: The Story of Black English* (38). The current discussion addresses this and related questions, specifically as the Rickfords frame their question in terms of the literary portrayal of African American English and in terms of the dichotomies faced by authors who choose to represent it. Representations of African American speech have been chosen as the focus here because of the literary, linguistic, and social importance of these representations and because of the controversy surrounding them, in particular with respect to the work of the authors discussed in this book. Attempts at representing African American dialectal speech are linguistically and artistically compelling, and, I believe, inextricably intertwined with racial attitudes and issues that help to define the American experience and, by extension, the national literature. A primary aim of this book is to show that while Rickford and Rickford's question may not be possible to answer conclusively in a single study, an approach to the problem that combines qualitative methods of literary criticism with technological approaches to text analysis can reveal new insights into the venerable problem of how to respond to dialectal representations of African American speech. But rather than simply joining the debate with opinions based on the kinds of impressionistic reactions that have hounded writers such as Dunbar, Hurston, Twain, and Harris, I believe that a methodology that incorporates computational tools, including text-analysis software programs such as LinguaLinks and WordSmith Tools, constitutes a unique approach to a persistent issue and therefore can contribute something new to the sometimes contentious debate over the representation of African American dialect in literature. Using computational tools, it is possible to analyze large amounts of textual data comprehensively, a difficult if not impossible task to complete by attempting even the closest of readings. By employing computational analysis in tandem with qualitative analysis into the artistic functions of literary dialect, it is possible to achieve both linguistic and literary purposes with respect to questions surrounding literary dialect.

This book is made up of two major components. The first, contained in chapters 1 through 3, consists of background and orienting material, including historical information and literature reviews of dialect writing itself and of literary dialect analysis, along with a discussion of theoretical and methodological assumptions. The second component consists of four original literary dialect analyses conducted on works of American fiction produced in the years between the Civil War and World War II, along with a concluding chapter.

Chapter 1 is an account of dialect writing in English from the oldest surviving examples of English texts through American modernism and the Harlem Renaissance. The review emphasizes the literature at the center of the current discussion, American fiction produced between the 1880s and 1930s, with particular attention to works containing representations of African American speech by African American and other writers, an overview of which concludes the chapter. The goal in chapter 1 is to provide literary and linguistic contexts for the controversies surrounding dialectal representations and especially those of African American speech. The chapter begins with a brief look at early British dialect writing before moving to a more in-depth discussion of literary dialect in the United States, beginning with the humorist traditions of the nineteenth century. Briefly discussed here are such writers as Augustus Baldwin Longstreet, William Tappan Thompson, Thomas Bangs Thorpe, Johnson Jones Hooper, and Hardin E. Taliaferro, all writers within the "Old Southwestern" genre, and New England writers Seba Smith and James Russell Lowell, along with Thomas Chandler Haliburton, a Canadian who wrote about New Englanders. The discussion next covers the period following the Civil War, when there was an explosion in dialect literature, which for a time continued in the American humorist tradition as in works such as George Washington Harris's Sut Lovingood tales and the yarns of Mark Twain, along with continued focus on characters in the South and West. However, postwar changes in the economy and demography of the United States as well as in literary trends resulted in the rise of the local colorists, including writers associated with the plantation tradition, and of realism, which resulted in increasing use of dialect as a mimetic device. Writers noted in relation to these trends include Mark Twain, Mary E. Wilkins Freeman, Harriet Beecher Stowe, George Washington Cable, Kate Chopin, and Stephen Crane.

The focus of chapter 1 next moves to a pivotal part of the discussion of American literary dialect traditions: the representation of African American speech in literature. Until late in the nineteenth century, most of the writers of African American dialect were white, and the social and linguistic issues surrounding this phenomenon, mostly concerning increasing diversity and the consequent desire of some Americans for a distinctly American language, are discussed. Mark Twain and Joel Chandler Harris are among the white writers considered, and critical questions about writers representing the speech of those outside their own communities, with critiques of Harris's work in particular, are raised and continue henceforth to be an important topic in the book. The critical views of Gavin Jones, Michele Birnbaum, and Dennis Preston are consulted here as sources of insight into the functions and effects of literary manipulation of spoken language, with attention to the problems inherent in representing language outside an author's social or ethnic community.

The significant development in the late nineteenth century of African

American writers representing African American voices is next covered, with attention to the work of Charles W. Chesnutt and Paul Laurence Dunbar as both innovative and controversial. Critical opinions concerning experimentation in the use of black dialect by black authors are explored, including those of James Weldon Johnson, Henry Louis Gates Jr., John Keeling, Joanne M. Braxton, and Gavin Jones. The discussion of Chesnutt and Dunbar leads into a review of African American literary dialect in the twentieth century, as created by African American as well as other writers influenced by modernist trends and the Harlem Renaissance. The work of Zora Neale Hurston and William Faulkner is emphasized here, but there is also attention to several of their literary contemporaries, including Langston Hughes and Ezra Pound, along with critical contexts from Houston A. Baker Jr., Michael North, and others.

Following the overview of literary texts that use dialect, chapter 2 reviews the scholarship on literary dialect and literary dialect analysis, beginning with early, now canonical, work on American literary dialect by George Philip Krapp and Sumner Ives. The review then considers some of the scholarly conflicts surrounding literary dialect analysis, focusing on sources for skepticism on the part of linguists, both with respect to the value of the data and on whether written language even constitutes "natural" language. Some literary theorists also have concerns about the traditional emphases on phonology and on accuracy of representation that they perceive as having long held sway in literary dialect analyses, to the detriment, they argue, of attention to the artistic functions of literary dialect. The scholarship review concludes with examples of analyses used to accomplish literary aims and others used as a means to accomplish linguistic aims, with a few attempting to achieve both. The goal of chapter 2 is to examine the purposes and strategies of literary dialect analysis as conducted by researchers with various scholarly orientations. In doing so, I hope to show that it is possible to build on the best of their approaches and incorporate new ones in order to achieve both linguistic and literary goals in literary dialect analysis.

Chapter 3 constitutes the final component of the introductory material, outlining the theoretical and methodological underpinnings of the four original literary dialect analyses that make up the remainder of the book. It also explains the specific techniques of data selection and analysis applied in each case study. The methods used in the analyses are based on techniques of empirical and computational linguistics, sociolinguistic theory, and qualitative critical analysis. The chapter emphasizes the practicality of focusing on particular linguistic components of language representation but also suggests tailoring an individual study according to the demands of the text under consideration. While computational methods are excellent tools for literary dialect analysis, an important part of this study's theoretical orientation is in its emphasis on the investigated texts as works of art. In other words, a key assumption here is that the goals of literary dialect analysis should reach beyond ideas simply about accuracy, a traditional emphasis. As the current discussion will attempt to show, however, the goal of determining accuracy should not be automatically discounted, as it may be a good place to launch an inquiry into literary and linguistic questions about literary dialect; ideally, though, it will not represent an end in itself.

The second major component of the book, the empirical section, is contained in chapters 4 through 7. The empirical component consists of four original literary dialect analyses, each of a different work of American fiction produced between the 1880s and 1930s, a significant period in American life as well as in American literary history, and with respect to dialect literature in particular. Each of the four works under investigation here is analyzed according to its use of literary dialect strategies and in some cases conventions to represent the speech of African American characters. The texts considered in the analyses, which are presented in chronological order according to the dates of publication of the literary works, are Mark Twain's *Adventures of Huckleberry Finn* (1884), Charles W. Chesnutt's "Dave's Neckliss" (1889), William Faulkner's *The Sound and the Fury* (1929), and Zora Neale Hurston's *Their Eyes Were Watching God* (1937). Each analysis incorporates the theories, methods, and assumptions described in the introductory material, but the subsequent directions taken in each are widely diverse, as the originality of each work demands and deserves. For example, chapter 4, "Articulating Jim: Language and Characterization in *Huckleberry Finn*," explores the relationship between characterization and dialectal representation in response to critical charges that the character of Jim is stereotyped and that his dialectal speech as represented by Twain has much to do with that characterization. The chapter explores the question of how dialectal representations can function in the construction of character stereotypes and whether the literary dialect functions in that way with respect to Jim. Chapter 5, "'A High, Holy Purpose': Dialect in Charles W. Chesnutt's Conjure Tales," takes a different approach, focusing on the speech of narrator Julius McAdoo in its exploration of Chesnutt's complex relationship with dialectal speech in the African American community—a community Chesnutt strongly identified with yet at the same time set himself apart from as a class-determined outsider and observer. Chapter 6, "Representations of Speech and Attitudes about Race in *The Sound and The Fury*," examines William Faulkner's complicated racial attitudes as well as those of the three first-person narrators of the novel as they impact the third-person representations of African American dialectal speech, which seem to vary more widely by narrator than by character. Chapter 7, "Community in Conflict: Saying and Doing in *Their Eyes Were Watching God*," examines Zora Neale Hurston's portrait of African American orality and community, qualities that are explored in large part by way of her representations of dialectal speech but that are also complicated by intra-community conflicts of class and gender. These conflicts are explored by Hurston with a subtle undercurrent that runs throughout the text, and they are also apparent in her representations of speech, as discussed in the chapter. Finally, chapter 8 offers conclusions with respect to the contexts surrounding the creation of the literary representations of speech discussed in chapters 4 through 7 and evaluates the effects of those representations.

An important objective in this book is to try to bring together literary and linguistic aims in the study of literature and especially in the study of literary dialect, using quantitative tools of linguistic analysis as well as qualitative methods of literary criticism, and it is my hope that the analyses included here achieve that objective. The specific audience for this treatment includes linguists who are interested in written language as a significant component of language itself and in literature as a unique application of language, but who would also still like to use methods from computational linguistics. The audience also includes literary researchers who are interested in language variation and intrigued by the idea of using linguistic methodologies to learn more about literary works, including but not necessarily limited to the ones discussed herein. The literary analyst who is drawn to literary studies in part because of lifelong fascination with words of all kinds, and the linguist drawn to linguistics for similar reasons, including a love for written language as well as spoken, may find literary dialect studies a compelling intersection of the artistic and technical sides of language and of themselves.

I

A Brief History of American Literary Dialect

Early Traditions of Dialect Writing in English

Everything scholars know about Old English, they know as a direct result of written sources. One thing we know from these sources is that for as long as there have been literary texts written in English, there has been written representation of variability in spoken language. The oldest surviving examples of Old English are literary texts dating as far back as the beginning of the eighth century, two and a half centuries after the Germanic invasions that began in the middle of the fifth century and that launched what we now know as the English language. Mostly in the form of epics of heroes and battles, such as those related in *Beowulf* and later *The Battle of Maldon,* the majority of the Old English texts that survive today were written in the West Saxon dialect. West Saxon had been on its way to becoming the standard variety of British English at the time of the Norman Invasion in 1066, which of course changed everything in Britain, linguistically and otherwise. The variation reflected in the written texts of Old English was largely the effect of immigrant (or conqueror) settlement patterns and consequent political and linguistic history, resulting in an English language that was far from uniform right from its inception.

In addition to the importance of British literature in efforts to reconstruct early varieties of English, there is also great literary significance in the use of dialect by British authors, as it represents the first literary dialect work in English and as such provides a context for literary dialect traditions in American literature. Perhaps more than in any other literary culture, the functions and traditions of literary dialect in the United States are closely associated with humor. However, this was not an innovation by American dialect writers. The Greek playwright Aristophanes, whose work dates back to the fifth century B.C.E., was perhaps the earliest writer to use dialect for humorous effect whose work survives. The Roman playwright Terence, active during the second century B.C.E., also provided an early model for the first writers of literary dialect in English. Later, British writers used literary dialect to humorous effect for centuries before there was an American literary tradition of any kind. Paula Blank notes a number of important uses of dialect in the work of British writers through the Renaissance, pointing out that the variation in medieval literary works, the earliest examples of English dialect literature, can be chalked up to writers simply writing in the varieties they knew rather than to deliberate artistic or linguistic goals (3). Blank acknowledges the exception of Chaucer, confirming that "The Reeve's Tale" may not only be the first literary work in English to use dialect deliberately as a humorous strategy but also that the tale may represent the first achievement by a British writer to incorporate several varieties of spoken English, which Chaucer accomplished by way of his differentiation between the dialects spoken by the miller and by the young clerks (Blank 172n).

Renaissance writers, Blank demonstrates, were more deliberate than their medieval predecessors in their applications of dialect. Observing that dialect comedy became popular during the Renaissance, Blank focuses on the function of British dialect literature of that period, arguing that it was written by authors who commanded several varieties of English, including especially "more elite forms" of the language, in efforts to determine and authorize a prestige form and to construct "the borders that separate one dialect of English from another" (6). In the Renaissance, Blank contends, and especially in the use of dialect in literature during that period, can be found the roots of the rise of English prescriptivism, usually associated with the eighteenth century. The goals of this incipient prescriptivism were "the differentiation of English forms, and the valuation of those differences" (Blank 9). The dialectal writing of the Renaissance, then, was concerned with negotiating the status of particular varieties of English, Blank maintains, with literature functioning as "an expression of an age engaged in a struggle for possession of the vernacular, a struggle in which linguistic authority was just as much at issue as linguistic freedom" (6). She points specifically to the work of writers such as Spenser, who incorporated a number of distinctively northern lexical items into his 1579 *Shepheardes Calender,* and Shakespeare— especially *King Lear,* in which Edgar assumes a southern variety of English as part of his disguise as a demented beggar, along with additional Shakespearean dialect experimentation in plays such as *Henry V* and *Love's Labour's Lost* as examples of literary contributors to the debate over dialectal supremacy. Interestingly, the issues of status and prestige that Blank describes as surrounding the Renaissance (literary) calls for standardization have some intriguing parallels in the climate of late-nineteenth-century American attitudes about language, as discussed below.

Norman Page further traces the long tradition of English dialect writing into the eighteenth and nineteenth centuries. Like Paula Blank, Page is interested in the social, political, and linguistic meanings encoded in dialect writing, but unlike Blank's analysis, Page's focuses on many types of literary representations of speech with literary dialect only one area under consideration. Rather, Page looks at the ways in which fictional dialogue in general functions as one of the ways characters can be "individualized substantially, and in some instances, almost entirely, through their speech" (16). Page argues that authors use dialogue, not to be confused with dialect but certainly at times including dialect features, to reconstruct various idiosyncratic types for reader recognition. Because of these conventions, Page argues, "fictional dialogue [has] a quality quite different from real speech" (17). With respect to literary dialect in particular, Page notes especially Fielding's and Smollett's use of dialect for humorous purposes and as a tool for illustrating the speech of non-Londoners, determining that for the two authors, "provinciality becomes equated with inferiority" (58–59). It is clear, then, that literary dialect continued to function both intra- and extratextually as a signifier of social status and hence continued the tradition of institutionalizing prestige linguistic varieties. Page also points to nineteenth-century English authors who used literary dialect, including Walter Scott, Emily Brontë, Charles Dickens, and Thomas Hardy, as well as D. H. Lawrence in the early twentieth century. He singles out Scott as the first to use dialect in nonhumorous situations (60) and also, if not especially, Dickens, whom he praises "among English novelists [as] the supremely original and versatile exponent of dialogue writing" (x).

By the nineteenth century, dialect began to appear more frequently in works by American authors after a few eighteenth-century forays into dialect representation, especially in novels and plays with colonial themes as well as in travel writing by Europeans exploring the colonies. The inception and growth of literary dialect as a significant tradition in the United States is usually identified with the nineteenth century and as a component of humorous writing. In the United States, the earliest publications of works within this dialect-humor tradition occurred before the Civil War. One of the first American contributors to the genre was the pioneering journalist, social critic, and travel writer Anne Newport Royall, who began publishing in the 1820s. By the 1830s, American dialect humor was well established. In fact, Walter Blair cites 1830 as the date that "American humor became a recognizable phenomenon" (xi). Prior to that decade, Blair adds, few American writers showed much interest or ability in trying to demonstrate "authentic popular speech" (xxiv).

In Britain, the premise of the joke was usually "juxtaposing a peasant dialect with the King's English" or depending on "provincials and foreigners being unable to speak the language properly" (Blank 3). By contrast, American dialect writing reflected an attempt at democratization of literature or at least a rebellion against more genteel literary forms that had been popular earlier in the nineteenth century and abroad, such as the "spiritual Romanticism, with its elevated language and sophisticated concerns" that James Nagel describes as having dominated during the earlier decades of the nineteenth century (xxii). However, juxtapositions similar to those Norman Page describes as having occurred in British dialect writing also appeared. Hennig Cohen and William B. Dillingham attribute the rise of American humor, and by extension dialect writing, in large part to the concurrent rapid disappearance of the Southern frontier, a frequent setting for prewar dialect humor, and to the rise of the "common man" (for this rise tended to be exclusively male). This common man, often associated with the Andrew Jackson administration (1829–1837), represented a challenge to the political power of the educated elite, with whom he was usually juxtaposed in the form of a standard-speaking narrator, and was a type which writers both celebrated and lampooned (Cohen and Dillingham 254).

The writing that came from this tradition is usually termed "Old Southwestern" humor, after the frontier that featured so prominently in the works. During these still relatively early decades in the existence of the United States, the "Old Southwest" included parts of Georgia and the Carolinas, Tennessee, Alabama, Mississippi, Missouri, and Arkansas (Blair xv). Distinguishing features of writing in this tradition included not only dialect, of course, but also boisterous and colorful characters and occasionally raunchy themes, including episodes of drinking, gambling, and sex. Also, Cohen and Dillingham stress the importance of another ubiquitous theme, politics, in Old Southwestern humorous writing, attributing the popularity of this theme among writers to their political involvement: "Many [authors] were staunch members of the Whig party, and their plainly stated views occur in their sketches" (xxxix).

One example Cohen and Dillingham cite of a politically identified writer is Augustus Baldwin Longstreet, a Georgian who was a superior court judge and later Methodist minister and college president. Longstreet was also briefly a member of the Georgia state legislature and a "strong advocate of states' rights" who later in his life supported Southern secession (Cohen and Dillingham 29). Longstreet was influential among the pioneers in the American humorist, and hence dialect, literature genre. His 1835 collection *Georgia Scenes* included humorous sketches with frontier settings and themes, as indicated by titles such as "The Horse Swap" and "The Shooting Match." The sketches were bolstered by dialectal representation of the speech of uneducated frontier characters, with characterizations and descriptions that critics continue to praise for their realism. Longstreet's work was enormously successful during his lifetime and according to Cohen and Dillingham, it "greatly stimulated other writers" (xvii), many of whom began to work within the genre of Old Southwestern humor after the publication of *Georgia Scenes*. Among these other writers were William Tappan Thompson, Thomas Bangs Thorpe, Johnson Jones Hooper and Hardin E. Taliaferro, all best known for works which appeared during the 1840s and 1850s.

A good example of the kind of writing produced during the "Old Southwestern" period is Thompson's *Major Jones's Courtship* (1843), sketches from the life of a young Georgia militiaman (a term that in Thompson's time had far different connotations than today, it may be worth mentioning). The author relies heavily on respellings, presumably in some cases to represent phonological characteristics but in others merely for humorous effect, and exaggerated grammatical features as sources of humor. The sketches usually place Major Jones, a young country dweller, in urban settings where his lack of sophistication is a source for humor as well as an opportunity for his unique linguistic features to stand out, recalling somewhat the regional and social juxtapositions that Paula Blank and Norman Page describe as having occurred in Renaissance and later British dialect writing, but with a distinctly American and Southern flavor. For example, in one of the letters from Major Jones in the 1848 epistolary novel *Major Jones's Sketches of Travel*, he describes a visit to the "opery," where he "couldn't hardly make out hed nor tail to it, though [he] listened at 'em with all [his] ears, eyes, mouth, and nose" (169), insisting finally that "A body what never seed a opery before would swar they was evry one either drunk or crazy as loons, if they was to see 'em in one of ther grand lung-tearin, ear-bustin blowouts" (172).

Another important example of the Old Southwestern tradition is Thomas

Bangs Thorpe's "The Big Bear of Arkansas" (1854), which according to Co-hen and Dillingham later heavily influenced William Faulkner and his own 1942 bear-hunting legend, "The Bear" (334). As in Thompson's portrayal of Major Jones, Thorpe also uses occasional humorous lexical innovation ("spontenacious"), respellings to indicate phonological variation or simply lack of education (as in "bar" for bear, "Arkansaw," and "Kaintuck"), and nonstandard grammatical features ("I knowd of") in his characterization of Jim Doggett, a legendary bear hunter. An important characteristic of the narrative form of "The Big Bear of Arkansas" is the standard-speaking nar-rator who encounters Doggett aboard a Mississippi River steamboat and whose educated speech is juxtaposed with the rather more organic vernacu-lar of Doggett. The narrator acts as observer and faithful reporter of Jim Doggett's stories, ostensibly as told to the passengers on the boat, including the narrator.

But Thorpe is not alone in incorporating this framing narrative device. In fact, the standard-speaking narrator is a convention many of the prewar humorists incorporated, perhaps in order to maintain a distance between the authors, who were generally educated, upper-class members of their communities—Thorpe was a newspaper editor and politician, for example—and the "folk" characters who people the stories. This dissociation was also shared with much of the readership of the literature, who, unlike many of the featured characters, were literate and had the means to purchase books and periodicals and the leisure time to read them. The middle-class status of Thompson's Major Jones was rather unusual among the protagonists of the humor genre. Hooper's shiftily opportunistic Simon Suggs, who Cohen and Dillingham note represents a "satire on the idealization of the Jacksonian common man" (254), and Taliaferro's Hamp Hudson, a moonshiner, and Ham Rachel, an Alabaman who "loves fur a man to be as plain as an old shoe" (Taliaferro 140), were rather more typical representatives of the kinds of people who were featured in the stories.

A consideration of the distance between the authors/narrators and the characters in the stories and sketches is useful in terms of the dialect repre-sentations in them. In their introduction to *Humor of the Old Southwest*, Cohen and Dillingham contend that "The Southwest humorist wanted to laugh at the earthy life around him and to enjoy it, but he did not want to be identified with it" (xxx). But they add that while some authors might have patronized their protagonists somewhat, prewar dialect humor was not meant to criticize the types of people its characters, their speech, and their values represent. Rather, they argue, many authors "respected the backwoodsmen for their manliness, their freedom, and their rapport with the natural world" (Cohen and Dillingham xxx). Additionally, they point out that the "framing narrator" was simply a matter of convenience for some authors, having long been a convention in American writing and storytelling. "The Old Southwestern writers were rarely sophisticated craftsmen, much less innovators of structural techniques," Cohen and Dillingham observe, adding that "They were innovators, however, in language" (xxxi). There is no question about Cohen and Dillingham's appraisal of the literary-linguistic innovation of the humorists, who were the first major American dialect writers. But the linguistic distance between author/narrator and characters may be more portentous than Cohen and Dillingham's analysis acknowledges, as discussed below.

In addition to the Old Southwestern tradition of dialect humor, with its frontier settings and occasionally raunchy themes and boisterous characters, Walter Blair observes that rural New England was also an epicenter for pre–Civil War dialect humor. He credits Seba Smith of Maine and Thomas Chandler Haliburton as important early contributors to the genre. Smith's Jack Downing character first appeared in 1830 in a long series of letters to a Maine newspaper, ostensibly written by Downing. Haliburton, a Nova Scotia resident, wrote about New Englanders under the guise of his Sam Slick character, whose musings also first appeared in newspapers in the 1830s. The work of these writers and also of James Russell Lowell, whose *Biglow Papers* first gave voice to Lowell's Hosea Biglow character, was keenly focused on political life, especially Lowell's writing, which as Blair observes first strongly protested the Mexican War and later ardently championed the Union cause during the Civil War (xii–xiv).

Following the Civil War came an explosion in dialect literature, still for a time part of the American humorist tradition, as in the tall tales of Mark Twain, including "The Celebrated Jumping Frog of Calaveras County" (1865), and George Washington Harris's Sut Lovingood tales (1867). And as with the prewar writers, some of the postwar writers, including Twain, Harris, and Mary Murfree, continued to focus on people in the South and West, and on their speech. However, as the frontier continued to dwindle and the postwar, Industrial Revolution–era economy resulted in increased immigration and ethnic and linguistic diversity, along with increasing literary attention to this evolving diversity, no longer was the Southwest the foremost setting for dialect writing. The rise of local color, a minor literary movement that was nonetheless vitally important to the continuing development of dialect writing and to the rise of realism in American fiction, concentrated on the idiosyncrasies of particular regions and their inhabitants. Twain's western writings, including *Roughing It* (1872) and shorter pieces like "The Celebrated Jumping Frog," along with some of his earlier stories of Mississippi River life, are associated with local color, as is Bret Harte's 1868 tale of California gold miners, "The Luck of Roaring Camp." The rise of local color resulted in the increasing use of dialect as a mimetic device, and incidentally marks the entry of women for the first time in any significant numbers into the formerly male-dominated genre of dialect literature, with Anne Royall a notable prewar exception. Now writers portrayed diverse localities, highlighting dialectal representations, in addition to continuing the New England–identified dialect-writing tradition, as in the work of writers such as Mary E. Wilkins Freeman, Rose Terry Cooke, and Harriet Beecher Stowe. New representations came from such writers as George Washington Cable and Kate Chopin, who portrayed the lives and language varieties of the Louisiana Creole population, Joel Chandler Harris, who wrote about his fellow Georgians, Indiana writer Edward Eggleston, and Stephen Crane, who illustrated the linguistic and other brutalities of New York City street life.

Other important developments in genre continued to occur after the Civil War, and these developments impacted significantly on the tradition of dialect writing. After the Civil War, James Nagel observes, "the short narratives of the humorous traditions and local colorism evolved into the realistic short story" (xxiv). This evolution continued through the early decades of the twentieth century, adds Nagel, resulting in "the maturation of the realistic 'novel'" (xx). Nagel points specifically to the increasing authorial use of "colloquial language . . . for the creation of literary art," rather than simply for the sake of humor, as characteristic of the trend toward realism (xx). He further explains that this increased use of vernacular language reflected the fact that the new realist literature "was fundamentally democratic, dealing with average characters in mundane situations, struggling with the social, racial, economic, and moral issues of terrestrial life" (xxv). These realistic characters and situations lent themselves easily to attempts at representations of realistic speech, as in the humorist and local-color traditions that helped to give rise to the new American fiction, only more so, because by this time the function of literary dialect was more likely to be realism than simply humor. A number of the authors associated with the local-color movement and rise of realism, including Twain, Stowe, Cable, Chopin, Crane and others, exemplify the late-century trend in their representation of dialect as a function of realism in short stories and novels. Along with Nagel, Walter Blair credits the American humor movement, whose "drift towards realism gave our fiction an important direction" (xi). The resulting trend, clearly influenced by the dialect humor tradition, was, as Nagel explains, that "the writers of Realism and Naturalism humanized American fiction" (xx). In doing so, those writers gave their characters the power of realistic speech.

Representing African American Speech in Literature

The work of the late-nineteenth-century dialect writers, like that of the prewar humorists, was enormously popular, making dialect literature an important component of American letters after the Civil War. In fact, in his analysis of Gilded-Age dialect literature, Gavin Jones contends not only that dialect writing was influential in terms of literary trends, but also that "the distinctiveness of late-nineteenth-century American literature lay largely in the generative role of dialect within it" (3). Jones further makes the important point that the sharp rise in dialect writing coincided with increasing attention to the idea of a distinctly American language, motivated in part by concerns about the possibility of "contamination" of that language by regional, social, ethnic, and foreign dialect influences. He observes that "the newly recognized dialects of America" resulted in "literature that sought to translate their implications" (Jones 36). This is an interesting parallel to Paula Blank's assertion, discussed in the previous section, that Renaissance dialect writing in Britain had normative functions with respect to the establishment of particular language varieties as preferred varieties. Jones observes that during the post–Civil War period in America, dialect writing had several social and linguistic functions, including

[to] explore the cultural and aesthetic politics of dialect difference: [by way of] regional stories that consider social aspects of rustic language; highbrow novels that react against the spoken idioms of mass culture; popular texts that experiment with humorous accents of ethnic interaction; southern romances that create racial hierarchies of speech; minority works that overturn linguistic hegemony; naturalist novels that depict the blasphemous degeneration of city talk; African American songs and stories that exploit the signifying alternative of vernacular discourse. (2)

In the context Jones describes, it seems to be little coincidence that representations of African American speech by white writers such as Twain and Joel Chandler Harris also began to appear during the latter part of the nineteenth century. And in fact, until quite late in the century, most of the writers who represented African American dialect were white. Michele Birnbaum, pointing to "the early political and pedagogical debates concerning a phonetic national language, marking linguistic independence from England" (36), attributes what she terms the "nineteenth-century preoccupation with the definition of a race-related dialect" (37) to the kinds of social and linguistic forces that Gavin Jones describes as having occurred during this period, again recalling forces that Paula Blank observes as having been in place in England during the Renaissance. Birnbaum takes the argument beyond issues of national linguistic identity, however, and contends that the rise in American dialect writing by the last decades of the nineteenth century, especially the representation of black speech by white authors, had less to do with realism in characterization than with the agitated reaction of some Southern whites to radical shifts in the social order resulting from Emancipation (36–37). Clearly Birnbaum refers here to the kind of politically motivated use of dialect that helped to define the plantation tradition.

The plantation tradition, a minor subgenre usually associated with the local-color movement, also incorporated dialect and strong regional identification, but it had political motives that reached far beyond simple nostalgia for the recent past in the face of changing times. The work of such writers as Thomas Nelson Page and Thomas Dixon is today usually interpreted as white-supremacist propaganda in the service of reconciliation between North and South in the wake of the Civil War and the discomforts for some white Southerners of Reconstruction. The stories were part of a strategy designed to reassure Northerners that conditions under slavery had been hugely exaggerated by former and escaped slaves and by abolitionists, and that the South could thus be counted on to make postwar conditions comfortable for blacks without further Northern intervention. In other words, as Eric J. Sundquist has noted, national reconciliation after Reconstruction was "predicated upon northern acquiescence in southern control of the 'Negro problem'" resulting in "an escalation of racial discrimination and violence" that proved disastrous to African Americans in the South (275).

In Thomas Nelson Page's best-known work, *In Ole Virginia* (1887), a white, standard-speaking narrator's voice frames each tale, a structural staple of the plantation tradition as it was of much of the Old Southwestern tradition, and the tale itself is then told by an African American speaker in dialect. According to Paul R. Petrie, "Page assumes unequivocal identification between his white narrator and his audience, and he produces unequivocal innocence and ignorance in his black speakers" (187). The white frame narrator functions in the plantation tradition to recreate and reinforce the distance between the white speaker who introduces the tale and the African American narrator who tells it, and consequently there is similar emphasis on the distance between that African American narrator and the predominantly white audience. Lorne Fienberg sums up the frame convention of the plantation tradition as an "illusion of distance for the comfortable reader, a kind of *cordon sanitaire* which makes it safe to contemplate the words and deeds of social and racial inferiors" (164). Fienberg further argues that because of the white control that is maintained at all times over the narrative context, "the frame is a strategy of containment which returns the freed slave to a state of narrative bondage" (164). In the work of Page, adds Fienberg, "The black narrator tells precisely the tale the white Southern listener would wish to hear" (165). Almost invariably, the tales of the plantation tradition portray former slaves still fiercely loyal to their masters and with sorrowful longing for the old plantation days. The representations of black dialect that were endemic to the stories of the plantation tradition, along with the dialect performed in minstrel shows, became in many white minds inextricably linked with reality and accepted as symptomatic of black inferiority, an image that proved persistent. Largely for this reason, many black writers of the late nineteenth and early twentieth century avoided representations of dialectal speech in their work. For African American writers who did use dialect, such as Paul Laurence Dunbar and Charles W. Chesnutt, writing during the last decades of the nineteenth century, along with such earlier twentieth-century writers as Langston Hughes and Zora Neale Hurston, the device, says Sundquist, "was fraught with the tension between capitulation to stereotypes and the desire to find an audience for African American literature" (304). That tension is particularly conspicuous in the work of Chesnutt, as discussed in chapter 5.

Questions about linguistic distance between authors, audiences, and characters, such as those Michele Birnbaum raises, are critical to an understanding of the functions of dialect writing during the period following the Civil War and beyond, especially in terms of the ways African American voices have been represented in literature, including in the works of fiction analyzed for the current discussion. Birnbaum maintains that white authorial representations of black speech in some (if not all) cases signify attempts to restructure, or rather restore, ideas about status and social hierarchy based on race and class that had been turned upside down in the aftermath of the Civil War and abolition of slavery. Birnbaum takes as her example the 1892 dialect representations of Joel Chandler Harris, pointing out that Harris was "an inveterate segregationist," despite his expressed desire to try through his Uncle Remus tales to deminstrelize the popular image of African Americans. She argues that his construction of African American dialect "provided a valuable *visual* ranking in a post-Reconstruction society in which race was no longer necessarily visible" (Birnbaum 36, emphasis in original). According to Birnbaum,

> The orthographic deviation from the standard clearly discriminates black from white, literally reinscribing an antebellum racial and social order threatened both by miscegenation (interracial sexual relations made physiognomy and skin color racially ambiguous cues) and Reconstruction legislation (the advent of black landowners left traditional class and status markers unclear). On the page, if not in the world proper, race appeared unproblematic and, most importantly, legible. (36)

Birnbaum argues that white representation of black dialect in general functions as "a kind of white blackface" (43) in which African Americans are stereotyped linguistically in order to relegate them to the social positions of "other" or "inferior," which generations of slavery taught many whites was the rightful place of African Americans.

Birnbaum raises a number of important questions, then, including about the relationship between white representations of black speech and the perceived decline of a visual racial identity, which she describes as being a major factor in the work of Joel Chandler Harris and his contemporaries. For these writers, Birnbaum argues, linguistic racializing was a response to shifting social roles. She also contends that black dialect in postbellum American literature, especially that of Harris, was not at all realistic but rather "directly reflects the white literary conventions . . . guiding its representation," which she reports were "well-standardized by the 1880s" (43). Walter M. Brasch offers a different view of Harris, arguing that "among White writers, [Harris] was among the best recorders of any of the variations of American Black English" (*Brer Rabbit* 78). The linguistic analyses Birnbaum relies on of African American and dialectal speech in general and Harris's work in particular are nearly all at least fifty years old, with several, such as those by Max Muller and William Dwight Whitney, more than one hundred years old. Birnbaum rightly criticizes the assumptions of linguists such as Muller and Whitney as racially and socially hierarchical as well as limited to comparisons of dialects in relation to a culturally dominant white standard, but the field of linguistics and especially scholarship on speech in the African American community has progressed substantially both in theory and in methodology since the days of those nineteenth-century linguists. Further, her assertion that all white representations of black speech are deliberately dehumanizing may oversimplify some of the more complex renderings of black dialect. But Birnbaum's argument is still compelling, especially in its observations concerning conventionalized strategies for representing African American speech and its questioning of whose speech is singled out to be represented "dialectally," that is, as orthographically or grammatically different from conventionalized standards of written English, and why.

As noted in the introduction, Dennis Preston has also raised questions about what social messages dialect representations send, not specifically in relation to literary authors but rather to "linguists, folklorists, sociolinguists, and others who provide written transcript of spoken language" ("Syndrome" 328). Preston's observations, however, especially taken alongside those of Birnbaum and Jones, offer substantial ammunition to a critique of the motives and strategies of dialect writers in general and, for the purposes of the current discussion, of white authorial depictions of black dialect in particular. Focusing specifically on "affective responses" to written representations of phonological variants of spoken language, using respellings to represent alternative or nonstandard pronunciations, Preston contends that even "in an albeit honest attempt to capture something of the spontaneous and natural character of a live performance," linguists, folklorists, and other researchers create false and negative impressions of the speakers whose language is represented with the respellings and "a negative or condescending attitude by the reporter towards his or her informant" (329). He asserts that "negative responses are attached to the spellings themselves and not to the pronunciations represented" (334). In other words, while an individual might not react negatively to a particular phonological variant in actual speech, the written representation of the same variant may engender a negative response. According to Preston, the represented speech need not even be "dialectal," necessarily, to engender negative reactions: "Totally unwarranted demotions of social status are brought about by honest attempts to imitate in writing something of the impression created by rapid, casual speech" (334). Preston's article does not treat literary dialect, but it does raise the questions of how respellings used to represent phonological variants in literary texts might be perceived, as well as how, as Preston notes, "attitudes may be productively manipulated by creative writers" (335). In chapter 6, "Representations of Speech and Attitudes about Race in *The Sound and the Fury*," an important issue discussed is how the narrator of each of the four sections of the novel perceives and represents African American speech and whether these representations stand for nonlinguistic racial attitudes the white narrators possess. Additionally, the observer of literary dialect must also consider what an author's use of dialect, including which characters are represented as speaking "dialectally" and to what effect the dialect is represented, might say about an author's social and racial attitudes, as well as about how authors perceive such attitudes as existing among his or her audience. Chapter 4, "Articulating Jim: Language and Characterization in *Huckleberry Finn*," also asks such questions as these as an integral part of the linguistic analysis.

Gavin Jones notes that dialect writing was frequently employed as a tool with which to claim authority, "not just over the quality of another's speech but over the nature of a dominant reality" (10), an idea he attributes originally to George Phillip Krapp, whose seminal but now almost universally criticized book *The English Language in America* (1925) included the first systematic treatment of literary dialect. But interestingly, Jones rejects interpreting all literary dialect as condescension and contends that the tool was double-edged, revealing the precariousness of the linguistic hegemony of the writers who wielded it as well as the subversive nature of the varieties themselves. This subversiveness, Jones shows, was enacted in the representations of dialectal speech in literature and thus in the "recording [of] voices in which alternative versions of reality were engendered" (11). This idea offers an interesting and useful context for the study of African American speech in literature, especially because white authors were not the exclusive interpreters of black dialect for long.

In a significant development, activated in large part by the 1887 publication of Charles W. Chesnutt's short story "The Goophered Grapevine" in the *Atlantic Monthly*, African American writers, including Chesnutt, were beginning to experiment with representing spoken varieties of American English, including the speech of African American characters, in their work for a variety of reasons and with interesting results and critical reactions.

With the publication of "The Goophered Grapevine," Chesnutt was not only the first African American writer to have his work published in the *Atlantic,* but he was also among the first published African American writers to represent uniquely African American speech. Yet with a few exceptions, Chesnutt has not been subject to the same kinds of criticism for his representations of black speech as his contemporary Paul Laurence Dunbar has been, despite Chesnutt's use of the same conventions some critics have interpreted as stereotypical in the work of Thomas Nelson Page, Joel Chandler Harris, Mark Twain, and Dunbar, including for example the ubiquitous and now nearly universally despised *wuz.* At the same time, for Chesnutt dialect frequently functioned as a signifier of class, in which only the speech of characters with a particular social, regional, and educational status is depicted with nonstandard orthography and grammatical constructions. Yet Chesnutt's use of dialect is more complex than it first appears.

Chesnutt's literary dialect is compelling because of the levels of meaning it enacts; what appears on the surface to be the tired linguistic stereotype of the uneducated plantation ex-slave standing for the whole of African American experience is actually, according to Houston A. Baker Jr., a "deep and intensive recoding of form" (41). Baker argues that Chesnutt deliberately "gives and takes in a single breath" (42), subverting even while apparently responding to the demands of his white publisher and many of the white members of his audience. Baker cites a letter from Chesnutt to his editor at the *Atlantic* magazine, Walter Hines Page, in which Chesnutt refers to his portrayal of African American dialectal speech as representative of how "an ignorant old southern Negro would be supposed to speak it" (qtd. in Baker 42). At first glance it might appear that Chesnutt himself assumes this stereotypical opinion of black dialectal speech, but he does not say in the letter that he shares this supposition and in fact his use of the passive voice is a skillful dissociation. As Baker indicates, it seems clear that Chesnutt is differentiating between the demands of his market and his own views, offering what may look like a work belonging to the plantation tradition but is rather "a world of sounds and sweet airs that resonates with . . . transformative power" (Baker 42). Baker attributes Chesnutt's transformation of black fiction from the plantation tradition to Chesnutt's view that "the plantation tradition in American letters and even more studied efforts by white authors to write about the Afro-American were inadequate and frequently idiotic . . . [and] radically opposed to the story he wanted to tell" (Baker 42). In other words, according to Baker, Chesnutt was successful for a time in balancing what he needed to do to be published, which was to make his work seem to fit into the plantation genre, while at the same time subtly subverting the genre. As Frances Smith Foster and Richard Yarborough note in their introduction to Chesnutt's work in *The Norton Anthology of African American Literature,* "Charles W. Chesnutt was the first African American writer of fiction to enlist the white-controlled publishing industry in the service of his social message, . . . reaching a significant portion of the national reading audience with his analyses and indictments of racism" (522). The question that remains for the current discussion is how Chesnutt used literary dialect to achieve this goal. As discussed in chapter 5, both Chesnutt's personal relationship with African American dialectal speech and his use of dialect as a literary device were far from uncomplicated.

Paul Laurence Dunbar, among the most important of late-nineteenth- and early-twentieth-century American writers, was with Chesnutt one of the most influential writers of black dialect, but as previously noted, according to some critics he did not share the success many readers credit to Chesnutt in subverting stereotypical ideas about blackness. Also like that of Chesnutt, Dunbar's work was not limited to dialect writing, and even his dialect work was not limited to portrayals of African American speech but also included representations of the dialectal speech of white Midwesterners. But Dunbar's representations of African American speech are particularly significant, not only because of his pioneering role in representing African American speech in literature, but also in large part because of the attention they received at the expense of his other work and the heated debate they continue to generate even one hundred years after their publication. Because of the important role Dunbar played in the development of twentieth-century dialect writing, and because his work and the reactions to it help to illustrate the complexity surrounding dialect writing and its functions, a few more words about Dunbar are in order.

For decades many critics have held that Dunbar's dialect poems, praised by early reviewer and supporter William Dean Howells and immensely popular among white readers of the day, make no attempt to subvert the plantation tradition and in fact perpetuate the persistent stereotypes of contented slaves and their romanticized post-Emancipation longing for a return to plantation life. James Weldon Johnson's 1922 commentary on Dunbar's dialect poetry in his preface to the first edition of *The Book of American Negro Poetry* praised Dunbar as "the first poet of the Negro race in the United States to show a combined mastery over poetic material and poetic technique, to reveal innate literary distinction in what he wrote, and to maintain a high level of performance" (877). Johnson even praised Dunbar's dialect poetry specifically, arguing that "Dunbar was the first to use [dialect] as a medium for the true interpretation of Negro character and psychology" (877). But Johnson's preface also marked the first serious criticism of African American dialect poetry, a medium, Johnson argued, which in its limitations, including "the fixing effects of long convention," was likely to trivialize and misrepresent African American life, even if attempted by African American writers, including Dunbar (880).

Since the appearance of Johnson's critique, a number of additional critics have, not surprisingly, been strongly critical of the unrealistic views they interpreted in Dunbar's representations of black life, which they argued and some continue to argue did not realistically represent the realities of most African Americans. John Keeling summarizes the critical position, which held that the dialect poetry "glosses over atrocities of slavery, conjures a static image of reality from a past that never was, and, most damaging of all, reinforces the marginalization of readers by adopting a regressive politics" (29). The plantation tradition Keeling describes was, as discussed above, part of a white-constructed view of black life that certain elements within white society could find palatable. Interestingly, however, many writers have focused specifically on Dunbar's representation of African American speech in their criticism of his dialect poetry. As noted, James Weldon Johnson was highly critical of African American dialect poetry, including Dunbar's, which he saw as not addressing a need for African American writers to "break away from, not Negro dialect itself, but the limitations of Negro dialect" because "there are phases of Negro life in the United States which cannot be treated in the dialect either adequately or artistically" (880). Clearly Johnson speaks here of urban life, specifically that of "the Negro in the Harlem flat," where "much of the subject-matter which went into the making of traditional dialect poetry, 'possums, watermelons, etc." presumably has no place (880). He contends that "this is no indictment against the dialect as dialect" but rather that the conventions of representation limit the writer only to "two full stops, humor and pathos" (881). In other words, Johnson makes a plausible argument that only the most stereotypical representations of African Americans emerge from those characters whose speech is represented by orthographic literary dialect conventions of the type Michele Birnbaum describes. However, his connection of dialect poetry to "'possums" and "watermelons" raises the specter of the "agriculture versus culture" controversy that persisted between African Americans who moved to the urban North after the Civil War, personified by W. E. B. DuBois, and those who stayed in the still mostly rural South or even arrived later in the North, represented by Booker T. Washington. Within this conflict of region, class, and ideology, Johnson's remarks concerning Dunbar's dialect poetry appear more problematic, calling into question his own views concerning the value of African American dialectal speech. More recently, Henry Louis Gates Jr., credits Dunbar for his "startling . . . use of black dialect as the basis of poetic diction" (*Signifying* 176) but only after arguing that Dunbar failed in "his attempt to register his authentic black voice in the tradition of Western poetry" and that as a result "he eventually gives up his black identity" (*Signifying* 115).

Despite some questions about unaddressed assumptions, especially in Johnson's observations, it is difficult to find fault with the interpretations of Dunbar's dialect poetry as sentimental if inexplicable longings for slave times because, superficially at least, that is precisely what the poems seem to be. However, despite these long-held views, recently a few critics have offered new interpretations of Dunbar's dialect poetry and discovered more complicated and subtle elements in his African American dialect depictions. Joanne M. Braxton, in her introduction to *The Collected Poetry of Paul Laurence Dunbar,* refers to the dialect poetry as "sophisticated dialect verse that located the black speaker, uniquely for Dunbar's time, at the center of experience" (x). Gavin Jones further asserts that "Rather than simply recapitulating a minstrel paradigm, Dunbar was a wily manipulator of literary conventions, a subtle overturner of racist stereotypes, and a sensitive recorder of the multiple facets of black consciousness at the turn of the twentieth century" (184). Another notable example is Keeling's position that the dialect poems are "subversive, acting against the dialect tradition they seem to mimic" (26). Keeling specifically addresses Dunbar's stereotypical representation of African American dialect, arguing that there is insufficient justification for dismissing the artistic and social significance of his work. Rather, he establishes that "Dunbar's adaptation of dialect . . . [can be taken] as a starting point for critical practice rather than as proof of the literature's dubious value" (27). He concludes, significantly, that "we should note that Dunbar wrote in dialect because it was the only form for which he had an audience" (34), a complaint Dunbar himself was known to have expressed, notably to James Weldon Johnson. And specifically on the subject of speech representation, Gavin Jones agrees that Dunbar's use of dialect is more complicated than it may appear to some critics. "Dunbar may not have been groundbreaking in his formal depiction of the phonemes of African American vernacular English," Jones observes, "but this does not mean Dunbar's work is thus politically retrograde or aesthetically deficient" (185). Further, Jones credits Dunbar with "the self-conscious use of different linguistic registers, [later] explored by Harlem poets of the nineteen-twenties" (186).

Dialect writing in the twentieth century continued to be a significant component of American literature, and as had been the case from some of the earliest examples of literary depictions of dialect, it continued to have both artistic and political implications. The two most significant literary trends associated with the early twentieth century into the 1920s and 1930s, modernism and the Harlem Renaissance, profoundly influenced and were influenced by these implications. However, the functions and strategies of literary dialect, especially in depicting African American speech, underwent major shifts. No longer used for minstrel-like entertainment purposes or for the mostly humorous intent of nineteenth-century dialect writing, literary African American English was wielded by twentieth-century authors in new forms, to enact new themes, and to represent changing social and political ideas. Because of the wide divergence between the political and social lives of blacks and of whites in the United States, divergence that also manifested itself in art and letters, the trends represented by modernism and by the Harlem Renaissance are usually considered to be distinct and unrelated. During this period, African Americans were still working to recover from the aftermath of slavery, continued racism, and the lack of economic emancipation, especially in the South, where the end of Reconstruction and rise of Jim Crow resulted in increased pressures for African Americans. Large numbers of African Americans continued the Great Migration from the South to the industrial cities of the Northeast and Midwest, with more than a half million and by some estimates closer to one million African Americans moving north between 1890 and the early 1920s. In other words, it is clear that black America was challenged by circumstances with which most non-immigrant whites were not similarly faced. However, it would be difficult to make the case that questions of race and civil rights were not a significant part of the consciousness of the nation as a whole, regardless of an individual's race, nor could one argue that they were not a major part of the national dialogue. As black America has never had the luxury of being able to ignore the influence of whites, neither has white America been since its inception outside the influence of people of color. To minimize or overlook the complicated and unbreakable bond between races and the influence of that bond on the national literature means to miss an important key to American life and letters. Similarly, to associate modernism only with white writers, as is usually done, ignores the social and artistic influences of African American experiences on the lives and art of others and ignores the influence of twentieth-century American life on African American artists.

In fact, such critics as Michael North and Houston A. Baker Jr. argue convincingly that American modernism is inextricable from race. North attributes much of the linguistic and thematic experimentation of white modernists to "white rebellion and escape by means of racial cross-identification" (9). He points to Wallace Stevens, William Carlos Williams, Gertrude Stein, Ezra Pound, and T. S. Eliot, all of whom at times adopted black personae or used dialectal features in their letters and literary works, a phenomenon North calls "racial ventriloquism" (9). The work of these writers exploited the linguistic fraternizing of races and classes that so alarmed the gatekeepers of American English. North observes the concerned responses of such linguistic critics, who dismissed both modernist literature in general as "rebellion against pure English and the great literature written in it" and anything written in "the despised dialect of African America" in particular as "racial treason" (27). North chalks this controversy up to a generational conflict, but also to a larger "confrontation between linguistic authoritarianism and American dialects," which he observes is "but one version of a more general conflict between repression and freedom" (26).

But at the same time, there is reason to be wary of the white modernist poets' co-opting of black vernacular, even if the motivation was, at least on the surface, rebellion rather than preservation of a linguistic and social status quo. North also addresses this issue as he describes the functions of African American dialect in the work of Pound and Eliot in particular. He argues that white modernist use of black dialect served dual political and artistic roles in contradiction to each other, functioning as a challenge to prevailing linguistic hegemony but also, paradoxically, as continued support for the social hegemony within which white males such as Eliot and Pound unquestionably benefitted. According to North, Pound "deploys dialect against the standard language to make way for an entirely new literature" (99). But he adds that "white masquerade behind black dialect became a well-established strategy that allowed for both rebellion and a reinforced conformity" (81), and that the "break with cultural authority" signified by white linguistic and literal blackface was made from behind a mask and thus perpetuated the social and artistic conventions that continued to name black as other. For white artists to disguise themselves as black in order to shock a white Victorian generation for whom racial roles had been clearly defined, perpetuates the view of black as outsider and hence of business as usual in terms of racial hierarchy.

Conversely, a white writer of the Modern era on whom none of the complexities of racial bonds and their influences seems to have been lost is William Faulkner. While there is no question that Faulkner's views on race issues were far from uncomplicated, as explored in chapter 6, Faulkner's experimentation with black dialect was very different from that of the modernist poets who were exploring personal and generational rebellion by way of disguises for themselves through their adoption of African American personae and linguistic devices. Rather than co-opting black speech as a way of flaunting the new generation in art and politics, Faulkner incorporated dialect in such works of fiction as *Absalom, Absalom!*; *Go Down, Moses*; *Light in August*; and *The Sound and the Fury* that show that in the wake of slavery Southern blacks and whites were still and would always be inextricably bound, even in the face of a divisive civil war and its devastating aftermath, including the rise and fall of Reconstruction and the entrenchment of Jim Crow. Further, Faulkner's Yoknapatawpha fiction seems to convey, for whites to betray that bond by denying it or by taking actions that exacerbate rather than right past wrongs can only result in disaster for themselves. Particularly in *The Sound and the Fury* and *Absalom, Absalom!*, Faulkner demonstrates the catastrophe that results when the evil engendered as the result of slavery is unleashed on its perpetrators and those who benefited from slavery. In doing so, he incorporates into both novels modernist characteristics of structure and form, such as frequent shifts in point of view, nonlinear representations of time and plot, and, most importantly for the current discussion, reliance on vernacular styles of language in his representation of dialogue, particularly African American vernacular. Both novels are also rich with modernist themes of fragmentation, disillusionment, and decay, as *Absalom, Absalom!* gradually reveals the story of the rise and collapse of the white Sutpen family, and *The Sound and the Fury* tells and retells the story of the self-destruction of the white Compsons in juxtaposition with the triumphant survival of the African American Gibson family. In the context of works such as *The Sound and the Fury* and *Absalom, Absalom!* that are steeped in racial issues, conflicts, and questions, Faulkner's representations of African American speech are important artistic and thematic strategies. His incorporation of African American dialect but not dialectal white Southern speech has interesting implications for the themes of his texts as well as for deeply held beliefs about racial hierarchy within and outside the texts.

In *The Sound and the Fury* in particular, Faulkner goes far in his idealization of the African American Gibson family, particularly Dilsey, but he brilliantly demonstrates the symbiosis between black and white, which the Compsons deny, take for granted, unconsciously rely on, and are incapable of survival without. Faulkner's use of dialect is ironic in this sense, as it seems to function as a device to segregate and differentiate the African American characters in relation to a white norm. But in reality, the Gibsons are the foundation on which the house of Compson is built. The Compsons are incapable of taking care of themselves but are equally incapable of acknowledging their limitations, bent on exacerbating past mistakes, and speeding toward annihilation. Their story disintegrates into Caddy's involvement with a Nazi officer and her daughter's certainly ill-fated elopement, Jason's failure to procreate, and Quentin's suicide, all while the wordless Benjy continues to bellow his grief and helpless rage. And yet the story of the fall of the Compsons is not simply their own story; rather, it is the story, Faulkner seems to declare, of every white Southern family who fails to come to grips with the infamy of slavery, an evil which like the curse on the house of Oedipus continues to be visited upon succeeding generations until there are no more generations left to punish. At the end of the novel, only the Gibson family thrives. These are curious conclusions in a text which represents the speech of the white Compsons as standard "normal" speech and that of the Gibsons as dialectal speech frequently stigmatized as "corrupt." Chapter 6 asks the question of how those representations of speech correlate with the themes of the text itself and with Faulkner's own attitudes about race.

Houston A. Baker Jr. also considers the themes of a modernism richly infused with African American art and life and deeply connected with the Harlem Renaissance. Baker notes the frequent association of modernism with white artists, indicating that the work of their African American contemporaries is frequently held up as a failed experiment, observing that "the 'Harlem Renaissance' has frequently been faulted for its 'failure' to produce vital, original, effective, or 'modern' art in the manner, presumably, of British, Anglo-American, and Irish creative endeavors" (xiii). Baker argues that this view of modern art and literature, evaluated in terms of its posing of inward-looking questions about personal and interpersonal contentment and self-actualization, is severely limited by its failure to consider that the criteria being applied are "descriptive only of a bourgeois, characteristically twentieth-century, white Western mentality. . . . Such questions presuppose at least an adequate level of sustenance and a sufficient faith in human behavioral alternatives to enable a self-directed questioning" (7–8). In other words, the precursors to the modern era for African Americans were slavery, Jim Crow, and the Great Migration, rather than rumblings in response to repressive Victorian artistic and social values. The conditions in place for African Americans during the late-nineteenth and early-twentieth centuries, Baker argues, when immigration to the United States boomed, technological and scientific discoveries proliferated, developments in psychological, theological, and economic theory abounded, and in the face of the Great War and its aftermath, resulted in a modern movement among African Americans, "a specifically Afro-American modernism" that was the Harlem Renaissance, which "included some of the earliest attempts by Afro-American artists and intellectuals to define themselves in 'modern' terms" (Baker 8–9).

Baker demonstrates, then, that the preexisting conditions for black and white artists were quite different, and that those differences were enacted in their art. African American writers were doing the important work of artistic "self-definition," as Baker (72) terms it. Part of this self-definition meant resisting definitions imposed by whites onto African American experiences and art and by black writers such as Paul Laurence Dunbar who were perceived as enabling the stereotypes, including by representing black dialect. James Weldon Johnson verbalized this resistance in his 1922 preface, expressing his concern that the African American artist had been categorized via dialect poetry, confined to a "niche" as a stereotypical "happy-go-lucky, singing, shuffling, banjo-picking being or more or less a pathetic figure" (880). Johnson's comment sets the tone for African American modernists who wanted to represent authentic African American experiences at the same time that they wanted to make the break Johnson advocated from limiting themselves and all African Americans in the eyes of predominantly white literary consumers to stereotyped images.

Poets such as Countee Cullen took, at least to some degree, Johnson's advice "to write *American* poetry spontaneously" (Johnson 881, emphasis in original). Johnson exhorted young poets "to work out a new and distinctive form of expression" in which poets would not "limit themselves to Negro poetry, to racial themes" (881). While Cullen's elegantly crafted poetry proclaims his strong desire to be accepted as simply a poet rather than as a "Negro poet," and according to Arnold Rampersad, the poet "shied away from being a racial writer" (1305), still Cullen's genius is in his fusion of traditional, classical poetic forms and language with the themes of racial disparity and pain. But Cullen did not write in dialect; in his use of language he was a traditionalist and in this respect successful according to Johnson's recommendations. In fact, Rampersad notes that Johnson greatly admired Cullen's work "because Cullen revolts against . . . 'racial' limitations—technical and spiritual" (qtd. in Rampersad 1305). For Johnson, then, and also for Countee Cullen, racial themes were in fact American themes, despite Johnson's earlier seeming resistance to the focus of the art of African Americans as distinctly African American, perhaps as long as the racial themes were not expressed using dialect.

As the work of Cullen and other writers shows, the disillusionment and rebellion identified with white modernists in response to earlier values and art forms was also being enacted, albeit differently and, as noted above, with different motives, in works by African American authors of the Harlem Renaissance. In contrast to Cullen, a number of Harlem Renaissance writers used dialect in their work, in part, to help reclaim African American voices for its speakers. Despite Johnson's highly influential recommendations, then, by no means did all Harlem Renaissance writers reject dialect as an artistic strategy. Langston Hughes experimented with dialectal phonology and grammar especially in his poetry, in which he championed the use of the African American musical languages of jazz and blues, which were deeply influenced by vernacular traditions. Some of his prose works also subtly incorporate dialectal grammatical features in the speech of African American characters, such as in his "Simple" stories, which use innovative tense markers, among other strategies: "'Virginia is where I was borned,' said Simple. 'I would be borned in a state named after a woman. From that day on, women never give me no respect'" (Hughes 1297). Claude McKay also used dialectal language in his fiction, including in his first novel, *Home to Harlem,* published in 1928 to become the first best-seller by an African American novelist. Rudolph Fisher was another Harlem Renaissance writer who surmounted the proscriptions against dialect writing in his attempts to create lifelike representations of language, including in his realistic and impressionistic story, "The City of Refuge" (1925), the story of Southern-born King Solomon Gillis as he begins a new life in Harlem. And Arna Bontemps's best-known short story, "A Summer Tragedy" (1932), used dialect in the characterization of Jeff and Jennie Patton, sharecroppers facing the agonies of aging and loss. Like Langston Hughes, Sterling Brown also wrote dialect poetry influenced by the language and rhythms of jazz and blues. According to Rampersad, Brown's work compelled James Weldon Johnson to reassess his position about the poetic use of dialect, with Johnson going so far as to praise Brown's dialect poetry above his more traditional work (1210).

However, despite the reemergence of the African American literary tradition of representing African American dialectal speech, a tradition associated with the Harlem Renaissance, critical reactions were not always favorable. Some of the negative responses to Zora Neale Hurston's use of African American dialect in her folklore collections and fiction, especially including her 1937 masterpiece *Their Eyes Were Watching God,* seem rooted in the idea that African American writers should eschew portrayal of any aspects of African American life that might raise the specter of stereotype in the minds of white readers, regardless of the level of realism of the portrayals. Like Dunbar, Hurston was criticized not only for her portrayal of characters in lower-class and rural situations that some urban black critics found unseemly, but also for her representation of African American speech, including in *Their Eyes Were Watching God.* Richard Wright in particular accuses Hurston, as Dunbar had also been charged, of selling a stereotypical image of African Americans and their speech to a white reading public. Wright does not use the word "dialect," but his critique clearly implicates Hurston's representations of speech: "[Hurston's] dialogue manages to catch the psychological movements of the Negro folk-mind in their pure simplicity, but that's as far as it goes" (17). Further, Wright adds, Hurston

> *voluntarily* continues in her novel the tradition which was *forced* upon the Negro in the theater, that is, the minstrel technique that makes the "white folks" laugh. Her characters eat and laugh and cry and work and kill; they swing like a pendulum eternally in that safe and narrow orbit in which America likes to see the Negro live: between laughter and tears. . . . In the main, her novel is not addressed to the Negro, but to a white audience whose chauvinistic tastes she knows how to satisfy. She exploits the phase of Negro life which is "quaint," the phase which evokes a piteous smile on the lips of the "superior" race. (Wright 17, emphasis in original).

Wright's critique fails to consider the realities reflected in the novel for many Southern blacks and recently transplanted Northerners, for whom an urban, educated life had until recently been or was still unimaginable, and it also fails to note specific instances of "minstrelization" as he alleges appear in the novel. Labeling Hurston an upholder of the minstrel tradition in terms of what is actually contained in the text is not accurate and seems to be designed more to punish her for failing to toe the party line than to describe her novel accurately. The party line for Wright would have required that Hurston "come to grips with motive fiction and social document fiction" (18), as Alain Locke put it in his 1938 review of *Their Eyes Were Watching God.* According to Sterling Brown, who also reviewed the novel, Hurston's characters inexplicably "escape the worst pressures of class and caste" (20). Conversely, Henry Louis Gates Jr. sees the views of Wright and many of his contemporaries as grounded in the theory of African Americans as "beings who only react to omnipresent racial oppression, whose culture is 'deprived' where different, and whose psyches are in the main 'pathological'" ("Afterword," 199). By that rationale, the art of African Americans should first and foremost be informed by the causes and act out the consequences of this oppression and its devastation. But Hurston did not accept the prevailing naturalistic view of blacks as existing only in relation to whites and a hostile white world. According to Gates, she "thought this idea degrading, its propagation a trap, and railed against it" ("Afterword," 199). Gates notes that her views were revolutionary for their time in their declaration of African Americans as whole persons, in relation to themselves and their communities, or as Alice Walker has described it, with "a sense of black people as complete, complex, *undiminished* human beings, a sense that is lacking in so much black writing and literature," presumably including Wright's (qtd. in Gates 200, emphasis in original).

In a time of modernist disillusionment for many writers both black and white, then, Hurston seems to have been criticized for not being disillusioned enough. However, as her fiction indicates, her views actually do subvert prevailing ideas about African American life and women in significant ways, even if these ways are not those prescribed by her literary contemporaries. In *Their Eyes Were Watching God,* African American characters live and speak authentically—working and telling stories and falling in love, having lives that are not lived every minute or even most minutes in response to the actions of whites—and Janie, the female protagonist, achieves love and selfhood. *In Their Eyes Were Watching God,* Hurston celebrates as well as critiques black life and portrays vernacular as poetry, all while challenging assumptions of black and white readers alike. As discussed in chapter 7, Hurston juxtaposes the communality of African American experiences with the gender and class divisions that make the community complex within itself rather than merely in constant reaction to pressures imposed from outside.

Between the time of Hurston and the present day, African American writers have continued the traditions established by Charles W. Chesnutt, Zora Neale Hurston, and other innovators in literary representations of authentic African American voices. Most notably in the work of writers such as Alice Walker and Toni Morrison, voices of diverse members of the African American community have continued to make themselves heard as they build new literary traditions and serve a variety of artistic, linguistic, and social functions. On the other hand, there seem to be far fewer examples today of white-authored representation of African American speech. Perhaps this is the result of increased sensitivity to the complications inherent in attempting to render black voices authentically, given the troubling history of these renderings. It is probably also an acknowledgment of revised critiques of nineteenth- and earlier-twentieth-century dialectal representations, critiques which are less accepting of speech representations as possible stand-ins for other strategies of stereotypical characterization. But these new attitudes do not mean that the voices of characters populating American literature are any less diverse or less realistic. Rather, the increasing diversity of writers promises a rich literary dialect tradition continuing into the twenty-first century.

2

Linguists, Literary Critics, and Literary Dialect

Returning to our earlier discussion, there is no question that everything that is known today of older forms of English and of other languages and varieties no longer extant comes from written sources. Thus, literature has long been companion to linguistic study. But despite this long relationship, considerable scholarly conflict exists between proponents of literary approaches and those of linguistic approaches to the study of language, including conflicts over whether such analyses should be performed in the first place, how to conduct them, and how to apply the results. Additionally, and perhaps more fundamentally, some linguists have been hesitant to consider the idea that written language constitutes natural language. Cynthia Goldin Bernstein notes that the Saussurean view, the idea that sound, "speech alone," is and should be the focus of linguistics, is still widely shared by linguists and largely responsible for the continued gap between linguistics and literary study ("Contextualization" 4). Walter M. Brasch also observes this proclivity, commenting on the "overwhelming number of contemporary researchers [who] have concentrated on the spoken language and on contemporary attitudes, but have neglected the written language . . . and its importance in historical analysis and development" (*Media* xvii). However, other linguists, such as Edgar W. Schneider, are skeptical of literary dialect in terms of its potential value for particular types of linguistic research. For example, Schneider argues that the depression-era Federal Writers' Project transcripts of ex-slave narratives, while not entirely reliable because of transcription inconsistencies and legitimate concerns about the possibility of editorial bias, are "clearly superior to literary dialect" as sources for earlier African American speech because of their internal linguistic consistency and similarity to other data ("Africanisms" 217–18n).

Schneider holds this view in contrast to J. L. Dillard's claim that the ex-slave narratives are seriously flawed as linguistic evidence because of critical questions about interviewee selection, lack of field-worker training, and heavy-handed editing practices. In fact, Dillard calls the speech representations in the narratives themselves "literary dialect," arguing that the literary dialect representations of gifted writers and observers like Frederick Douglass and Charles W. Chesnutt are at least as valuable as those of field-workers poorly trained in linguistic transcription. Contending that literary representations of speech are not necessarily without value simply because they are literary, Dillard asks, "If attestations from black author[s] . . . are to be dismissed because of the literary reputation of the recorder, what are we to say of the Louisiana ex-slave narratives collected and elaborately edited under the direction of the [white] novelist Lyle Saxon?" (224) He concludes, "If we throw out everything which can be considered tainted by the dialect fiction tradition, we may simply wind up throwing out everything," including the ex-slave narratives (227). Attempting to draw conclusions as to the reliability of the narratives is of course beyond the scope of the current discussion, but Schneider's argument and Dillard's response offer some perspective into the opposing schools of thought.

On the other hand, literary critics interested in literary dialect research may be reluctant to use methodologies devised by linguists, feeling that such methods are not relevant to the analysis of artistic creations. The perceived tendency for some linguists to privilege accuracy of representation over artistic functions, a perception that is valid to some degree, can be a major sticking point. But before analyzing the critiques of the accuracy issue, it may be helpful to look first at the original sources for many of the prevailing ideas about how to look at literary dialect.

Sumner Ives's "A Theory of Literary Dialect" (1950) is frequently cited as a landmark work in the field, replacing George Philip Krapp's *The English Language in America* (1925), which prior to publication of Ives's work was one of the first, as well as still one of very few, systematic studies of literary representation of speech and hence is still a significant work. However, Krapp's analysis has since been widely and justly criticized for his reduction of all dialectal variation in American English to "the more or less formal standard" and the so-called "low colloquial" (243) and for his acceptance of the view that "there are no true dialects in America" (228). That is, his theory of literary dialect was based on the idea of a single national standard for American English and the position that variation from that standard was fairly uniform, adding that literary dialects "represent on the whole relatively slight departures from the forms of standard speech" (228). The existence of multiple regional standards has subsequently been demonstrated by numerous scholars, including in Raven McDavid's "The Dialects of American English" (1958), in which the longtime director of the Linguistic Atlas Project acknowledges that the precepts of the Atlas projects in the United States are predicated in part upon "such typical American cultural phenomena" as "the lack of any single prestigious form of speech that may be considered a national standard" (488).

Despite the abandonment of the basis for Krapp's evaluation of literary dialect, however, his work is of value in the sense that it illustrates the starting point for literary dialect studies in American English. Additionally, he was among the first to observe that literary dialect was not always intended to represent reality nor did it always show respect for the linguistic varieties represented or its speakers, but rather that it could indicate a condescension shared between author or narrator (or both) and reader toward the characters whose speech is represented dialectally. However, his claim that "In *all use of dialect* there is probably present some sense of amused superiority on the part of the conventional speaker as he views the forms of dialect speech" (229, emphasis added) is controversial because it reduces the functions of literary dialect to a single motive. The dialect in Hurston's *Their Eyes Were Watching God*, for example, is difficult to view in terms of Krapp's theory, but of course that 1937 novel had not been written yet when Krapp's 1925 treatment appeared. However, Hurston was not the first writer to represent dialect with an eye (and an ear) toward dialect being something other than a curiosity or a boundary between representer (and audience) and represented. Krapp's statement, then, indicates a limited view that corresponds primarily to the Old Southwestern humorist functions of dialect, in which there is some evidence of "amused superiority on the part of the conventional speaker" (Krapp 229). Conversely, Ives's "Theory," which outlines methods and guidelines for literary dialect analysis, is still widely cited in even recent analyses (see, for instance, Cooley, 1997; Ellis, 1994; Tamasi, 2001; and chapters 4 and 6 herein).

In his "Theory of Literary Dialect," Sumner Ives formulates a set of procedures for researchers to consider, limited mostly to phonological analysis of literary speech representation. He stresses the importance of researcher awareness of recent scholarship on social and regional variation, especially scholarship that describes and analyzes the actual speech production of real speakers, citing in particular data gathered as part of the Linguistic Atlas projects. Additionally, Ives emphasizes the importance of determining what the author's speech sounds like or might have sounded like in determining the level of accuracy. While he does not overtly address his (apparent) theory that phonology and accuracy should necessarily be the central (and, some critics charge, sole) objects of attention, he offers specific steps to follow when performing a literary dialect analysis, which he demonstrates using his own analysis of literary dialect in the work of Joel Chandler Harris. The steps include "phonetic interpretation of the spelling devices" used to represent dialectal speech, determining phonological relationships between respelled words and "standard" pronunciations, and evaluating features for authenticity. The final step, according to Ives, is to "determine what degree of individuality the dialect has, whether it is a truly restricted type, and whether the restriction is regional, social, or both" (173–75).

While some of Ives's strategies may be useful, and in fact several are incorporated into the discussions of *Huckleberry Finn* and *The Sound and the Fury* included herein, the notions that 1) phonology is the most important category of features to investigate, and 2) determination of accuracy is or should be the ultimate goal of every analyst, both warrant further discussion. Roger W. Cole argues that the Ives approach is seriously flawed both in its overemphasis on phonological representations and in its preoccupation with authorial accuracy as a prerequisite for artistic success. He anticipates Bernstein's observation in attributing the first flaw to the influence on Ives and others of what he calls the "well-known 'phonological bias' of structural linguistics," and he contends that the focus on accuracy results in studies that "tend to divert attention from the central artistic problem a writer faces when [attempting] to represent human speech in . . . fiction" (4). Cole does not address the significance of phonology for linguists as an important component of speech, focusing on its privileging by linguists without exploring, as Bernstein does, the reasons behind that privileging. He further dismisses both the extensive reliance on phonological representations by literary authors that demand the attention of the analyst and the orthographic limitations of phonological representation in writing that make it an interesting subject for analysis. However, Cole is correct in maintaining it is neither the only nor necessarily the most important category of feature to consider in an analysis. He argues that "artistic success . . . in any representation of human speech must obviously be judged in terms of function or purpose of that speech within [a work's] overall artistic scheme: that is in terms of the artistic work as whole" (4).

Cole's charge that the literary-dialect analyst must look at how the dialect functions in the work is an important point. However, his wholesale dismissal of structural analysis will not make sense to linguists interested in what an author's representation of features, including but not limited to phonological features, can say about language variation and change or about perceptions of and attitudes toward language varieties and their impact on social organization, for example. His position also comes up short for literary theorists interested in what the representations might indicate about characterization and narrative strategies as well as about relationships between characters. In other words, as this book is intended to demonstrate, linguistic methodologies can engender exactly the kinds of results Cole demands: Linguistic analysis of literary dialect can and does lead to conclusions about the artistic functions of the literary dialect in a given work. The category or categories a researcher decides to investigate need to be determined by the specific literary or linguistic goals of the analysis as well as by the categories attended to by the author of the literary work itself. It is not entirely clear why Ives chose to focus exclusively on phonology. It may be because in the works he analyzed, respellings used to denote alternative pronunciations are the most salient of authorial choices for representation. But as Lee Pederson has demonstrated, syntactic analysis of the Uncle Remus tales of Joel Chandler Harris, the same literature as Ives explores, yields interesting and surprising results that an examination of phonology alone simply cannot uncover. Pederson shows that Uncle Remus's narration "is distantly removed from the observed patterns of American folk speech and bears little resemblance to the received forms of colloquial English spoken by any American social group" ("Language" 293). He argues that it is rather a "carefully developed mode of poetic language" that he traces back to "a literary tradition that has its roots in the old fields of Athens and Rome" (294). Pederson poses the intriguing questions of how and why so many readers and analysts, including Ives, interpret "the neoclassical diction of Uncle Remus" (294) as authentic African American folk speech and concludes that it is largely a result of preoccupation with phonology.

But for Cole, the preoccupation with accuracy is also a major point of contention. As noted above, he points out that the still widely accepted methods of analysis, as espoused by Ives's seminal study, "do not address the central artistic problem of dialect representation" because of what he views as their "implicit assumption . . . that accuracy of representation is equivalent to artistic effectiveness in representation" (3–4). His challenge to the traditional focus on accuracy is welcome. Accuracy investigated simply as an end in itself adds little either to literary or linguistic understanding of language, to borrow from Cynthia Bernstein's title, within "the text and beyond." That is, such investigations of accuracy per se cannot contribute much to discussions of issues either within the literary text itself or of issues about language variation and change, the varieties portrayed, or the social relationships of speakers, real or fictional. Presumably, these are some of the major issues in which students of literary dialect are interested.

On the other hand, an analysis for relative accuracy as a component of a literary dialect analysis raises important and intriguing questions. Because of these questions, an evaluation of literary dialect for accuracy can be important and useful. Some of the issues raised may include questions about the significance of the level of accuracy with which the dialect is represented. Consideration of how a character's speech is represented, including by way of linguistic analysis of specific categories of features and attention to relative accuracy, can lead to insights about how writers perceive linguistic and social characteristics and what their attitudes are. It is possible that a dialect depiction that is clearly inaccurate is designed to ridicule and degrade, as Preston argues most written representations have the potential to do and Birnbaum argues most written representations of African American speech do deliberately. A corpus-driven survey of phonological and grammatical features, the methodology advocated here, to determine whether the dialect is represented with some level of relative accuracy is a useful starting point for formulating discussions about how literary dialect functions inside and outside the texts in which it appears. These discussions can lead to insights about characterization and also about attitudes toward speech and speakers held by authors, and by various characters toward one another. To dismiss accuracy entirely as irrelevant ignores the artistic meanings generated precisely because of the author's choices about how to represent the dialect as well as about whose dialect to represent.

For these reasons, the methodology advocated and used in this book, as outlined in the following chapter, includes emphasis on the relationship between literary dialect and real speech, without claiming that it is possible to reproduce spoken language exactly in writing. The best practitioners of literary dialect create effects that are linguistically and artistically believable. Thus for linguists, many of whom are concerned with applications beyond the text itself, a comparison with the real speech of people regionally and socially similar to the characters can add depth to the discussion by shedding light on whether a representation is realistic or stereotypical. This question of veracity is important to address because dialects and perceptions of them are not, of course, neutral and equal but rather laden with subjective perceptions and consequent social meanings. Cole seems unaware of such alternate approaches to literary dialect analysis as suggested here, citing as negative examples of literary dialect analysis in the Ives tradition papers published no later than 1971 and most several decades earlier, rather outdated even at the time of his own article's publication in 1986. Fortunately, the field of literary dialect analysis has matured considerably since its inception, and today much rigorous, diverse, and innovative work exists and continues to be produced, including that by scholars discussed in this chapter.

Another contentious issue raised in the debate over the theories, methods, and functions of literary dialect analysis is that some literary theorists have argued, Bernstein explains, that "linguistics lacks the tools needed to examine anything but features within the texts" ("Contextualization" 3). She finds this conclusion surprising, however, arguing that "linguists have been developing the tools to study precisely those cultural and psychological features of language that concern literary theorists today" (3) and that linguistic tools and methods can help the literary critic "in seeking meaning outside the text" ("Text" 2). Perhaps it is for this reason that, despite some resistance from literary critics, a reasonably wide sampling of published studies using linguistic approaches to literature indicates that the research aims are as often literary as linguistic. That is, the tools of linguistic analysis are frequently used to provide insight into the literary texts under investigation rather than into how people use and respond to language. In other words, it seems that researchers with both literary and linguistic aims in mind are coming around to the idea that study and understanding of the functions of written and spoken language can both be of value.

For example, Helmut Esau, Norma Bagnall, and Cheryl Ware stress the importance of understanding sociolinguistic and variation theory for critics interested in evaluating literary dialect. Such understanding, they argue, "can deepen the critic's appreciation of the nature and function of literary dialects" (8). In their article "Faulkner, Literary Criticism, and Linguistics," they interpret Faulkner's fictional speech representations in *Intruder in the Dust* as components of characterization through the theoretical lenses established by the work of Hans Kurath and others in dialect geography and the work of sociolinguists and variationists including William Labov and C.-J. Bailey. In doing so, Esau, Bagnall, and Ware emphasize the existence of regional standards and the power of social influences on linguistic behavior, including the effects of interlocutor status and speaker attitudes on intra-speaker variability. Their idea of a "gradient pattern of polylectal speech outputs" contrasts with earlier ideas promoted by Krapp and Ives with respect to their reliance on "simple dichotomies" such as "'standard' vs. 'non-standard'" and "'educated' vs 'noneducated'," respectively (Esau, Bagnall, and Ware 15). In actual speech as well as in literature, the authors note, variation "reflects the social stratification of the speech community, is used as a tool to establish social dominance, camouflages complicated patterns of overt and covert prestige, and indicates that opposing value systems may be linked to social class membership" (12–13). According to Esau, Bagnall, and Ware, more important than determining accuracy and mapping the fictional dialect, which they, like other critics, claim is the legacy of early literary dialect analysis theory, is determining the social and linguistic "hierarchy of values" among the characters, or whether the variation patterns among the characters correlate to the social class structure of the fictional community (44). They derive a socioeconomic hierarchy for the major characters based solely on representation of dialectal features in each character's speech, which they then apply to a critical analysis of the interaction and relationships between the characters, determining these relationships largely if not entirely through their linguistic features and concluding that "the patterns of dialect shifting are central to an interpretation of the meaning of the novel" (40). "The more readers understand the nature and function of linguistic varieties," assert the authors, "the more they will appreciate the subtle dimensions of meaning that an author can build into a work of literature by using literary dialects effectively" (44).

Lee Pederson's studies of the dialect in Joel Chandler Harris's Uncle Remus tales represent distinctive linguistic approaches toward accomplishing both literary and linguistic aims. His "Language in the Uncle Remus Tales" dismisses conclusions about the widely perceived accuracy of Harris's work, arguing that "Harris's literary mastery of Piedmont Southern pronunciation" (293) has distracted readers and critics from syntactic constructions that represent neoclassical literary styles and have little in common with the folk speech portrayed in dialect writing. Beginning with Uncle Remus's first utterance in the 1880 book *Uncle Remus: His Songs and His Sayings,* Pederson shows that his syntax, particularly in that passage but also in other parts of the text, resembles an "elaborately symmetrical Ciceronian style [incorporating] parallelism, antitheses, anaphora, tricolons, and metrical prose" and also at times imitates "the studied realism of the Senecan style" (295). Pederson allows that the Greek and Roman rhetorical styles may "have precedents in ordinary speech, but their manipulation and recurrence in the Uncle Remus tales create a rhetorical and emotional impact that has no counterpart in ordinary language" (295–96). Despite problems this conclusion may present for the linguistic critic concerned with Harris's accuracy, for Pederson the rhetorical achievements of Uncle Remus place him "among the most ingenious storytellers in Anglo-American literature" (296) and position his creator as an author who "synthesized three cultures and their heritage in this narrative": the cultures of rural Middle Georgia, as enacted through "the sounds and words of a regional dialect," African American traditions in the South "through the beast fables and the occasionally vulnerable trickster rabbit," and "the classical tradition of English prose through the syntax and prose style that elevate the spoken word to literature" (298).

Pederson's "Rewriting Dialect Literature: 'The Wonderful Tar-Baby Story'" also moves beyond questions about accuracy to questions of artistic motivation. The study takes the approach of analyzing the publication history and revision process of the story as Pederson raises questions about the "century-old assumption about Harris as a dialect writer . . . that [he] was transcribing exactly what he heard" (57–58). Pederson compares the text of "The Wonderful Tar-Baby Story" as published in the *Atlanta Constitution* in 1879 with three subsequent revisions produced between 1880 and 1895, including unpublished notations in Harris's personal copy of his own 1880 book, *Uncle Remus: His Songs and His Sayings,* noting specific changes from one version to the next. Carefully analyzing the changes, including with attention to dialectal elements, Pederson dispels the widely held view that the revisions represent Harris's attempt to achieve transcriptive reality, noting that Harris's revisions, even when they have to do with the representation of particular dialect features, result in more effective "prose style, not dialect" (61). Pederson does not rule out the possibility raised by critics such as R. Bruce Bickley that Harris revised the dialect in his personal copy of *Songs and Sayings* because "he was afraid that he had not been accurate enough" (qtd. in Pederson 64), simply because there is no way to know for certain what motivated those notations. However, Pederson suggests that the revision history indicates rather that Harris's dual roles as literary author and newspaper editor resulted in "a conflict of editorial and artistic responsibilities," in which his "inclination as a reader differed from those as copy editor of the second edition" (68). Pederson determines that "Harris's revisions move consistently in the direction of universal art. He makes no concessions to scientific folklore study and shows little concern for systematic phonography" (63). The implication here is that if transcriptive reality had been Harris's goal, he could have achieved it but only at the expense of the artistic quality of the work.

Barbara A. Fennell and John Bennett use linguistic means to literary-critical and linguistic ends in their "Sociolinguistic Concepts and Literary Analysis." Like Esau, Bagnall, and Ware, the authors argue that "approaching the social systems which are set up in literary works through the medium of linguistic analysis, rather than looking at the social system alone, is often a much more concrete and revealing approach" (372), a theory they demonstrate via an analysis of John Kennedy Toole's *A Confederacy of Dunces*. Not specifically an analysis of literary dialect, the article instead focuses on functional aspects of the characters' speech, situating the discussion in discourse theory, especially as outlined by Grice's maxims of cooperative conversation. In addition to the emphases on discourse as well as on basic sociolinguistic theory, through which they note the "direct and indirect reference to linguistic competence as a social marker" that occurs throughout the novel, Fennell and Bennett also ground their discussion in part in social network theory as outlined by Lesley Milroy (372). Social network theory incorporates ideas similar to those raised in the theoretical basis of the study by Esau, Bagnall and Ware, in which variation within the production of a single speaker occurs in response to social contexts, but goes further in its focus on the specific social patterning that occurs in a community. *A Confederacy of Dunces* offers particularly interesting raw material for literary analysis, because the protagonist, Ignatius J. Reilly, deliberately uses linguistic strategies to maintain his isolated social position. Fennell and Bennett sum up his goals and strategies: "Ignatius aims to seal himself off from the other characters in a speech community of one, consistently employing verbal obfuscation and breaching linguistic conventions in order to stifle effective communication with those he considers inferior" (372–73). In terms of social network, as Fennell and Bennett demonstrate, Ignatius uses language deliberately in order to maintain distance from others in his ostensible community. He achieves this goal by flouting all the Gricean maxims of cooperative conversation: He lies frequently, deliberately obscures meaning, goes off on long-winded tangents, and in his interaction with others is impolite and even openly hostile. The authors conclude that viewing the novel through the lens of discourse and social network theory "enables [researchers] to give credence to the mechanism by which the author is able to convey and maintain [the social differences between characters], that is, by the sociolinguistic factors in speech" (378). In other words, in addition to the analysis itself, another stated goal of Fennell and Bennett's study is to make the arguments that "sociolinguistic concepts apply to the analysis of literature" and that sociolinguistic theory can be demonstrated "in the context of literary analysis" (371).

Fennell continues to make arguments in support of linguistic applications to literature by using linguistic methods to achieve literary understanding, but in contending that "literature is linguistic data" (242), she is also one of several researchers open to exploring the intersections between the two fields of study, offering an intriguing approach to studying the language(s) of bi- and multilingual immigrant workers in Germany. In her article "Literary Data and Linguistic Analysis: The Example of Modern German Immigrant Worker Literature," she demonstrates that analyzing the literature of immigrant authors such as Jusuf Naoum and Aras Oren, whose works indicate important choices in the language(s) used, including a creole-like Immigrant Worker German, can lead to increased understanding of language contact theory, linguistic awareness, and attitudes toward language varieties. Fennell's article is unique in its attention to the literary significance of the linguistic choices the authors have made, claiming that "knowledge of the specific structural characteristics of Immigrant Worker German as well as of its political, socio- and psycholinguistic context brings a fuller appreciation of the skills of the writers involved" (242–23), thus bringing together both literary and linguistic goals of linguistic applications to literary data.

Other works that use literary dialect as linguistic data while incorporating linguistic methods and theories include William Evans's "French-English Dialect in *The Grandissimes*," which offers a linguistic analysis of the varieties of Louisiana Creole spoken by the characters in George Washington Cable's 1879 novel. The article contains some impressionistic analysis but it also provides useful insights into prevailing attitudes toward speech varieties and, by extension, their speakers. In addition to looking at particular linguistic features in the speech of several of the major characters and determining, based largely on historical information about Cable and his knowledge of dialect rather than on a comparison with actual speech data, that the varieties the characters are represented as speaking are realistic, Evans focuses on the reactions of several of Cable's contemporaries to the ways the characters are depicted as speaking. Several of Cable's critics reacted strongly to what they viewed as his "inappropriate" and socially "misleading" linguistic characterizations. Evans cites an 1893 review of *The Grandissimes* that charges Cable with attributing to "accomplished women and cultured cavaliers . . . a jargon unreal and impossible beyond conception in people of their class" (qtd. in Evans 216–17). But classism is not the only motivator for such alarmed critiques. Evans also cites Charles Gayarre, a white Creole historian, who decried Cable's efforts to represent the speech of the white Creoles in his novel, charging that the author insulted them by depicting their language as the "broken, mutilated africanized English of the black man" (qtd. in Evans 215). But Evans shows that white Creoles of French descent, regardless of their social standing, did indeed speak varieties of the creole language Cable represents, and that those varieties were very likely at least shared by black speakers if not in fact directly influenced by them.

Using the data of real speakers, and in contrast with the predominantly literary aims of his work on the literary dialect of Joel Chandler Harris's Uncle Remus stories, Lee Pederson's articles on Twain's *Huckleberry Finn* offer useful models of empirical methods for linguistic ends. Pederson based studies such as "Negro Speech in *Adventures of Huckleberry Finn*" and "Mark Twain's Missouri Dialects: Marion County Phonemics" on field interviews with actual speakers followed by analysis of interviewee data and Twain's textual material. As the director of the Linguistic Atlas of the Gulf States, Pederson advocates the use of field data in analyzing literary dialect, and his work is important in the history of literary dialect analysis in its application of Atlas data in tracing the geographical and dialectal roots of Twain's speakers. The focus in these articles is largely on the social and geographical distribution of the features Twain represented in the novel, and the idea of using Atlas and other field data originally advocated by Ives but perhaps best exemplified in Pederson's work is an approach that is still of considerable value today, including in the methods followed in this book.

Additionally, historical reconstruction has been a function of literary dialect analysis for linguists open to the idea. A particularly notable example is Walter M. Brasch's comprehensive study *Black English and the Mass Media*. Brasch argues persuasively that speech data gathered from literary sources and other media is invaluable in reconstructing earlier varieties of African American English and in evaluating the influence of media representation on perceptions about the varieties. In support of his hypotheses, first that "the only strong evidence available as to the existence of Black English historically in America is what appeared in the mass media," especially in the days before African American English became an important area of academic inquiry, and secondly that "the mass media reflect the state of knowledge, concern, and awareness of Black English," Brasch analyzes media portrayals of black speech in public performances, travel writing, newspaper and magazine selections, and literary sources from the seventeenth through twentieth centuries (*Media* x). His analysis focuses on black- and white-authored representations of black speech, with attention to numerous major and minor dialect writers and their works. Brasch's determinations are carefully researched, with close attention both to the original primary sources and to critical and popular responses to them. Many of his conclusions about the linguistic representations are impressionistic, perhaps fittingly so, given his emphasis on the role of attitudes about African American English and its speakers in the production and consumption of dialect writing.

Similarly, Michael Ellis's "Literary Dialect as Linguistic Evidence: Subject-Verb Concord in Nineteenth-Century Southern Literature" assumes that literary evidence is valuable as linguistic data, suggesting that literary data has "two distinct advantages": accessibility and retention of features that would otherwise have been lost through the use of a written standard. He addresses the limitations of literary evidence, however, and offers an interesting analysis of subject-verb concord in the works of seven authors, including William Gilmore Simms, A. B. Longstreet, and George Washington Harris, making the point that comparative analyses, such as those using the data of actual speakers, can help establish the level of authenticity of literary data.

Katherine Wyly Mille's article, "Ambrose Gonzales's Gullah: What It May Tell Us About Variation," also uses literary dialect for comparative purposes, focusing on the fictional dialect "as a resource to the study of Gullah's history and a background against which to evaluate present-day variation in the creole" (98). Mille incorporates computational linguistic methodologies in her analysis of tense-mood-aspect markers in Gonzales's literary Gullah in an effort to provide evidence for the view that Gonzales, a white man "reared by and among Gullah speakers," who has unfortunately been known to misrepresent his black fictional creations for humorous and patronizing purposes, was despite his social shortcomings, "exceptional in his ability as a white man to write the language in a manner faithful to its models" (99). Marianne Cooley represents another example of a linguist using literary dialect for historical-reconstructive purposes, including in her article "An Early Representation of African American English." She echoes the caveat originally articulated by Raven McDavid, however, who cautioned that literary dialect is more likely to be "suggestive rather than representational," in part because of authorial "selectivity for a literary purpose" ("Design" 2). Cooley reiterates this view and concludes that literary data should therefore be used as "suggestive, corroborative evidence, not as definitive historical evidence" (57).

These are but a few examples of literary dialect analysis undertaken for a variety of purposes, including literary, linguistic, and combinations of both. Certainly there are many other examples of the use of linguistic applications to approach literary texts, with nearly as many goals, theories, and methods as there are analyses. Additional examples with specific applications to the analyses contained in this book are addressed in the appropriate chapters. These sources include, but are not limited to, studies by David Sewell and Sylvia Wallace Holton of Jim's speech in *Adventures of Huckleberry Finn,* analyses by Thadious M. Davis and Mark Lencho of Faulkner's dialectal depictions in *The Sound and the Fury,* an analysis by Charles W. Foster of Charles W. Chesnutt's portrayal of the speech of Julius McAdoo in the conjure tales, and discussions of the black vernacular tradition in literature and Zora Neale Hurston's contributions to that tradition by Karla F. C. Holloway, Barbara Johnson and Henry Louis Gates Jr. in relation to *Their Eyes Were Watching God.* Questions about the linguistic and literary applications of literary dialect analysis need to be discussed in the context of the theories and methods used in the preparation of the analyses contained in this book, as outlined in the next chapter.

3

Methodology

The methodological and theoretical principles developed and advocated here have been informed by several interconnected approaches. Experimentation with quantitative methods borrowed from empirical and computational linguistics, in conjunction with qualitative critical analysis, has made it possible for me to develop a unique approach to analyzing literary dialect. In my research, I have used software programs that allow for rapid, efficient, and accurate analysis of data, and this chapter focuses in part on the technologies and strategies implemented in the analyses of literary speech data that constitute chapters 4 through 7. Additionally, it outlines the principles informing my text and corpus selection, analysis of the data, and application of the results to a discussion of each literary text under consideration.

The methods used across the four individual text analyses are based on a set of shared principles: comprehensive analysis, selection of comparable data across the four analyses, benchmarking or referring to sources outside the literary texts for verification of features, use of sociolinguistic methods for interpretation of data and inferential statistics for analysis, and acknowledgment of the creative nature of the literary texts by employing qualitative methods in the experimental design and application of results.

The first principle is my decision to conduct a comprehensive analysis of the literary speech data for a given text. This means that all of the direct speech data produced by each character whose language use is under consideration is analyzed, rather than only a selected sample. Because computational methods make it possible to analyze large amounts of speech data in a corpus, and because analyzing all the available speech data can provide more accurate results than can anecdotal reports or analyses of smaller samples of the data, there is no reason not to apply the more rigorous standard of comprehensive analysis.

The next principle is the emphasis on comparable data from each of the selected literary texts. There are several components involved in developing comparable corpora for each text. First, the data analyzed for each of the four literary works under consideration here is limited to fictional representations of African American speech by American authors. The rationale for this selection is discussed elsewhere in this book, including in the previous chapter, and it has much to do with the significant influence of the African American presence in American life and letters. Another component of the comparable data principle is my decision to limit analysis exclusively to direct speech from each text. This decision reflects my interest in authorial attempts to reproduce how real people actually talk. Analysis of indirect or reported speech can also be an interesting pursuit, but such analyses raise questions, such as how one character might reproduce the speech of another, beyond the scope of the current discussion. Next is my decision to focus on both phonological and grammatical features of African American dialectal speech in each analysis. The emphasis on grammatical analysis comes as a result of the influence of such scholars as Lee Pederson, who advocates attention to grammar despite the traditional emphasis on phonology in literary dialect analysis, as well as in response to the demands of each of the four texts analyzed, in which grammatical features are deployed as major components of each author's artistic and linguistic strategies. But phonological features are also treated in this discussion as crucial components to literary dialect construction because of extensive authorial reliance in all four texts on alternative respellings of words to denote alternative pronunciations. Finally, there is considerable overlap with respect to the particular linguistic features selected for investigation in each of the four analyses, as shown in tables 3.1 and 3.2 at the end of this chapter. Fifty-two features are considered in the analyses, with about a third of these, or seventeen of the fifty-two, shared among all four texts under consideration. The demands of each individual literary text influenced feature selection, and so in this case, the comparable data principle required flexibility. The methods for feature selection as well as a discussion of the selected features appear below.

The reliability of my analysis and interpretation of the particular linguistic features is supported by benchmarking, which constitutes the third principle. Since one of the goals of my study is to draw conclusions about the effectiveness and relative realism of literary-dialectal depictions of African American speech, reference to external sources provides documentation for the features reproduced in the literary texts and analyzed in the following chapters. In other words, comparison of the literary speech data with the data of real speakers provides a basis for evaluation of the literary data. The sources for real-speaker data include community-based studies and analyses conducted by leading scholars in language use in the African American community as well as corpora of African American speech data, such as those provided by way of survey research, particularly the Linguistic Atlas projects. These sources are discussed in greater detail below.

The fourth principle reflects the importance of using rigorous methods for counting and interpreting the data and includes the use of basic sociolinguistic counting methods as well as the application of inferential statistics. For phonological data, it is possible in many cases to conduct type-and-token counts. This approach, a staple of sociolinguistic analysis, makes it possible to determine relative frequencies of usage of a particular feature. The procedure involves counting the number of occurrences, or tokens, of a particular feature, or type, and counting the total number of possible places in which the feature could occur. By dividing the number of tokens (actual occurrences of the feature) by the number of possible occurrences of a type within a corpus, the resulting percentage is the frequency. For the grammatical features, on the other hand, creating a type-and-token analysis was generally not feasible, in part because of lack of consensus regarding constraints on where features might occur. Such uncertainty, of course, makes it nearly impossible to count the number of opportunities for the feature to occur. For this reason, in most cases grammatical features have been noted as occurring or not occurring in a character's speech, and when feasible, occurrences have been counted and totals given, but statistical testing has not been applied. For the phonological features, however, inferential statistics are engaged as a probability measure to determine whether the distributions of features are indicative of deliberate action on the part of the literary author rather than simply the result of chance or random variation. The statistical methods used are discussed in greater detail below.

Finally, the fifth basic principle is emphasis on the artistic quality of the literary text. At the same time that the methods used here recognize the importance of employing a systematic means of investigation, based on a set of operating principles that apply to each analysis, they also recognize the need for tailoring an individual study to the demands of the text under consideration. While computational methods are excellent for literary dialect analysis, a key consideration here in both selecting the corpora and applying results is emphasis on the investigated texts as works of art rather than simply as sources for data. Thus, the unique qualities of a literary text are not only not ignored but are also essential to the experimental design. Further, foregrounding the artistic value of literary dialect involves a rethinking of some of the traditional goals of literary dialect analysis, particularly in terms of its traditional emphasis on accuracy. Artistic success in terms of language use, characterization, or development of theme, for example, is not the inevitable result of strict linguistic accuracy, or authenticity, as some researchers term it, which can in fact raise artistic problems for a literary text. That is, it is possible for a linguistically valid representation to have unintended literary consequences in terms of readability, believability, and aesthetic value; excessive use of radical respellings, phonetic symbols, or apostrophes to represent sound alternation or deletion, for example, could sabotage an otherwise valuable literary work. These are concerns with which the literary author must be engaged, and therefore the analyst must also be mindful of them. As Cynthia Bernstein observes, "some inaccuracies reflect prejudice or ignorance on the part of the writer, [but] it is fair to say that accuracy is constrained by the very nature of the creative process. A writer uses dialect to convey a message about character or setting in the very limited space of the text" ("Misrepresenting" 340). However, it is equally important to consider that an artistic representation that lacks believability or readability because it resorts to stereotype necessarily fails no less as an artistic achievement than as a linguistic representation. Such a theoretical orientation as the one proposed here, then, requires attention to accuracy but only as one complex factor of literary representations of speech, especially in relation to a writer's artistic goals. This artistic-quality principle is illustrated more specifically below.

For the linguist, the thematic and artistic concerns of the literary analyst as considered herein may not be of central importance. The methods discussed here, however, can also serve goals of linguistic researchers, especially if they are interested in investigating older forms of spoken language, such as those Charles W. Chesnutt seems to have been particularly adept at reproducing and therefore preserving in his literary dialect. Additionally, sociolinguists and variationists might well be interested in what literary dialect can tell them, for example, about how spoken language and variation can function as tools for maintaining solidarity or distance, or collectivity versus individuality, between and among characters within a text. These functions are demonstrated in the upcoming chapters. Further, the chapter on *Huckleberry Finn* offers a perspective on how critical reaction to literary dialect representations can help to illustrate attitudes within and outside of the text; that is, it illustrates how the character of Jim may be interpreted in terms of his speech, and conversely how his speech is perceived and evaluated based on other components of his characterization. For the perceptual dialectologist, this can be compelling information.

In light of the persistent controversy among linguists regarding the value of literary dialect as linguistic evidence, whether the focus is historical reconstruction, language as a marker of social identification, or perceptions and attitudes about variation, it is important to consider that literary evidence need not replace other types of linguistic data and evidence. Rather, as has frequently been the case with more recent, but still historical, varieties of English, the literary data can be used as a supplement, not only bolstering the discussion by adding a new perspective on what constitutes evidence but also by adding depth and dimension to an examination of these most human of activities: production of speech and of art. Especially in cases in which other types of evidence are scarce or nonexistent, spoken forms interpreted by literary authors can be of great value. Additionally, linguists may be less skeptical of the corpus approach proposed here, incorporating computational methods that were until recently not ordinarily applied to literary studies.

Literary researchers wary of linguistic methods as appropriate means for approaching literature may eventually come to appreciate the linguistic methods upon realizing that there need not be (and should not be) a one-size-fits-all approach and that the approach need not (and, again, should not) reduce a work of art merely to a list of numbers and percentages, even though these numbers can provide a useful new approach to considering a literary text. Another key assumption here is that decisions about what constitutes corpora for analysis are based on the individual characteristics of each text, and the corpora are then analyzed not in isolation but as tools for providing new insights into the literary work under consideration. A deliberate aim of the analyses included in the following chapters is to advocate the application of theories and methods traditionally associated with linguistics in the service of enabling richer understanding of literary texts.

The analyses in the following chapters share the basic methodological and theoretical principles outlined above, but beyond that the approaches are diverse because of the diversity of the works under consideration. Each of the four analyses begins with an investigation of a large corpus of literary speech (or corpora in some cases) using computational methods, but consideration of the artistic components of each individual text leads to a unique approach to each analysis. Since my primary interest is in fictional representations of African American speech, there is some commonality among the corpora created for the four studies herein. But there are also important differences in the approaches to corpus selection for each study. For chapter 4, "Articulating Jim: Language and Characterization in *Huckleberry Finn*," the analytical focus is on the speech of Jim, a major character in the novel and producer of the most speech by far by an African American character in the novel. The corpus for that study consists of Jim's direct speech in its entirety, approximately four thousand words, enough data to generate statistically significant results. Also, this data on a single speaker opens a discussion on Jim's functions in the novel and the way speech can be used as part of a characterization strategy while at the same time offering a new approach to analyzing critical reactions to the portrayal of Jim and his language.

Similarly, in chapter 5, "'A High, Holy Purpose': Dialect in Charles W. Chesnutt's Conjure Tales," the data of a single speaker, Julius McAdoo, comprises the corpus. Julius functions as the narrator of all but one of Chesnutt's conjure tales and related stories, from which "Dave's Neckliss" was selected as the source of speech data to investigate. As the narrator of the tales, Julius tells each story in what is presented as his own dialect. Julius reproduces the speech of a variety of characters within each story, including women, men, slaves, free blacks, wealthy white slave owners, uneducated overseers, and others, apparently without any differentiation among the varieties of speech those characters might be imagined to speak. For this reason, Julius's speech in the telling of the tales is interpreted for the purposes of the study as belonging uniquely to him. That is, no attempt has been made to discern variation among speakers within Julius's stories. Rather, his speech, including his representation of dialogue, has been taken at face value and analyzed as if it is simply his own normal speech. Julius's speech in the telling of "Dave's Neckliss" amounts to approximately 4,500 words, again enough to produce statistically significant results.

Conversely, for *The Sound and the Fury* and *Their Eyes Were Watching God*, corpus preparation procedures were more complicated because in each of those novels, there are several characters whose speech data had to be considered. In *The Sound and the Fury*—in which several members of the Gibson family function prominently throughout the novel, as do several other significant African American characters—one corpus consisting of the speech of a single character is not sufficient for a thorough and meaningful analysis. Also, because a different character narrates each of the first three sections of the novel, with a third-person narrator for the fourth and final section, and because the speech of African American characters who appear in more than one section is represented somewhat differently by the narrators of each section, the speech produced by characters who appear in more than one section had to be separated into individual corpora according to the sections in which they appear. For example, four corpora were created for the speech of Dilsey Gibson, who produces approximately 5,000 words: one corpus each for her speech in each of the three sections in which she appears and one corpus for all her speech across the entire novel. In this way it was possible to look at the effects each narrator has on how African American speech is represented as well as how each narrator's representations fit into the portrayal as a whole.

Finally, *Their Eyes Were Watching God,* unique because nearly half of its total text is direct speech, required that the speech of several characters and groups of characters be analyzed in separate corpora in large part because of the sheer amount of talk produced. The protagonist, Janie, produces over 7,000 words; Tea Cake, Janie's third husband, produces nearly 6,000. Additionally, the Eatonville men, whose speech data is analyzed in the aggregate for reasons explained in chapter 7, produce nearly 5,000 words; four other characters produce between 1,300 and 2,800 words apiece. In order to analyze the distribution of features found in the novel and to compare the characteristics of speech produced by different characters, the speech of any character who produced a meaningful amount of talk was analyzed individually and then compared to the results of other speakers in the novel.

Despite the diversity with respect to corpus selection, however, the initial procedures for processing the speech data are similar for all of the texts under consideration here according to the basic principles. After the corpus (or corpora) of speech was selected from the text on the basis of considerations such as the significance of a particular character or characters to the literary work as a whole, the speech data of the selected characters was then digitized if not already available in electronic form. The University of Virginia's Electronic Text Center was the source for the electronic text of *Adventures of Huckleberry Finn* used for the analysis in chapter 4. The University of North Carolina Libraries' online literature project, Documenting the American South, was the source for the electronic version of "Dave's Neckliss," the tale selected from among Chesnutt's conjure stories for the analysis of the speech of narrator Julius McAdoo. For *The Sound and the Fury* and *Their Eyes Were Watching God,* digital texts were not available and both novels were therefore electronically scanned in their entirety. The electronic versions of the texts, whether scanned or already available in electronic form, were then converted to text files. Once the text was in editable, digital form, the specific parts of the text under investigation, that is, the direct speech of the selected characters, had to be extracted and placed into text files established for each corpus.

In analyzing phonological features in the speech of the fictional characters, the next step after corpus selection was to use a text-analysis program to look for unusual spellings. For the first of the four analyses included here, the *Huckleberry Finn* study, which functioned as the pilot study for the research questions addressed in the current discussion, I used the Summer Institute of Linguistics' LinguaLinks program. This program requires an additional step, that the data be marked up (I used SGML markup language for the Twain data) prior to being imported into a LinguaLinks language project set up to accept the data and prepare it for analysis. For the remaining three studies, I used the Oxford University Press WordSmith Tools program, for which there is no further data preparation required before the data from the corpus files can be loaded into the program. That is, plain text can be loaded into WordSmith, eliminating the marking-up step that LinguaLinks requires, a step that can become time-consuming if a researcher has a large corpus or several corpora. With both programs, though, once the data was imported, the programs were used to index and count the number of occurrences of each word in a corpus.

For the analysis of *Huckleberry Finn,* I reviewed the text and made what seemed the logical distinction of differentiating between Jim's direct speech and his reported speech, related by Huck in his narration (e.g., "Jim said we could take deck passage on a steamboat now," 70). While an analysis of Jim's reported speech may be useful, especially if analyzed separately from his direct speech, I decided to focus only on the direct speech. It is possible to be certain that the direct speech represents Twain's portrayal of Jim's language; this is not the case for the reported speech, which depends on Huck's secondhand and possibly unreliable interpretation of Jim's phonological and grammatical features. Similarly, according to the principle of comparable data outlined above, I analyzed only direct speech in each of the other three analyses as well. An interesting issue arises with respect to the free indirect discourse in *Their Eyes Were Watching God,* which Hurston uses throughout the novel to allow the voices of characters to mingle with the narration in highly innovative ways, but given the considerable amount of direct speech also available in that novel for study, I made the decision to limit the discussion to direct speech, once again in accordance with the basic principle of comparable data for each analysis.

Once the data was imported, with LinguaLinks I created a wordform inventory using Jim's speech data to index each occurrence of every word Jim speaks in the novel. Similarly, after importing the corpora of speaker data gathered from the other three texts into files in the WordSmith Tools program, I was able to create wordlists, which like wordform inventories list in alphabetical order each word that appears in the corpus along with the number of occurrences. The lists generated by both programs are useful for analysis of phonological features as represented in literature because the primary strategy available to authors, including those discussed in the chapters to follow, is to use alternative respellings to represent various alternative pronunciations. Not only, then, do LinguaLinks and WordSmith Tools make it possible to view each word separately, but they also allow the analyst to compare variation within a person's speech. For example, it is possible to see how many times Jim in *Huckleberry Finn* reduces the final consonant cluster in a word such as *and* (223) and how many times he does not (6) because LinguaLinks classifies the three variant spellings (*and, an'* and *en*) into three separate entries in the wordform inventory. WordSmith functions similarly. In both programs, a word's spelling is of course the determining factor of placement in the alphabetized inventories, while the LinguaLinks inventory and the WordSmith concordance tool display the sentences in which each instance of a variant appears. This makes it possible to check the environment surrounding the represented feature in order to verify whether it is incorporated appropriately according to descriptive rules developed by linguistic researchers. It also makes it possible to be certain, for example, of the number of times *en* stands for *and* and not for something else, and therefore it is a simple task to review phonological variation in the corpus.

Tracking grammatical features, whether using LinguaLinks or WordSmith Tools, is another story. It is more difficult to search for grammatical features than for phonological items, which rely almost entirely on spelling for representation. For grammatical features, it was necessary to use multiple approaches. These approaches included computerized searches of the texts in electronic form (to look, for instance, for question marks in order to analyze question-formation constructions), as well as use of the LinguaLinks wordform inventory or WordSmith Tools wordlists to search for words that tend to appear in certain grammatical constructions (such as variants of *ain't, no, didn't, don't, wasn't,* and *never* for negation constructions). Additionally, the text had to be perused the old-fashioned way, then tagged by hand and finally searched electronically to count and classify the tags. In general, the grammatical features authors use to denote dialectal speech are difficult to find in a corpus even using a good analysis program. But through close and careful perusal of texts and judicious search-and-tag missions, it is possible to incorporate a variety of tags by building an inventory of characteristics for which to search and strategies for searching. For example, each occurrence of copula deletion could be tagged by typing a notation such as [+cd] directly onto the text file next to the occurrence. In this way, each occurrence of a particular grammatical feature could be noted directly on the electronic text. Once tagged, the marked-up text can itself be imported into the analysis program, which will then sort the corpora by tag using the program's concordance tools. This way, numbers of occurrences can be counted and environments in which the features occur can be evaluated in order to determine whether they have been applied in accordance with established rules and standards of usage among real speakers. Any feature that appears to violate documented rules or standards of usage is of course not included in the counts, although it is a testament to all four authors whose work is analyzed in the following chapters that in their work, such occurrences are rare. Specific instances of any questionable usage by an individual author are discussed in the chapter focusing on that author.

The process of determining which features should be considered in an analysis is similar to making decisions about corpora, in that such decisions can and will vary by literary text. However, regardless of which feature or features are under consideration, knowledge of the real speech characteristics the authors are trying to represent is crucial. The studies included here are based in part on that principle. Lee Pederson (personal communication) notes that an ideal approach is to use field data gathered from real speakers socially and geographically similar to the fictional speakers in order to draw conclusions about the quality of the literary-dialectal representation. Today there is substantial data available for comparison, the result of decades of work by scores of linguistic researchers. For African American varieties of English in particular, there is an excellent array of documentation of phonological and grammatical features. Some notable examples, and the sources used for the four studies discussed here, include the work of Pederson, who gathered data from Missouri speakers with the goal of determining the real-life geographical and social counterparts of speakers in *Huckleberry Finn,* and Geneva Smitherman, whose *Talkin' and Testifyin': The Language of Black America* (1977) documents specific features associated with African American varieties of English. Also consulted is the work of Marianne Cooley and Edgar Schneider, both of whom explore earlier varieties of African American speech, Cooley via the study of dialect as represented in colonial plays and Schneider in part by consulting the tapes of African American speakers made in the 1930s for the Archive of Folk Songs. Sources for verifying syntactic and morphological features of African American varieties of English include Stefan Martin and Walt Wolfram, Salikoko Mufwene, Lisa Green, Ralph Fasold, and William Labov. Additionally, the work of Wolfram, Green, Donald Winford, and Guy Bailey and Erik Thomas provides documentation of phonological features, as does the voluminous data from the Linguistic Atlas projects. Especially useful for the studies included here were the *Linguistic Atlas of the Middle Atlantic States* (*LAMSAS*), directed by William A. Kretzschmar Jr., and the *Linguistic Atlas of the Gulf States* (*LAGS*), directed by Lee Pederson. *LAMSAS* provides substantial data for speakers who would have been neighbors and contemporaries of the fictional North Carolinians who people the conjure tales of Charles W. Chesnutt, first published in book form in 1899. Similarly, the Florida speakers interviewed for *LAGS* were geographically and generationally similar to the characters in Zora Neale Hurston's *Their Eyes Were Watching God* (1937), and other Gulf States residents interviewed for *LAGS* provide data useful to an evaluation of the dialect spoken by the fictional Gibson family of *The Sound and the Fury* (1929). For verification of the dialect in *Huckleberry Finn,* published in 1884 and set "forty to fifty years" earlier, according to the original title page, finding data from real speakers who were Jim's contemporaries is nearly impossible, but the Atlas data from speakers only a few generations younger supports much of what Twain represents, as does more recent data. Please see table 3.1 at the end of this chapter for a list of the phonological features considered in the analyses, the sources used to document them, and literary examples of the features. Similarly, table 3.2, also at the end of the chapter, describes the grammatical features investigated in the analyses, notes the sources consulted to document each feature, and provides examples.[1]

The selection of features analyzed in each of the four texts was determined iteratively, by reviewing the scholarship documenting phonological and grammatical features of African American English (AAE) and then looking in the text for those features, as well as by examining the literary texts for any nonstandard representations and then looking to the scholarship in order to determine whether the representations coincide with documented features. As explained above, the resulting list of features studied for each analysis varies somewhat from one text to the next according to what is in each text and also because the methodology continued to refine itself as I became more adept at analyzing texts. For the analysis of Jim's speech in *Huckleberry Finn*, after reviewing the scholarship and considering the contents of Jim's speech, I selected thirty-four phonological and grammatical features to focus on. The goals were to try to confirm Twain's representations with the existing scholarship and to examine the data in order to determine how Jim's language contributes to his overall characterization and, consequently, how the representation and responses to it reveal interesting attitudes toward some spoken varieties of English. In the analysis of "Dave's Neckliss," which may be the most complex of the four works discussed here in terms of how dialect is represented as well as with respect to the author's relationship to African American vernacular speech, more than forty features are considered. Additionally, Chesnutt's use of dialect seems to provide useful data regarding earlier linguistic forms, which significantly impacts which features are analyzed.

For *The Sound and the Fury,* the focus is on the distribution of features that Faulkner uses in representing the speech of his characters and whether or not there is variation by character and by section of the novel in the features and frequencies of occurrence. The analysis considers the ways language can be made to function as a tool to create distance or solidarity and, as the analysis of Jim's language and critical reactions to it and to him also shows, how attitudes about language varieties and their speakers are sometimes inseparable. Dialect figures prominently in Faulkner's character development, and the features considered have much to do with the function of dialect in illuminating the relationships between characters. Finally, in the analysis of *Their Eyes Were Watching God,* various features are compared among characters in order to determine how spoken language functions simultaneously to build and maintain community and to perpetuate social divisions based on class and gender. The emphasis in the novel on the value of oral tradition is subtly juxtaposed with the revelation that not all members of the community are free to participate in the same ways in this celebrated component of African American life. Hurston's emphasis results in an analysis that focuses less on individual features than on other characteristics of language.

For the phonological data, tables in each chapter, supplemented by additional tables in the appendix, where necessary, illustrate the type-and-token ratios and the frequencies of occurrence of the selected features for each character under consideration. According to the methodological principles set out above, *t*-tests were performed for each analysis in order to determine whether the frequency is statistically significant for each feature at a ninety-five percent or greater level of confidence, and, where applicable, whether differences between characters or between sections are statistically significant, also at a ninety-five percent or greater level of confidence, and tables are annotated accordingly. For the grammatical features, on the other hand, as discussed above, because creating a type-and-token breakdown was in most cases not feasible, the tables simply indicate occurrence or non-occurrence of a feature and in some cases provide occurrence counts.

The ways the frequencies and other data provided in the tables are used and interpreted in the analyses in the following chapters vary in terms of what the dialectal features indicate about their function in the particular work of literature being analyzed. It is important to note that data is not being used here to argue that the feature distributions and frequencies are necessarily comparable with those of real speakers, or that they indicate that some literary speakers are more "authentic" than others. Also, I have not compared frequencies to try to determine whether any particular feature is more or less authentic an indicator than any other, in part because such value seems nearly impossible to assign with any kind of objectivity. Perhaps the data will be useful to researchers interested in trying to make such determinations. In most cases, the frequencies for phonological features indicate what I think are believable frequencies for feature production. Instead of simply sprinkling the dialogue with dialectal features to give the speech the "flavor" of dialect, each of the four authors has produced what appears by virtue of their consistency at representing features, sincere attempts to represent real speech. Working from this assumption, which itself was reached by way of the quantitative analyses, I have applied the results toward establishing new ways of thinking about literary-linguistic data, including what can be learned about the literary text but also what can be learned about how writers and readers interpret and understand language variation. The data in all four of the analyses could conceivably be applied to a discussion of the prevalence of particular features at a particular time and geographical

Table 3.1 Phonological Features of AAE Considered in Analyses

Feature	Sources of Documentation	Authors Using Feature* (Examples from Literature)
Vocalization of postvocalic /r/	Bailey and Thomas, Cooley, Smitherman	All (before→befo': Hurston)
Loss of /r/ after consonants and in unstressed syllables	Pederson (1965)	All (from→fum: Faulkner)
Intervocalic /r/ loss with syllable loss	Pederson (1965), Smitherman	All (different→diffunt: Twain)
Vocalization or loss of unstressed syllabic /r/	Bailey and Thomas	Chesnutt, Faulkner, Hurston (doctor→doctah: Hurston)
Stopping of syllable-initial fricatives	Cooley, Pederson (1965), Smitherman, Wolfram	All (that→dat: Faulkner)
Stopping of voiceless interdental fricatives	LAGS, LAMSAS	Chesnutt, Faulkner, Hurston (with→wid: Faulkner)
Labialization of interdental fricatives	Bailey and Thomas, Smitherman	All (both→bofe: Chesnutt)
Consonant cluster reduction, especially word final	Green (2002), LAMSAS, Pederson (1965), Wolfram	All (child→chile: Hurston)
Deletion of initial or medial unstressed syllable	LAMSAS, Pederson (1965), Smitherman, Wolfram	All (about→bout: Twain)
Final unstressed /n/ for /ŋ/ in present participle	LAGS, LAMSAS, Pederson (1965)	All (saying→sayin: Hurston)
Other alternation of final unstressed /n/ for /ŋ/	LAGS, LAMSAS, Pederson (1965)	All (evening→evenin: Hurston)
Alternation of /b/ or /ß/ for /v/	LAMSAS	Chesnutt (evening→ebening)
Metathesis of final /s/ + stop	Cooley, LAGS, LAMSAS	Chesnutt (ask→ax)
/t/ in final position	Pederson (1965)	Twain (across→acrost)
/j/ after velar stops /k/ and /g/ before vowels followed by /r/	Pederson (1965)	Twain, Chesnutt (care→k'yar: Twain; care→keer: Chesnutt)
Word-initial addition of /h/	LAMSAS	Chesnutt (it→hit)
Word-initial loss of /h/	LAMSAS	Chesnutt (house→'ouse)
Alternation of word-initial unaspirated /w/ for /hw/	LAMSAS	Chesnutt (while→w'ile)
Alternation of diphthongs /aI/ for /ɔI/	LAMSAS, Pederson (1965)	All (boiler→biler: Twain)

Continued on the next page.

Table 3.1 Continued

Feature	Sources of Documentation	Authors Using Feature* (Examples from Literature)
Alternation of /e/ for /ɔ/	LAMSAS, Pederson (1965)	Twain, Chesnutt (because→ bekase: Twain)
Merger of /ɛ/ and /ɪ/	LAGS, LAMSAS, Winford	All (get→git: Faulkner)
Glide reduction of /aɪ/ to /a/	Smitherman	Chesnutt, Hurston (I→Ah: Hurston)
Alternation of /a/ for /ɛ/ before /r/	Common in 19th-century literary sources	Chesnutt (learn→l'arn)
Alternation of /ɑ/ for /æ/	LAMSAS	Chesnutt (master→marster)
Alternation of /e/ for /i/ before /r/ and /l/	LAMSAS	Chesnutt (real→rale)

*Author is listed here only if the given feature is analyzed for his or her text.

location, for example, but I have attempted only limited such applications here. My approach is mindful of the data sources as works of art and as potential linguistic evidence; therefore, I do not attempt to argue that a particular feature, combination of features, or frequency signifies the same set of meanings in every literary work.

As I hope the following chapters will show, analysis of literary dialect using computational methods can add new dimensions to the study of both spoken and literary language. Additionally, the combination of methods borrowed from empirical linguistics, motivated by my interest in language variation and text analysis, with qualitative approaches generated by an appreciation for the artistic value not only of the dialectal representations but also of the works of literature themselves, represents the ultimate goal of this book, which is to integrate two approaches to studying language into one.

Table 3.2 Grammatical Features of AAE Considered in Analyses

Feature	Sources of Documentation	Authors Using Feature* (Examples from Literature)
Auxiliary and copula deletion	Smitherman, Wolfram	All (What he gwyne to do?: Twain)
Be + done for habitual, future, or conditional states	Green (2002), Labov, Smitherman	Hurston (If Ah wuz, you'd be done woke me up callin' me.)
Completive been for SAE have been	Smitherman	Hurston (we been kissin'- friends for twenty years)
Done + been (perfective)	Smitherman	Hurston (Ah done been on mah knees)
Done + verb (resultant states)	Green (1998), Labov, Smitherman	All (I s'pose yer all done hearn befo' now: Chesnutt)
Simple past done	Labov, Smitherman	Twain, Chesnutt, Hurston (So I done it: Twain)
Multiple negation	Martin and Wolfram	All (He couldn' tell no lie: Chesnutt)
But negative	Smitherman	Chesnutt (Dey wa'n't but th'ee er fo' poun's lef'.)
Negative inversion (negative auxiliary before negative indefinite NP)	Green (2002), Martin and Wolfram	Chesnutt, Faulkner, Hurston (Dey didn' nobody answer: Chesnutt)
Noninverted questions	Martin and Wolfram	Chesnutt, Faulkner, Hurston (w'at fer yer won' speak ter me?: Chesnutt)
Subject-verb nonconcord (includes 3rd-person singular s-deletion, 1st-person singular/plural -s, and leveling to was or weren't)	Labov, Schneider (1997), Smitherman, Wolfram	All (Ef she say anything: Faulkner; I knows: Faulkner; You wuz los': Twain; He warn't no wise man: Twain)
Unmarked past	Fasold, Smitherman, Wolfram	All (he didn' tel Dilsey come on the plantation: Chesnutt)
Regularized past	Fasold, Wolfram	All (he seed dis gal a-cryin': Chesnutt)
Relative pronoun deletion or alternation	Martin and Wolfram	Chesnutt, Hurston (a gemman over on Rockfish w'at died: Chesnutt)
Possessive they	Mufwene, Smitherman	Chesnutt, Hurston (dey wicked ways: Chesnutt)
Pronoun apposition	Smitherman	Hurston (And Sam, he know so much into things.)
Undifferentiated pronoun reflexives	Mufwene, Smitherman	Chesnutt, Hurston (deyselves: Chesnutt)
Object pronoun them for subject pronoun those	Smitherman	Chesnutt, Hurston (one er dem big waggins: Chesnutt)

Continued on the next page.

Table 3.2 Continued

Feature	Sources of Documentation	Authors Using Feature* (Examples from Literature)
Plural -s deletion	Kessler, Smitherman	Twain (Not if it's forty year!)
Hypercorrect plural -s	Smitherman	Hurston (Folkses, de sun is goin' down.)
Regularized plural	LAGS, LAMSAS	Hurston (usin' yo' body to wipe his foots on.)
A-prefixing	Wolfram	Twain, Chesnutt (I see a light a-comin': Twain)
Existential it/they with indefinite subject	Green (2002), Martin and Wolfram, Smitherman	Chesnutt, Hurston (It's so many people never seen de light at all: Hurston)
Tell + say serial verb construction	Martin and Wolfram	Hurston (mah husband tell me say no first class booger would have me.)
Indignant come as semiauxiliary with verb + -ing	Martin and Wolfram, Spears	Hurston (You come makin' out ah wuz dreamin'.)
Counterfactual call with reflexive pronoun and verb + -ing	Martin and Wolfram	Hurston (if dat's what you call yo'self doin', Ah don't thank yuh for it.)
For-to constructions	LAGS, LAMSAS	Chesnutt (he'd be glad fer ter do w'at he could)

*Author is listed here only if the given feature is analyzed for his or her text.

4

Articulating Jim

Language and Characterization in *Huckleberry Finn*

Mark Twain's *Adventures of Huckleberry Finn* (1884) remains an icon of American literature in part because of its standing as a flashpoint for debates about art and about politics, especially the politics of race, in American life. While no single analysis can hope to address every level of complexity embodied in the novel itself as well as in the discussions and debates surrounding it, it is possible to add an interesting dimension to the discussions of race generated by *Huckleberry Finn,* specifically in this case with respect to the character of Jim, using the methods described in the previous chapter. In response to the persuasive interpretations of Eric Lott, Toni Morrison, Frederick Woodward and Donnarae MacCann, and others who conclude that Jim is represented negatively and stereotypically, this chapter explores the characterization of Jim through an analysis of his speech as represented by Twain. The procedures used, as outlined in chapter 3, combine a quantitative linguistic inquiry with a more traditional critical approach in an attempt to determine how representations of speech can be used in characterization in general as well as in the characterization of Jim in particular. As discussed in chapter 3, the quantitative approach allows for an empirical analysis of the actual language used, while the qualitative critical approach makes it possible to keep in mind the artistic value of the work. As a novel long noted for the complexity of its themes, *Huckleberry Finn* not only lends itself, but also demands that attention be paid, to the relationships among its artistic, linguistic, and even political intricacies.

One of the great contradictions in *Huckleberry Finn* is in its interpretation as social commentary. For some readers, it is a manifesto against racism, culminating in the scene in which Huck chooses his friendship with Jim over what he believes to be the well-being of his own soul. It is hard to argue that Twain is not in fact making such a statement in light of the power of that scene. On the other hand, critics such as Morrison, Lott, and Woodward and

MacCann point to what they view as Twain's frequent lapses into stereotype in his formulation of Jim's character. The question arises as to whether it is possible for a work that in many ways attempts to take an antiracist stance also to contain unexamined racial assumptions of its own. A more recent analogy may help to illustrate this dichotomy as well as to introduce the main part of the discussion.

The example comes from a 1969 *New York Times* article about poverty and hunger in the rural South. The story profiles Dr. Donald Gatch, a white South Carolina physician who was forced to leave his job at Beaufort County Memorial Hospital when his reports of serious malnutrition among African Americans living in poverty in South Carolina were met with hostile skepticism by his white colleagues and patients. It is surprising today to read this decades-old feature story that describes, without exactly naming, the deep denial in which much of middle-class white America was then apparently mired with respect to the existence of poverty and hunger in the United States. Dr. Gatch was the subject of a statement signed by every other white doctor in Beaufort County condemning what they called his "unsubstantiated allegations," insisting that the "rare cases of infant malnutrition" in Beaufort County were the result of "parental inexperience, indifference or gross neglect" (qtd. in Bigart 1:1). Dr. Gatch's white patients responded to his carefully documented and easily verifiable reports of widespread hunger and disease with a permanent boycott.[1] The *Times* attempts to explain:

> Chronic hunger seems so remote in this bounteous land that reports of extreme malnutrition among Negroes in the rural South, among migrant farm workers, among Mexican-Americans and reservation Indians have been set down as exaggerations and lies, the observers frequently assailed as charlatans or do-gooders who would sap the initiative of the hungry poor by expanding "giveaway" Federal food programs. (Bigart 1:1)

The article reports but does not challenge the questionable basis for the widespread denial of Dr. Gatch's observations. The belief that hunger could not possibly exist in a land of plenty is unconvincing and illogical in its failure to consider unequal access to food and other resources. Such inequality exists, of course, regardless of the overall abundance of resources and is apparent in the areas of poverty that occupy cities and rural areas throughout the United States, then as now. However, the article's failure to question the shaky rationale of Gatch's opponents or offer an alternative explanation raises questions about the newspaper's own editorial position. Indeed, the article relates the shocking unfairness and even cruelty, without naming it as such, of the reactions to reports of extreme poverty and consequent malnutrition and disease in its typical "objective" style of reporting and without ever mentioning the word "racism." A reader today may begin to question the *Times*'s stance upon viewing a large photograph accompanying the article. The photograph's caption identifies only (white) Dr. Gatch and not the three African Americans also pictured: a tiny girl whose limbs are bent by rickets, a young woman gazing down at the girl as the doctor examines her, and an elderly man sitting behind the doctor with his eyes nearly closed. The caption accompanying the article's other photo also fails to identify its subjects, an African American woman and little boy. Today it seems to be a clearly racist editorial decision not to identify non-white subjects of photographs, perhaps indicative of the *Times*'s racism even while that newspaper, ironically, chronicles and critiques the racism of others. It appears that the *Times* was earnestly attempting to chronicle the consequences of racism, but at the same time it was apparently oblivious to its own racist practices.

The *Times* article offers an interesting parallel to *Adventures of Huckleberry Finn,* in many ways an antiracist text, but also one which even as it questions bigotry still is perceived by many as falling short of challenging the liberal racism of the predominantly white Northerners who comprised much of its first audience. Those readers, possibly like many readers of the *Times* article, may have found reassurance in the novel's portrayal of the overt racism of white Southerners without having to challenge their own possible racist views. Also, contradictions within Twain's own racial attitudes are apparent in *Huckleberry Finn,* analogous with those of the *Times* in the article under discussion here.

Additionally, the hostile responses of many white South Carolinians to Dr. Gatch's words and actions may sound to modern readers a lot like some of the initial reactions to *Huckleberry Finn.* Evan Carton relates Philip Foner's 1958 account of the indignation of some whites at the time the novel was published, who took offense at the novel's depiction of "endemic lying, the petty thefts, the denigration of respectability and religion, the bad language, and the bad grammar" (qtd. in Carton 155). Carton argues that such objections "reveal[ed] deeper motives through references to Twain's 'hideously subversive' depiction of brutal, corrupt, and exploitative white characters and of a heroic, morally superior black one" (155). Twain, as Arnold Rampersad reminds us, "wrote as a Southerner in a period of intense reaction against blacks" (*"Adventures"* 109). But critics of Twain's representation of Jim are not limited to those who believe he is portrayed in an unrealistically positive way. A number of critics, such as Eric Lott, Frederick Woodward and Donnarae MacCann, and Toni Morrison, charge rather that Jim is portrayed as a racist caricature, a "buffoon" in a "clownsuit" in Morrison's words (388). Their treatments of *Huckleberry Finn* take Twain to task for what Morrison calls his "over-the-top minstrelization of Jim" (388), a charge which, as we will see, is not without justification. On the other hand, most critics, including many of the same writers who are critical of Twain's depiction of Jim, acknowledge the superiority of Jim's moral character over nearly every other character in the novel. David L. Smith sums up this view in his description of Jim as portrayed by Twain as a man who is "compassionate, shrewd, thoughtful, self-sacrificing and . . . wise" (92).

While many critics have considered how Jim is represented in the text of *Huckleberry Finn,* whether that representation is discussed with respect to racial stereotypes or morality or both, and whether it focuses solely on Jim's qualities or also on those of other characters and their behavior toward him, few have approached the question of how Jim is characterized via an examination of Twain's representation of his speech. Some of those who have, such as Walter M. Brasch, Sylvia W. Holton, William E. Lenz, David Sewell, Arnold Rampersad, and Shelley Fisher Fishkin, offer interesting and useful discussions, but with the exceptions of Holton and Sewell have emphasized the significance of the literary dialect more than the specific linguistic features Jim exhibits in his speech. Sewell notes only three features, offering no discussion of the linguistic significance of the features as opposed to the literary function the features are described as serving. Holton offers a list, if not an analysis, of five phonological features and three grammatical features that she identifies in a short passage of Jim's speech that have also been identified in real speakers.

There are a number of critical treatments of *Huckleberry Finn* that focus on the accuracy of Twain's representation of language varieties as his characters speak them. Much attention has been given to Twain's note at the outset of the novel that his characters' dialectal variation has not been represented "in a haphazard fashion, or by guesswork; but painstakingly, and with the trustworthy guidance and support of personal familiarity with these several forms of speech" (xxxii). More linguistically oriented treatments of *Huckleberry Finn,* such as those by David Carkeet, Lee A. Pederson, and Curt Rulon seek to verify Twain's assertion or to discredit it. Some of those treatments, especially Pederson's, which consult the data of actual Missouri speakers, do so more effectively than others, but in general the treatments tend not to concern themselves with critical applications with respect to characterization. That is, they do not address the way the representation of a character's speech serves to identify his or her nature, if it does. Holton comes close, briefly discussing what she calls the "fusion of dialect speech and characterization" (89) in her discussion of *Huckleberry Finn.* She argues that Jim's speech "individuate[s]" him (88), but her linguistic analysis in support of the statement is limited, perhaps befitting a literary/nonlinguist audience as well as reflecting the wide scope of her study, which documents African American speech as it is represented in American fiction since 1790.

As noted above, a principal aim of this chapter is to attempt to incorporate into the traditional critical approach a comprehensive linguistic inquiry into African American English (AAE) as it is spoken by Jim and by real speakers in order to reach a place where conclusions about Jim's characterization based on his language can conscientiously be made. In doing so, the first step is to look specifically at linguistic features of Jim's speech to determine whether or not they correspond substantially to documented features of AAE. Access to examples of real speech produced by African Americans of the 1830s and 1840s, when the novel takes place, is of course limited, but there are a number of good sources available of examples of older AAE, as reviewed in chapter 3.

After determining the level of accuracy at which Jim's speech is represented, the next step is to analyze the portrayal of features to try to determine if the character of Jim is stereotyped by the depiction of his speech, and if he is, how. One question addressed here is whether an author can stereotype a character through the representation of the character's speech. Also, there is the related question of whether the presence of particular linguistic features might cause readers to perceive a character as embodying a stereotype. Also addressed are the complicated interactions between actual linguistic characterization and stereotyped characterizations that have nothing to do with speech representation, or whether it is possible for critics to make judgments about Twain's use of dialect that may be based on nonlinguistic factors. Finally, there is the question of what the depiction of Jim, including his linguistic behavior, might say about Mark Twain. The pages to follow consider these issues.

In addition to the methodological discussion in chapter 3, it is necessary to add a qualifier here. In the analysis of Jim's speech data, there are certainly documented features of AAE that were not selected for consideration but that can be found in Jim's speech. There are also documented features that do not occur in Jim's speech. Conversely, there are features present in Jim's speech which do not correspond to documented features of AAE, including features associated with Standard American English (SAE) but also a few occurrences of what some critics interpret as eye dialect. More about this claim later. But for the most part, variation within Jim's speech is not particularly problematical to the analysis because such variation is of course common to real speakers. Further, no speaker of AAE, real or fictional, will incorporate every possible feature associated with AAE into his or her speech, produce speech that contains no non-AAE features or AAE features shared with other American English varieties, or produce speech that contains the same AAE features as every or even any other speaker. Therefore, I decided to focus on specific features, a determination I also followed in the remaining three analyses in chapters 5 through 7. For the analysis of Jim's speech, the initial goal was to determine whether or not Jim's speech is represented accurately in order to pursue the question of whether the speech contributes toward an overall negative or stereotypical characterization of Jim. The results of the analysis show that it is possible to do so without tracking every possible AAE feature or looking for every possible deviance from AAE in Jim's speech.

For the thirty-one features under investigation, I selected some of the more salient features associated with dialectal AAE, such as final consonant cluster reduction and auxiliary and copula deletion, according to the sources reviewed in chapter 3. Jim's speech data itself also yielded features for investigation, and features both salient and in some cases intriguing were selected in order to determine whether or not they can be documented as coinciding with those of real speakers. For example, a particularly interesting feature because of its apparent rarity among speakers today is the alternation of /e/ for /ɔ/, as documented by Lee Pederson in his fieldwork in Missouri and by the *Dictionary of American Regional English* (*DARE*). This feature, which also occurs in Charles W. Chesnutt's conjure stories and is discussed further in the following chapter, occurs in the work of both Twain and Chesnutt

Table 4.1 Syllable-Initial Fricative Stopping in Jim's Speech

Examples (Number of Occurrences)	Nonoccurrence (Number)
dah (16)	there (0)
dan (1)	than (0)
dat (87)	that (2)
de (238)	the (1)
dem (7)	them (0)
den (26)	then (0)
dese (4)	these (0)
dey (64)	they (0)
dis (14)	this (0)
Total=457 (99%*)	Total=3 (1%*)

*Significant at p<.05.

exclusively as a variant of the stressed vowel in *because,* represented by Twain as *bekase, 'kase,* or *'kaze.* Jim uses this vowel pronunciation exclusively when expressing the meaning *because,* with fourteen occurrences of the variants using /e/ and no occurrences using /ɔ/, which it was assumed for the purposes of this analysis would be represented with the standard spelling *because.*

As with the alternation of /e/ for /ɔ/, the other thirteen phonological features investigated also tend to occur in Jim's speech at high relative frequencies. In other words, an analysis of Jim's speech indicates many occurrences of the targeted features and far fewer instances of nonoccurrence. It should be noted that for the phonological data, rather than reporting every example that fits a particular feature description, a number of words were highlighted to illustrate each of the features under investigation, and occurrences of dialectally represented forms were then compared with occurrences of their standard counterparts. Jim's complete phonological data is shown in appendix A, but an example is in order here. For one particular feature, stopping of syllable-initial fricatives, I selected nine words that provide environments in which this feature might be articulated and analyzed them for occurrence of the feature, as shown in table 4.1. Because of this procedure, there may be a few additional items that Jim pronounces in ways that correspond to the scholarly documentation as well as items that do not. However, of the words selected for investigation, every occurrence and nonoccurrence in places where occurrence is possible has been included in the data counts so that relative frequencies for Jim's use of a variant can

Table 4.2 Phonological Features in Jim's Speech

Feature	Example from Text	Tokens/Types	Frequency*
Vocalization of postvocalic /r/	hear→heah	47/103	46%
Loss of /r/ after consonants	hundred→hund'd	13/13	100%
Intervocalic /r/ loss with syllable loss	different→diffunt	7/8	87.5%
Stopping of syllable-initial fricatives	that→dat	457/460	99%
Labialization of interdental fricatives	both→bofe	11/12	92%
Consonant cluster reduction	ain't→ain'	313/346	90%
Deletion of unstressed syllable	about→'bout	42/48	87.5%
/n/ for /ŋ/ in present participle	going→goin'	57/59	97%
Other alternation of /n/ for /ŋ/	evening→evenin'	11/13	85%
/t/ in final position	across→acrost	9/11	82%
/j/ after velar stops /k/ and /g/	care→k'yer	6/7	86%
Alternation of /aɪ/ for /ɔɪ/	point→p'int	48/51	94%
Alternation of /e/ for /ɔ/	because→bekase	14/14	100%
Merger of /ɛ/ and /ɪ/	again→agin	52/54	96%

*Significant at p<.05.

reasonably be assessed. Table 4.2 provides an example for each of the selected phonological features from Jim's speech and shows the relative frequency of occurrence for each feature, along with the type-and-token ratio for the total number of occurrences out of the number of possible occurrences.

For grammatical features, twelve of the seventeen documented features considered for the analysis are found to be present in Jim's speech. Table 4.3 lists the seventeen grammatical features investigated here, provides an approximate count of occurrences for each of the twelve features found, and lists examples of the feature from Jim's speech data. For grammatical features that lend themselves to frequency counts, those that occur in one hundred percent of the places where occurrence is possible are so noted. When a feature occurs fewer than ten times, the number of occurrences is given. For more than ten occurrences, the presence of the feature is noted as "frequent." The consistency with which Twain incorporates dialectal features in Jim's speech throughout the novel, along with minimal examples of stereotyped features, reveal that Twain was a sensitive (if not flawless) interpreter of the phonology and grammar associated with black speech.

Table 4.3 Grammatical Features Investigated in Jim's Speech

Feature	Presence in Jim's Speech (Occurrences)	Example from Text
Auxiliary and copula deletion	Yes (frequent)	What he gwyne to do?
Be + done	No	
Done + verb	Yes (2)	She done broke loose.
Done + been	No	
Simple past done	Yes (4)	So I done it.
Multiple negation	Yes (frequent)	I couldn' get nuffn else.
Noninverted questions	No	
3rd-person singular s-deletion	Yes (frequent)	How much do a king get?
1st-person singular/plural -s	Yes (frequent)	I knows what I knows.
Leveling to was	Yes (100%)	You wuz los'.
Leveling to weren't	Yes (100%)	He warn't no wise man.
Unmarked past	Yes (frequent)	I begin to git oneasy.
Regularized past	Yes (1)	I knowed [they] wuz goin'
Plural -s deletion	Yes (2)	Not if it's forty year!
Hypercorrect plural -s	No	
Tell + say	No	
A-prefixing	Yes (frequent)	I see a light a-comin'.

Relative frequencies such as those given for the phonological data can be used to compare the speech of particular speakers. But the goal here is not to compare Jim's speech to any other speaker; there is no "ideal speaker" of AAE or of any other language variety, for that matter, to whom other speakers can be said to measure up or not measure up. Rather, the intention is to look for occurrences of AAE features in order to try to determine whether Twain represents Jim's speech authentically, that is, in a way that indicates a real rather than stereotypical awareness of and sensitivity to the speech of real speakers of AAE. After reviewing Jim's direct speech in its entirety and comparing it to features of AAE as identified by some of the top scholars in the field, it is clear that Twain's statement, that his dialectal representations "have not been done in a hap-hazard fashion, or by guesswork; but pains-takingly" (xxxii), is a defensible one. In both phonology and grammar, Twain incorporated features that have been identified with African American speakers in the scholarship, and he did so in a way that reveals his understanding of how these features functioned in real speech. But the controversy surrounding the characterization of Jim and of his speech can by no means be resolved solely by way of a determination of the level of accuracy achieved in dialectal representation. Rather, the data must be applied to a wider analysis of the text itself as well as to critical responses to it.

There are a number of credible critical accounts that argue that Jim is in some ways represented unfairly or stereotypically in *Huckleberry Finn*. However, if the results here are considered, such a representation is not created by way of Twain's depiction of Jim's actual linguistic behavior. It is important to note, though, that this conclusion, assuming that Jim's speech is represented with reasonable accuracy as argued herein, necessitates acceptance of the linguist's view that all language varieties are rule-governed and that all are equally valid as systems of expression. Unfortunately, many individuals do not accept this assumption, and African American English is among the varieties of American English most frequently stigmatized, especially by nonspeakers but not exclusively so, just as is the case with many American regional and social varieties. For example, Dennis Preston demonstrates the prevalence of unfavorable evaluations of particular, especially Southern, varieties of American English, including by speakers of those varieties. He cites in particular negative self-evaluations of Indiana speakers, whose "linguistic insecurity," according to Preston "stems from associations with Southern speech" ("Folk" 348). It therefore follows that a reader who believes that AAE is not an acceptable variety may perceive Jim to be negatively portrayed by way of his speech simply because it contains features associated with AAE. Further, Preston has also argued that folklorists' respelled representations of any kind of dialectal variation may result in possible negative perceptions by readers, such as that the represented individuals are from lower-ranked social classes than those they are actually from and that they possess lower levels of education than they actually do, presumably without regard to the accuracy of the speech representation ("Syndrome" 334). I contend that such perceptions are the result of attitudes about class, region, and race, attitudes with which language has little more to do than guilt by association. Unfortunately, these kinds of attitudes represent deeply held beliefs that are difficult to separate from language and even more difficult to overcome.

Not every critic would agree with my assertion that Jim is not negatively portrayed by his speech, nor with my assessment of the accuracy with which Twain represents Jim's speech. For an example of the latter, David Sewell, while asserting that Jim's speech is "part of a positive characterization" (205) rather than a component of the minstrelization of Jim that Toni Morrison and others describe, resists arguments that Jim's speech is in many ways representative of AAE: "The fact that . . . Jim does not speak the exaggerated farcical dialect of the blackface minstrels has misled critics into describing his speech as 'realistic' black dialect. It is, in fact, romanticized folk speech" (207). In attributing to critics a dependence on a questionable either/or relationship between exaggerated speech and realistic speech, Sewell asks for acceptance of an in-between interpretation of Jim's language without offering linguistic evidence, such as features analysis, and ignores studies that produce such evidence, especially including the linguistic surveys of older speakers in Missouri conducted by Lee Pederson in the 1960s. And as I have tried to show, my analysis also seriously challenges Sewell's view that Jim's speech is not realistic.

Even though a good case can be made that Twain accurately represents the speech of Jim, a man barred from literacy because of his status as a slave, and whose speech contains a number of features associated with AAE, some critics charge that Twain uses "eye dialect" to characterize him. According to James S. Leonard and Thomas A. Tenney, eye dialect

> pretends to represent nonstandardness by variant (in some cases, merely phonetic) spellings, though the pronunciations represented may actually be regionally acceptable. The speech of Jim and other black characters in the novel is marked by extreme forms of eye dialect, while that of whites usually is not; the result exaggerates the ignorance and/or deviance of black speakers as compared to white. ("Introduction" 5)

A linguistic analysis of Jim's speech both can and cannot challenge such a view. It can answer the charge of Twain's use of "eye dialect": Most of Twain's respellings for Jim, and also for Huck and the other characters—nearly all of whom, regardless of race, are represented as speaking something other than Standard American English (SAE)—actually do in most cases indicate alternative pronunciations that have been documented as regionally or socially distributed, including in the speech of some African American speakers. With a few exceptions, such as *wuz* for *was,* although this could indicate a phonological variant, /wʌz/ compared to /wəz/, or be an indicator of stress, most representations are not simply misspellings that would be pronounced the same as in SAE, or even necessarily as in regional standards.

A linguistic analysis cannot defend Twain if the question is about whether

Jim's speech is "marked by [more] extreme forms" of variation than that of white characters. The answer to that question may well be affirmative. In a recent analysis of the speech representations of the character of Huck Finn in the two novels in which he appears, *Adventures of Tom Sawyer* (1876) and *Huckleberry Finn,* Susan Tamasi found that Twain reduced considerably the frequency of dialectal articulations in Huck's speech between the two novels. In *Tom Sawyer,* Huck is not the main character but rather functions as an adjunct to Tom; Huck is a colorful but ultimately illustrative character "who does not attend school," which his dialectal speech seems intended to reflect, and "who just plays the side-kick to Tom" (Tamasi 141). Jim can be seen to serve similarly illustrative purposes in *Huckleberry Finn.* Tamasi found in her analysis of several grammatical and phonological features that Huck's frequency of nonstandard feature-articulation dropped from 92 percent in *Tom Sawyer* to just over 73 percent in the novel that bears his own name. This may indicate a deliberate move by Twain toward increased standardization for his protagonist. Still, among the dialectal features analyzed by Tamasi in the speech of Huck in *Huckleberry Finn,* there are several that coincide with those found in Jim's speech. For example, both Jim and Huck produce several occurrences of simple-past *done* (Jim: *So I done it*). Also, both Jim and Huck produce *was*-leveling (Jim: *You wuz los'*) in 100 percent of possible occurrences. These similarities appear to support the position that Twain did not act deliberately to single out Jim as a linguistic inferior or deviant as charged by Leonard and Tenney. However, a closer look at the data of the two speakers yields more controversial results.

A particularly interesting observation in the speech samples analyzed by Tamasi is that Huck does not produce a single occurrence of alternation of /n/ for /ŋ/ in present-participle forms (*doing*→*doin'*) or in other final unstressed /ŋ/ constructions (*anything*→*anythin'*), or g-dropping, in either novel, notwithstanding his very high frequency of nonstandard articulations in general in *Tom Sawyer.* Huck produces /ŋ/ in all fifty-nine opportunities in the data sample Tamasi analyzed for the later novel (140). On the other hand, in the same novel and as shown above in table 4.2, my findings are that Jim rarely articulates /ŋ/ in present-participle forms and other final unstressed /ŋ/ constructions. For present-participle constructions, Jim produces the /n/ variant fifty-seven times, compared to only two /ŋ/ articulations, or in 97 percent of possible occurrences. For other final unstressed /ŋ/ forms, he produces eleven /n/ variants to two /ŋ/ variants, articulating the nonstandard variant 85 percent of the time. It is curious that the barely-schooled Huck would produce the /ŋ/ variant exclusively, even in *Tom Sawyer*, in which his speech is represented as highly dialectal according to Tamasi. A possible explanation raises substantial questions about how Twain uses dialect to characterize Jim.

It might appear initially that Twain would not have bothered to represent the /n/ variant in Huck's speech by respelling words without the final *g*, conventionally with an apostrophe in its place, because of the widespread distribution of the feature among many varieties of American English, probably including the one Twain himself spoke. At first glance, it could be interpreted that Twain might have just assumed that the reader would "hear" the *-ing* spellings as /n/, with the dropped-*g* variant based on his awareness that the feature is persistent in the speech of many Americans. In his "Theory of Literary Dialect," Sumner Ives argues that "the accepted criteria" of the literary dialect author's "own region" had to be considered by the author, and that authors would then use nonstandard respellings not to represent dialectal variants that occur in their own speech varieties but only those that do not (158). According to Ives, "It follows, then, that an author will fail to represent many features of his character's speech which may be regionally characteristic but which carry no implication of inferiority or 'difference' within those regions in which they are found" (163). Viewed alongside Huck's speech data as presented by Tamasi, the position Ives articulates might initially seem to be a reasonable explanation for the lack of respelled /n/ variants in Huck's speech. However, this explanation does not hold up when Jim's speech data is considered. Twain respells nearly all Jim's articulations of *-ing* words as *-in*, which indicates a pronunciation that according to the findings of Lee Pederson was common among Missouri speakers regardless of race and level of education, and therefore was probably also quite similar to that of Huck and even to "the cultivated Midland dialect of Mark Twain" himself (Pederson "Speech" 3). The question is why Twain represented the variant with respellings for Jim but not also for Huck.

In his general discussion of literary dialect, Ives raises another issue that may also be applied to Twain: "By the very fact that he has represented the speech in unconventional spellings, the author has passed judgment; he has indicated that it is *not*, in his definition of the term, standard English" (165, emphasis in original). For the discrepancy between the speech data of white protagonist Huck and black supporting-character Jim, the issue of language representation appears to be inextricable from other components of characterization. Twain might not have intended to pass judgment, as Ives puts it, on Jim as inferior or deviant, a view which is in fact difficult to reconcile with an otherwise mostly positive characterization. But it seems clear that to represent features that Jim and Huck unquestionably share with respellings for Jim and in standard orthography for Huck, is to mark Jim as other. For Twain, this may have been racially motivated, as some of his critics contend. Or it might have been part of a strategy for establishing Huck's position as narrator-protagonist, a major shift from his second-banana status in *Tom Sawyer,* using dialect to distinguish the other characters in relation to him, as it seems apparent that Twain also did in his linguistic marking of Huck in relation to Tom in *Tom Sawyer.* As Tamasi concludes, Twain uses Huck's "new voice" in the later novel as part of a strategy for reflecting the "major developmental changes" that Huck undergoes between the two novels (141). Linguistically and otherwise, *Huckleberry Finn* represents Huck as norm, defining others in relation to him.

While the position of Leonard and Tenney rightly highlights the contrast between Twain's representations of black and of white speech, it falls short in their position that Twain's representation of Jim's dialectal features amounts to "extreme forms of eye dialect" ("Introduction" 5). As noted above, my analysis turns up minimal examples of eye dialect. However, when Tamasi's data on the dialectal representations of Huck's speech are considered, it appears that Twain may have included a greater number of dialectal features in the speech of Jim and had Jim produce higher frequencies for shared features. But this is not the same thing as eye dialect. Had Leonard and Tenney considered a features analysis, they might well have found greater dialectal representation in the speech of Jim than in that of the white characters, but they would not necessarily find more "eye dialect," which Twain seems actually to keep to a minimum, lapsing only rarely into the stereotypical conventions of dialectal representation. Perhaps the more legitimate question is whether Twain might have concentrated his dialectal representations on Jim to a greater degree than he did for the white characters, and if so, why.

Twain might have expended more effort in relating the speech of Jim and other African Americans more meticulously, although some might say disparagingly, than that of the white characters, or he might have simply portrayed Jim as using more features and producing higher frequencies of occurrence as a way of acknowledging Jim's limited educational opportunities under a system of slavery that included forced illiteracy. David Carkeet finds in his analysis of the original manuscripts of *Huckleberry Finn* that Twain made hundreds of revisions to the dialectal representations, confirming the author's desire for what he must have felt was realistic representation (319). The evidence that Twain actually uses the depiction of Jim's speech to disparage him is simply not found in the text of the novel, according to this analysis, nor in the articles produced by critics of Twain's version of AAE. A possibility is that those critics are responding negatively to the appearance of respelled dialectal representations on the page. As noted above, Preston has demonstrated the prevalence of a negative "affective response" to the way representations of dialectal features look in print. He also comments that the viewer might not find the identical features as offensive upon actually hearing them in a person's speech ("Syndrome" 328). What is also likely is that such critics find other textual evidence that Jim is portrayed negatively or stereotypically, evidence that has nothing to do with the actual linguistic features Jim uses. The view may be that if Jim is stereotyped, then so must be his speech. Again, this may well be an example of how the stigmatization of language varieties could simply be standing in for expression of other attitudes.

And, in fact, a number of writers have made strong cases against Twain that argue that Jim is represented negatively and stereotypically. Most such writers focus on the influence upon Twain of nineteenth-century minstrel shows, which contributed greatly to popular stereotypes of African Americans and which Twain is known to have regularly attended and enjoyed. They maintain that these minstrel shows had considerable impact on the author's depiction of African American characters, including Jim. One frequently cited example of that influence in the characterization of Jim is his reaction to seeing Huck alive after he was believed dead, interpreted as a denigration of Jim for his belief in and reaction to the supernatural, which some critics have described as a staple of minstrelsy. In this scene, which occurs early in the novel, the two meet unexpectedly on the island where they are both hiding, Jim after escaping when he fears he is to be sold, and Huck after faking his own death in order to escape his violently abusive father. When Jim sees Huck, the latter reports,

> He bounced up and stared at me wild. Then he drops down on his knees, and puts his hands together and says: "Doan' hurt me—don't! I hain't never done no harm to a ghos'. I awluz liked dead people, en

done all I could for 'em. You go en git in de river agin, whah you b'longs, and doan' do nuffn to Ole Jim, 'at 'uz awluz yo' fren'." (53)

It is entirely possible that Twain might have intended for this to be a comic scene based on the minstrel genre. But Shelley Fisher Fishkin, in her analysis of *Huckleberry Finn* as the work of an author deeply influenced by authentic black voices and culture, argues persuasively that Jim's beliefs in ghosts and the supernatural "may turn out to have their roots in his African and African-American past" rather than in minstrelsy (86).

Also, Jim's reaction to finding Huck alive is remarkably similar to a scene that occurs toward the end of the novel, in which Tom Sawyer appears and is equally and comically surprised to see Huck alive. According to Huck,

> [Tom's] mouth opened up like a trunk, and staid so; and he swallowed two or three times like a person that's got a dry throat, and then says, "I hain't ever done you no harm. You know that. So then what you want to come back and ha'nt me for?. . . . Don't you play nothing on me, because I wouldn't on you. Honest injun, now, you ain't a ghost?" (234)

It may well be that Twain uses the minstrel stereotype to make fun of Jim in the earlier scene. But Tom's belief in ghosts and reaction to seeing Huck alive might also be indicative of Twain's penchant for making merciless fun of anyone, regardless of race, whenever he could. Further, the section at the end of *Huckleberry Finn,* centered around Tom's scheme to free Jim, is often considered one of the novel's major weaknesses, and it also portrays Tom in a far more negative light than any in which Jim is portrayed.

But this is not the only example of apparent minstrelization of Jim, and it is not possible to explain them all away so easily as simply the products of Twain's sometimes insensitive sense of humor. The conversation in which Jim and Huck discuss Jim's past financial exchanges, which also occurs early in the novel, similarly seems to fit into the minstrel tradition, and again, there is little question that this scene, along with a later scene in which Jim is disguised, complete with face paint, and the exaggerated responses to real or perceived supernatural phenomena, mimicked staples of the minstrel shows Twain frequented. According to Eric Lott, instances in the novel such as these provide evidence that "[b]lackface minstrelsy indeed underwrote" *Huckleberry Finn,* the text of which, he adds, is "shot through with blackface thinking" (133). Frederick Woodward and Donnarae MacCann cite similar examples and conclude that "Twain's use of the minstrel position undercuts serious consideration of Jim's humanity beyond those qualities stereotypically attributed to the noble savage" (142). They, along with other writers such as Arnold Rampersad and Toni Morrison, insist with considerable justification that readers and scholars pay attention to the serious racial issues of the novel beyond the often-discussed confusion of Huck over whether he should adhere to what a racist society has taught him is right or to what his own emerging principles tell him to do.

Despite a textual presentation that privileges Huck, Jim emerges as far more significant than simply a foil to Huck's beliefs and a convenient temporary father to Huck. Rather, Jim even more than Huck represents the overarching theme of the pursuit of freedom in the novel. In Huck's case, the quest for freedom takes places against a rapidly disappearing frontier and is an attempt to escape from the consequently increasing control of a violent and hypocritical (white) society, culminating in his decision at the end of the novel to "light out for the territory" (296). Jim's quest, on the other hand, is for freedom from the ultimate example of American hypocrisy: slavery. But it is not Jim's story that gets told. Ultimately, Jim is returned to a reality that exists primarily in relation to Huck, and so Jim's story goes unfinished. This is a consequence of the characterization of Jim and one of the novel's greatest flaws.

David L. Smith argues that Twain's portrayal of Jim identifies the author as "an antiracist writer oriented toward the [progressive] tradition" (123), who at the same time possesses a "commonplace racist attitude" (122). Still, Twain's use of dialectal language as a means for Jim to communicate his own humanity is an unequivocal statement of the author's belief in dialectal black speech as a legitimate means of expression. Jim's scenes are certainly not all comic, and in one of the book's most powerful passages, he expresses his pain at being separated from his family and remorse over his misunderstanding of his daughter's deafness with eloquence and dignity. But perhaps just as significantly, the evidence exists that Twain uses stereotypical situations with Jim to attempt to create humor. This is of course ironic in a novel that just as clearly satirizes and criticizes racism, and it raises questions about the credibility of the text. Like the *New York Times* story that offered up for (justifiable) reader condemnation the white Southerners who refused to believe Dr. Gatch's reports of African American suffering in South Carolina, *Adventures of Huckleberry Finn* pits its readers against a hostile, overt racism.

But also like the *Times* article, some of the assumptions and attitudes of the author and the predominantly white—and in some cases liberal white— readership at its time of publication remain unaddressed in the text.

Like everyone in America then and now, Twain struggled with and against the influences of a racist society and, like most of us, did not always prevail. The flaws in his art may simply represent the flaws in his character, which are no less human than those of any of his critics. Finally, I have to argue on behalf of the enormous artistic, historical, and linguistic value of Twain's greatest work. The complexity of the art and politics of *Adventures of Huckleberry Finn,* and its propensity for generating heated critical discourse as well as deeply emotional human reactions, are simply products of the greatness of the novel. As no human being is without complexity or contradiction, neither is great art. A quantitative analysis of linguistic features can offer a useful and interesting dimension to the discussion of a literary text, but ultimately, as with all other interpretations and critiques, it cannot come close to resolving or containing the artistic representations of that which William Faulkner described in his Nobel prize speech as "the human heart in conflict with itself."

5

"A High, Holy Purpose"

Dialect in Charles W. Chesnutt's Conjure Tales

For Charles W. Chesnutt, the questions of whether and how to incorporate African American dialectal speech into his fiction were complicated by artistic, political, and commercial tensions imposed by the interrelations between post-Reconstruction social conditions and Chesnutt's personal goals as a writer. Publishing during the last decades of the nineteenth century and the first decade of the twentieth, Chesnutt faced unique challenges as an African American artist. Perhaps most significant among these challenges was in his effort to have the antiracist messages he unabashedly promoted as a primary goal of his fiction accepted by the white-dominated publishing establishment and disseminated to the then predominantly white reading public.

Chesnutt was from early childhood a precocious learner, voracious reader, and highly motivated student of academic subjects and personal self-improvement, and the contents of his journals reveal that he wrote poetry and fiction beginning in his teens. In his early twenties, he began to consider seriously the possibility of making his living as a writer of fiction, and in a journal entry dated May 29, 1880, Chesnutt clarified his principal motive as an artist:

> If I do write, I shall write for a purpose, a high, holy purpose, and this will inspire me to greater efforts. The object of my writings would not be so much the elevation of the colored people as the elevation of the whites—for I consider the unjust spirit of caste which is so insidious as to pervade a whole nation, and so powerful as to subject a whole race and all connected with it to scorn and social ostracism—I consider this a barrier to the moral progress of the American people; and I would be one of the first to head a determined, organized crusade against it. (Chesnutt, *Journals* 139–40)

Given the racism Chesnutt experienced and wanted to work to eradicate, an important challenge for him was to determine how best to construct his message in order to "open the way" for African Americans to achieve "social recognition and equality," a challenge he planned to meet, according to the May 29, 1880, journal entry, by "amusing [the white audience] to lead them on imperceptibly, unconsciously step by step to the desired state of feeling" (Chesnutt, *Journals* 140). A related challenge was to persuade the white-controlled publishing industry to disseminate the message. Capitalizing on the popularity of literary representations of African American dialectal speech, Chesnutt deployed them as a central part of his strategy for persuading the publishers to support his work, encouraging readers to buy it, and "lead[ing] them on imperceptibly" toward "a moral revolution" (140). However, the complexity of Chesnutt's use of dialect and how it functions in his fiction cannot be accounted for sufficiently simply by way of attention to his stated political goals. Chesnutt's work as well as his personality are far more complicated than that.

What is known of Chesnutt's own relationship with African American dialectal speech raises interesting questions about his use of vernacular styles in his fiction, and this information makes highly implausible any theory that Chesnutt meant to celebrate his own heritage and linguistic traditions through the dialect tales of his invented narrator, former slave Julius McAdoo. In 1873, at age fifteen, the exceptional young student discontinued his own formal education in order to become a teacher himself, earning his teaching certificate in 1874, a move Charles Duncan attributes to Chesnutt's desire to help improve his family's finances (xvii). However, the move probably also reflects the youth's powerful ambition, self-confidence, and desire to help improve the lives of African Americans in Fayetteville, North Carolina, his home from age seven through twenty-five. Significantly, Chesnutt considered one of his major responsibilities as an educator to be to "re-educate others in the proper use of English," that is, in the variety he spoke, according to Richard Brodhead (Intro. to *Journals* 14). Brodhead further notes that as a young teacher, Chesnutt was acutely aware of the differences between himself and many of his African American neighbors in and around Fayetteville, observing that at this time, "Chesnutt's response to the culture of his illiterate black countrymen is usually one of estrangement, embarrassment, and an anxious attempt to guard his distance from it" (23).

Chesnutt's conjure tales—those works among his short fiction that took as their themes the conditions of slavery and the survival techniques of slaves—are an interesting product of this highly educated and class-conscious writer born of free parents in North Carolina in 1858. The conjure tales include seven stories published by Houghton Mifflin as a book in 1899 under the title *The Conjure Woman* but also seven additional stories, six of which Chesnutt submitted for possible inclusion in *The Conjure Woman* but which the publisher declined to include. In 1993 Richard Brodhead brought all fourteen of the stories together in a complete collection, *The Conjure Woman and Other Conjure Tales.* The first thirteen stories were written between 1887 and 1898, with six tales penned in 1898 alone with the specific aim of being included in the volume of conjure tales that became *The Conjure Woman,* a project suggested by Walter Hines Page, editor of the *Atlantic* magazine. By then Chesnutt had already published several stories in the *Atlantic,* including the conjure story "The Goophered Grapevine," which appeared in 1887 and made Chesnutt the first African American author to have his fiction published in that magazine. Two other conjure stories, "Po' Sandy" (1888) and "Dave's Neckliss" (1889), had also previously appeared in the magazine and were generally well received.

However, the artistic, critical, and, to a lesser degree, popular successes of the conjure tales do not negate Chesnutt's self-recorded ambivalence toward the language and customs of his characters. Further, as recently as the 1960s, Henry B. Wonham observes, several African American critics, including Amiri Baraka, have challenged Chesnutt on his views, focusing specifically on the dialect, superstitions, and perceived racial stereotypes in the conjure tales. Baraka saw these elements as symptomatic of Chesnutt's identification "with an assimilationist black middle class that 'wanted no subculture, nothing that connected them with the poor black man or the slave'" (qtd. in Wonham 56). While Chesnutt's contemporary, admittedly mostly white, critics were kinder, and later African American critics including Houston A. Baker Jr. continue to offer justifiable praise of the conjure tales, Chesnutt's earlier attitudes toward African American speech and culture are important to an analysis of the tales, and so critiques such as Baraka's merit serious consideration.

At Reconstruction-funded schools in North Carolina, Chesnutt was schooled according to a northern white educational and social ethic. As a young man he possessed feelings that were, at best, ambivalent about African American dialectal speech and openly negative about the African-rooted supernatural beliefs and traditions that comprise conjure, traditions that were, ironically, later to distinguish some of his best fiction. The journal entries that express Chesnutt's ambivalent or negative feelings seem to have been written largely in response to a difficult period in his life, which not incidentally was also a period during which he was far from having achieved the maturity of an experienced adult, despite his intelligence and education. At age seventeen, spending the summer of 1875 teaching in rural South Carolina, which the unhappy Chesnutt called "this much-abused negro-ruled state" (*Journals* 76), he contended with poor pay, difficult students, and frustration with local administrators who, according to a journal entry dated August 20, 1875, "say they'll pay your board, and then don't do it. They accuse you indirectly of lying, almost of stealing, [and] eavesdrop you" (*Journals* 82). In an entry dated a week earlier, he mocks what he saw as the administrators' lack of responsibility and also their speech: "The 'committee' said they were going around to see about my board this week, but they 'hain't' gone yet'" (81). In the same entry, he is critical of one of the several families with whom he boarded that summer, exclaiming,

> Well! uneducated people are the most bigoted, superstitious, hardest headed people in the world! Those folks down stairs believe in ghosts, luck, horse shoes, cloud signs, and all other kinds of nonsense, and all the argument in the world couldn't get it out of them. It is useless to argue with such persons. (81)

Such views anticipate those of John, the white frame narrator of the conjure tales, a liberal but limited Ohioan displaced to the warmer climes of North Carolina because of a chronically ill wife, Annie, and a seemingly insatiable desire to exploit the plentiful resources of the American South. By the time Chesnutt composed the conjure tales, however, beginning in 1887, his views had matured considerably to the point where both dialectal speech and conjure are represented with greater complexity than the teenage Chesnutt would have been willing or able to allow was possible. In the conjure stories, Brodhead observes, Chesnutt "combines the occult properties of magic with the this-worldly, even businesslike properties of a social administrations system," with conjure functioning "above all" as a survival mechanism for the slave characters in the stories, or "as a recourse, a form of power available to the powerless in mortally intolerable situations" (Brodhead, Intro. to *Conjure* 9).

But questions still remain about how Chesnutt came to his appreciation of conjure and, more importantly for this discussion, whether that appreciation extended to African American dialectal speech. Looking at Chesnutt's work in the context of literary trends in force during his career offers a useful perspective. Some critics, including Walter Blair and Raven McDavid, have classified Chesnutt's conjure tales along with the local-color movement of the late nineteenth and early twentieth centuries. This may be an appropriate classification because of Chesnutt's emphasis on the east-central North Carolina setting of the tales, including its topographical and agricultural idiosyncrasies, and perhaps especially because of his incorporation of dialectal representations of speech. The local-color writers had established dialect representation as a major convention of the tradition, which James Nagel notes as having its genesis in the 1860s with the 1865 publication of Mark Twain's "The Celebrated Jumping Frog of Calaveras County" and later Bret Harte's "The Luck of Roaring Camp," which appeared in 1868 (xxiii). The frontier settings, a staple of the "Old Southwestern" tradition of humorous writing of the 1830s through 1850s, a trend which also usually included representations of dialectal speech and from which the local-color movement is arguably descended, did not continue to define the work of many of the local colorists who came after Twain and Harte. However, the strong regional identifications and the preservation in fiction of changing ways of life continued to define the work of New England local colorists such as Harriet Beecher Stowe and Sarah Orne Jewett, Southern writers such as Joel Chandler Harris of Georgia and Thomas Nelson Page of Virginia, Indiana writer Edward Eggleston, and other regionally identified writers. Chesnutt's tales of life in North Carolina under slavery, most of them narrated in the first person by Julius McAdoo—a former slave on a plantation in the fictional Patesville, North Carolina, a locale based on Chesnutt's hometown of Fayetteville—seem to fit into the genre of regional portrayals of, what was at their times of publication, the recent past.

But by the time Chesnutt began publishing his dialect tales in 1887, the local-color movement was beginning to decline from its prominence in American letters, to be superseded by realism and naturalism, the roots of which are clearly present in the local-color literature, especially in the continuing trend of dialectal representation in the service of realistic portrayals of setting and character. According to James Nagel, "By the 1890s, the central concept of Realism was well established in American literature" (xxvii), and therefore by the time Chesnutt's two collections of short stories, *The Conjure Woman* and *The Wife of His Youth and Other Stories of the Color Line*, appeared in book form a few months apart in 1899, local color no longer dominated the American literary scene. Chesnutt came late to the local-color tradition, then, and for different reasons from those of the other local colorists; and for these reasons, the simple classification of Chesnutt as a local colorist is too limited. But the association is still relevant, since it is clear that Chesnutt found in his apparent adoption of the popular literary conventions of local color ways of subtly manipulating the popular forms in order to achieve his well-documented political goals, his "high, holy purpose" of freeing African Americans from continued postslavery racism (Chesnutt, *Journals* 139). In other words, Chesnutt deliberately employed popular means in the hope of achieving potentially unpopular ends in the days after the demolition of Reconstruction and entrenchment of Jim Crow, with much of his work, including the conjure and related tales, built around indictments of slavery and criticism of Southern racial relations, all in the guise of local color. Or perhaps it would be more accurate to say that Chesnutt's work seems to mimic conventions of that subcategory of local color, the plantation tradition.

The plantation tradition can be distinguished, for the purposes of this discussion, from local color in general in two major ways. First, as in the local-color movement, the plantation tradition sought to preserve or at least document ways of life that were disappearing after the Civil War with the rise of industrialization and modernization. But unlike most local-color literature, the plantation tradition had a specific political agenda, and that was to create a mythologized Southern antebellum past, in which slavery was benign and familial rather than cruel and degrading. Second, as with the rest of the local colorists, dialect representation was used to a large degree to evoke a particular region and moment in time, but for plantation writers such as Thomas Nelson Page and Thomas Dixon, politics also impacted this device of regional writing. The political aims of plantation-tradition writers such as Page, Dixon, and, some critics argue, Joel Chandler Harris, were to evoke nostalgia for slavery by romanticizing it, to argue that freedmen and women had been better off as slaves by creating fictional ex-slaves to say so in their "own words" (and dialect), and generally to absolve the South for slavery and pave the way for continued racial inequality. Within the plantation tradition, a key function of the dialectal representations seems to have been designed deliberately to act as evidence that freed African American former slaves were innocent, ignorant, submissive, and inferior, and hence in need of continued white control and supervision. Unfortunately, this view became for many African American writers inextricable from the dialectal speech of many real African American speakers, and along with the minstrel tradition, a publicly performed version of the plantation tradition and other racist themes, became a principal reason why African American writers of the late nineteenth and early twentieth centuries avoided representing African American dialectal speech in their writing. Those who did not avoid it, such as Paul Laurence Dunbar and later Zora Neale Hurston, were accused of perpetuating and profiting from the stereotype. For some reason, perhaps because of the subversive themes in his writing, Chesnutt has not garnered as much negative attention as Dunbar and Hurston received for their representations of dialect from black critics through the Harlem Renaissance, but on the surface at least, it is no more clear that Chesnutt is not in fact perpetuating and profiting from the plantation tradition, and on first glance, in fact, it appears that he is, just as Amiri Baraka claimed.

An educated member of the middle class, Chesnutt was a writer of conflicting goals and loyalties. On one hand, his journal entries and the harsh depictions of slavery in the stories themselves leave no doubt that Chesnutt's conjure tales share only a superficial resemblance to the literature of the plantation tradition. On the other hand, however, the narrative structure of the white standard-speaking narrator framing the narration of a former slave, along with heavy reliance on dialectal features in the speech of the latter, bear far more than merely a passing resemblance to work of the plantation tradition. Chesnutt's well-known frustrations with the educational and professional limitations exerted upon him by a racist society solely because of his African blood clash with his equally well-documented desire for middle-class respectability according to a white middle-class model. This clash is apparent in a journal entry dated October 12, 1878, in which Chesnutt wrote bitterly: "As to procuring instruction in Latin, French, German, or Music, that is entirely out of the question. First class teachers would not teach a 'n——' and I would have no other sort" (93). Henry Louis Gates Jr. points to Chesnutt's negative review of William Wells Brown's 1867 history of African American participation in the Revolutionary War, *The Negro in the American Rebellion, His Heroism and His Fidelity,* as further evidence of Chesnutt's concern with middle-class virtue. Declared Chesnutt, "This book reminds me of a dirty shirt. You are rather apt to doubt [Brown's] gentility under such circumstances. I am sometimes doubtful of the facts for the same reason—they make but a shabby appearance" (qtd.

in Gates, *Signifying* 117). According to Gates, through his observations, "Chesnutt means to connote images of middle-class respectability and gentility" (117).

Chesnutt's preoccupation with class and his own social position keeps the specter of his distaste for African American dialectal speech constantly hovering over his portrayals of Julius McAdoo's speech. But there is no question that the conjure tales are designed to be indictments of slavery and continuing racism, a clear response to literary nostalgia for plantation life and to increasingly harsh political realities of African American life as Reconstruction evaporated into a new institutionalized set of racist policies and practices. Paul R. Petrie emphasizes that Chesnutt deliberately exploited the plantation tradition "for racially progressive purposes" (184). According to Petrie,

> if plantation-dialect fiction, because of its familiarity to white readers, presents itself as a logical choice for seeking to alter white racial attitudes, Chesnutt asks, "To what extent can that familiarity be made to yield white readerly sympathy with black folk and black experience, beyond the accustomed generic boundaries of a condescending pity or an amused toleration?" (184)

Chesnutt's mission, argues Petrie, was "to exploit plantation-dialect regionalism's capacity for cultural mediation while ridding it of its white racist values" (187).

For further convincing, we need only look at the cruelties suffered under slavery by Sandy and Tenie in "Po' Sandy," in which Sandy's work ethic and valuable skills keep him in constant circulation among his master's relatives and thus away from his own family. He and his wife, Tenie, eventually agree that she should use her conjure skills to turn him into a tree so that he can stay in one place, near Tenie. The couple makes it appear as though Sandy has run away, and Tenie secretly turns him into a man every night and back into a tree in the mornings, until she is sent from the plantation to care for her master's ailing daughter-in-law. Tenie returns in time to find the tree that is Sandy has been cut down and sent to the sawmill to make lumber for a new kitchen. Forced to watch the sawing process and hear the tree's cries of agony, Tenie dies of grief not long afterward as the new kitchen is abandoned as haunted and the lumber removed to make a schoolhouse nearby.

Similarly, in "Sis' Becky's Pickaninny," Becky suffers the loss of her husband when he is sold away to a Virginia plantation owner and later is cruelly separated from her infant son as her master trades her for a racehorse in order to try to improve his fortune at the track. And in "Dave's Neckliss," the title character learns to read and preach and is well respected among the slaves and even the whites on the plantation, until he is falsely accused of stealing meat from the plantation's smokehouse. As punishment, he is brutally whipped by the overseer, stripped of his bible and permission to read and preach, and forced to wear a ham around his neck. Dave is so demoralized and dehumanized by these events that he ultimately loses his own sense of humanity, identifies himself as a piece of meat, and commits suicide by hanging himself in the smokehouse. Nowhere in these stories is there any feeling of nostalgia for slavery.

Chesnutt's genius was in his ability to outline the cruelest realities of slavery—families torn apart and marriages ignored or forbidden, whippings, forced illiteracy—while framing them in the mysticism of conjure. The juxtaposition of magic with harsh reality made Chesnutt's conjure tales palatable to members of a white reading public who might otherwise have responded with hostility to literature that was openly critical of slavery or of continuing racial inequality. Many of those readers might have been able to tolerate, forgive, or, like the white narrator John, dismiss or fail to notice the legitimacy of Julius's testimony to the evils of slavery contained in the tales because of the appeal—and seeming unreality—of the elements of conjure and fantasy. A response similar to John's may not have been the result Chesnutt had in mind for his audience, but there is no question that Chesnutt acted deliberately in his attempt to get his antiracist message out in a subtle, and for a mostly white readership and white-controlled publishing industry, nonaccusatory way. Dialect functions similarly, mitigating for publisher and reader the pointed criticism the tales contain by couching the criticism in what Chesnutt once sarcastically described as "English pronounced as an ignorant old southern Negro would be supposed to speak it" in an 1898 letter to his editor, Walter Hines Page (qtd. in Baker 42). According to Houston A. Baker Jr., Julius McAdoo tells the stories to his white interlocutors, John and Annie, with full awareness of "the sounds that are dear to the hearts of his white boss and his wife, and he presents them with conjuring efficaciousness" (44). The result, continues Baker, is that Julius, and by extension Chesnutt himself, "presents a world in which 'dialect' masks the drama of African spirituality challenging and changing the disastrous transformations of slavery" (44).

The complexity of Chesnutt's art and politics presents an intriguing set of challenges in terms of his use of dialect in the conjure tales. A look at his procedures and methods in representing Julius's speech dialectally may help to illustrate what Chesnutt's attitudes might have been toward dialectal varieties of African American speech, how his portrayals of dialectal speech function in the stories and in the literary marketplace, and what relationship might have existed between Chesnutt's opinions about African American dialectal speech and his perspectives on class and race issues. For my analysis, I selected the story "Dave's Neckliss" as the source for the sample of Julius McAdoo's speech. First published in the *Atlantic* in October 1889, "Dave's Neckliss" was Chesnutt's fourth conjure tale and also the fourth published story of his writing career. As in all but one of the other thirteen conjure stories ("The Dumb Witness" is narrated by John), Julius McAdoo narrates within a frame established by the white, standard-speaking John. In "Dave's Neckliss," Julius produces more than 4,500 words as he narrates the tragic story of the wrongfully accused Dave. The 4,500-word corpus was analyzed in its entirety using WordSmith Tools and yielded substantial results, perhaps most significantly that Chesnutt was meticulous and thorough in his documentation of speech characteristics. Additionally, eye dialect, questionable respellings and malapropisms, while not entirely absent from the data, are generally infrequent. Finally, the high number of dialectal features, along with their generally high frequencies of occurrence, result in the portrayal of a variety of speech that is radically different from the standard speech of the white frame narrator, a standard that was apparently shared by the author and presumed to be shared by the predominantly white readership.

Chesnutt's representations of dialectal speech are notable in part because of the meticulousness with which they are constructed. As illustrated in table 5.1, in "Dave's Neckliss" alone, numerous documented phonological features of African American English and other Southern varieties are present in Julius's speech, with frequencies for twenty-four features included in the table. Many of the phonological features Chesnutt incorporated into the speech of Julius McAdoo are still familiar to speakers and scholars of more recent Southern speech, including Southern varieties of AAE. But Chesnutt also included several features that have since become less common in African American speech, with most of them confirmed by data from older African American speakers, especially those interviewed in North Carolina for *LAMSAS* during the 1930s.

Table 5.1 Phonological Features in Julius McAdoo's Speech

Feature	Example	Tokens/Types	Frequency*
Vocalization of postvocalic /r/	before→befo'	128/176	73%
Loss of /r/ after consonants	from→fum	40/40	100%
Intervocalic /r/ loss with syllable loss	curious→cu'ous	3/3	100%
Vocalization or loss of unstressed syllabic /r/	Master→Mars	51/223	23%
Stopping of syllable-initial fricatives	there→dere	383/384	99%
Stopping of voiceless interdental fricatives	with→wid	21/21	100%
Labialization of interdental fricatives	both→bofe	19/19	100%
Consonant cluster reduction	hold→hol'	542/561	97%
Deletion of unstressed syllable	about→'bout	171/200	86%
/n/ for /ŋ/ in present participle	looking→lookin'	109/109	100%
Other alternation of /n/ for /ŋ/	morning→mawnin'	12/13	92%
Alternation of /b/ or /β/ for /v/	evening→ebening	47/49	96%
Metathesis of final /s/ + stop	ask→ax	3/3	100%
/j/ after velar stops /k/ and /g/	care→keer	5/5	100%
Word-initial addition of /h/	it→hit	5/64	8%
Word-initial loss of /h/	house→'ouse	17/22	77%
Word-initial /w/ for /hw/	while→w'ile	97/102	95%
Alternation of /aɪ/ for /ɔɪ/	going→gwine	22/22	100%
Alternation of /e/ for /ɔ/	because→caze	5/5	100%
Merger of /ɛ/ and /ɪ/	get→git	59/60	98%
Glide reduction of /aɪ/ to /a/	like→lack	16/111	14%
Alternation of /a/ for /ɛ/ before /r/	learn→l'arn	11/11	100%
Alternation of /ɑ/ for /æ/	Master→Marster	58/58	100%
/e/ for /i/ before /r/ and /l/	real→rale	4/4	100%

*Significant at p<.05.

In his 1971 monograph *The Phonology of the Conjure Tales of Charles W. Chesnutt,* Charles W. Foster attributes Chesnutt's success at representing realistic speech both to his training as a stenographer, which enabled him to transcribe, according to Foster, a remarkable two hundred words per minute, as well as to Chesnutt's "opportunities to observe speech in the Negro community under conditions not possible for a white man" (2). Foster's analysis uses data from *LAMSAS,* focusing on North Carolina interviews completed between 1934 and 1937 of speakers born during the 1850s and 1860s to verify the pronunciations of Julius, much as my own analysis also relies on data from *LAMSAS*. Interestingly, however, Foster uses Atlas data collected from white informants to verify the "folk" speech Chesnutt attributes to Julius. Also, on the basis of the Sumner Ives model, which presumes a need for establishing the author's speech in order to determine what he or she considers to be "standard" and therefore what will be represented as dialectal, Foster consults the data of white speakers of the cultivated variety that he believes the highly educated Chesnutt must have spoken. Foster concludes that "there is no reason to believe that the phonology of the Negro differs significantly from that of whites on the same economic and educational level" (3). While some scholars today might find this conclusion surprising because of particular features or clusters of features that have been documented as being associated specifically with AAE, a look at recent scholarship and at Atlas data shows overlaps between some features associated with African American speakers and with white Southern speakers especially, overlaps that are not surprising because of the influence of the Southern speech varieties on one another resulting from close interactions among speakers under the system of slavery and continuing after the Civil War. However, it may be going too far to assume that dialectal features of whites are generally interchangeable with those of black speakers. But it is clear that Foster's use of white informant data is a result of the limited amount of *LAMSAS* data collected from black speakers in the region of interest.

Foster does consult the speech data of two African American speakers interviewed for *LAMSAS,* one a male farmer, age seventy-seven at the time of his 1937 interview, a resident of Harnett County, the next county west of Cumberland County, which is the site of Chesnutt's hometown of Fayetteville and probable location of the fictional Patesville. The other, a sixty-year-old woman at the time of her 1934 interview, also a farmer, lived in Sampson County, adjacent to Cumberland County to the east. Foster could also have consulted the data of two additional Atlas sources interviewed in 1937, both African American men and former slaves. They are slightly less similar geographically to the fictional Julius McAdoo but much closer to him in age and with respect to their shared experiences under slavery. One of these interviewees was eighty-nine at the time of his interview and a resident of Brunswick County, approximately seventy miles southeast of Fayetteville. The other was eighty-one and interviewed at his home in Franklin County, approximately seventy-five miles north of Fayetteville.

It is difficult to determine Julius's exact age, but there are enough clues to make a reasonable approximation. Chesnutt's fictional Julius makes his first appearance in "The Goophered Grapevine," first published in 1887, or twenty-two years after the end of the Civil War. The tale takes place "[s]ome years ago," according to the white frame narrator, John, "a sufficient time after the war for conditions in the South to have become somewhat settled" (Chesnutt, *Conjure* 31). Presumably, then, it is possible to estimate that the telling of Julius's stories probably takes place sometime between 1870 and 1880. Upon their first meeting, which occurs within that window of time, John describes Julius as a "venerable-looking" man, and "though slightly bowed by the weight of years, apparently quite vigorous" (34). In subsequent stories, including "Dave's Neckliss," John continually refers to him as "the old man" (123). There is no question, then, that Julius was born before even the eighty-nine-year-old Atlas speaker, who was born in 1847 or 1848. Granting the conjure stories a telling date of approximately 1875, and granting Julius an age of between fifty and seventy years, he would have been approximately twenty to forty years older than the oldest interviewee. However, perhaps more important than this relatively slight age discrepancy is that they would both have experienced slavery, Emancipation, and life as freedmen in North Carolina.

There remains the possibility that there are features in Julius's speech that cannot be corroborated by even the oldest surviving documents of African American speech—such as *LAMSAS* data as well as data from the slave narratives collected during the 1930s as part of the Federal Writers' Project—but these should be viewed as opportunities to add to the existing store of knowledge concerning earlier African American English rather than as problematical to the authentication of literary dialect. For example, at least one lexical item with two grammatical forms occurs in the speech of Julius McAdoo that seems so far to have no other surviving written corroboration. The words "junesey," meaning "sweetheart," and "juneseying," meaning "courting," are credited only to Chesnutt and his conjure stories in the *Dictionary of American Regional English* (*DARE*), the only written source I have located so far in which either form appears at all.

But distinctive variants are not limited to lexical items. As shown above in table 5.1, Chesnutt preserves in Julius's speech a number of interesting phonological features that are unusual today but were apparently more common in speakers in the nineteenth and early- to mid-twentieth centuries. One of these features is the alternation of /e/ for /ɔ/, represented in "Dave's

Neckliss" and elsewhere in the speech of Julius as *'caze* (five occurrences in "Dave's Neckliss") for *because* (zero occurrences). Julius's pronunciation is similar to one in Jim's speech in Twain's *Adventures of Huckleberry Finn,* as observed in chapter 4, represented by Twain in the alternates *bekase, 'kase,* and *'kaze,* of which there are a total of fourteen occurrences, with zero occurrences of *because.* Despite the geographical distance between Julius and Jim, who have more in common with respect to their ages and experiences as slaves, both articulate this variant, and in the speech of both men it occurs in the same environment, exclusively as a variant of the stressed vowel sound in *because.* As Lee Pederson indicates, the variant does not occur in the speech of any white speaker in *Huckleberry Finn,* even though the speech of many white characters, including first-person narrator Huck, is represented as dialectal. In the conjure tales, no white speech is represented dialectally, and so there are no occurrences of the feature in Chesnutt's white speakers. The 1964 interviews of African American and white speakers in Marion County, Missouri, on which Pederson's observations are based, found that the alternation of /e/ for /ɔ/ was "remembered as fairly common in all rustic speech of a generation or two" prior to the interviews, in both black and white speakers (Pederson 3). Further, *DARE* documents a number of occurrences of the variant, mostly recorded in literary sources, with most examples articulated by Southern speakers or characters, many but not all of them African American.

Similarly, in his phonological analysis of the conjure tales, Charles W. Foster found that the /e/ variant was also elicited during Linguistic Atlas interviews of North Carolina speakers living in or near Cumberland County, home of Fayetteville and the fictional Patesville. Foster also found that both African American and white Atlas interviewees used the variant, including the sixty-year-old African American woman in Sampson County and the seventy-seven-year-old African American Harnett County man mentioned above, and a seventy-year-old white woman interviewed in 1937 in Johnston County, about twenty miles from Fayetteville. Additionally, a fourth Atlas interviewee, a white Cumberland County woman, age seventy at the time of her 1937 interview, reported familiarity with the variant, according to Foster, but considered it "old-fashioned" (11). Further, the Franklin County and Brunswick County men whose Atlas data I consulted both also produced /kez/ in response to questions designed to elicit *because* or its variants. In fact, only one African American speaker interviewed for the Atlas in North Carolina, an eighty-year-old man in Martin County, produced a variant other than /kez/, articulating a sound resembling the now-standard /ɔ/ for the stressed vowel in *because,* without being prompted. One other, the Sampson County woman whose data Foster also consulted, produced it in response to field-worker Guy Lowman's suggestion and referred to it as a "new" form. She had previously articulated /kez/, also in response to interviewer Lowman's prompting, calling that form "old." From the Atlas data, it is possible to see that the /e/ variant was preserved in North Carolina speakers at least through the 1930s, and Pederson's data show that it persisted in Missouri through the 1960s. The *DARE* data is consistent with the positioning of the /e/ forms in Southern and South Midland speech, citing examples documented through 1961. However, *DARE* provides no North Carolina attestations of the variant, aside from its citation of Chesnutt's literary use.

The Atlas contains no data for North Carolina speakers of any race beyond 1937, by which time Guy Lowman, who single-handedly conducted all 160 of the North Carolina interviews, had already completed that impressive task. Looking outside North Carolina to neighboring states for additional data is of little help, because there is no data from African American speakers in Virginia or South Carolina beyond the 1940s. Surprisingly and unfortunately, despite plentiful data from nine African Americans interviewed for *LAMSAS* in Georgia between 1965 and 1972, not a single response was recorded for the target item *because.* This is probably the result of variation among the worksheets used in conducting those interviews and the ones Guy Lowman and other field-workers used in their earlier *LAMSAS* interviews. In all nine of the interviews with African American speakers in Georgia (and in a number of the interviews with white Georgia speakers as well), a combined questionnaire was used rather than the South Atlantic or Preliminary South Atlantic worksheets used in the North Carolina interviews. Even though data from Georgia speakers may be less reliable as evidence for the continued presence of forms found earlier in North Carolina, such data still could have been useful, as we have already seen evidence provided by the *LAMSAS* east-coast data and Pederson's Missouri findings that indicate that geography might not be as strong an influence on the variant as social factors seem to be. Most of the speakers who produced the variant in the *LAMSAS* data are identified as Type I, or folk speakers, according to the Atlas criteria, and Pederson's data indicates similar distribution. Chesnutt's documentation of the /e/ for /ɔ/ variant, along with that of Twain, supported by the data from socially similar speakers, provides an interesting and credible source for this apparently disappearing or extinct variant. Also, the clues provided by both Pederson's speakers and the *LAMSAS* interviewees concerning the venerability of the /kez/ forms and apparent subsequent rise of /ɔ/ forms, together with the literary representations of the form, contribute substantially to the possibility of observing language change in action.

Other older phonological variants found in Julius's speech and attested in the North Carolina Atlas data include the substitution of a low unrounded or slightly rounded back vowel similar to /ɑ/ for the now-standard /æ/ as in Julius's pronunciation of *Master* as *Marster*. Foster and other researchers, including Sumner Ives in his work on the literary dialect of Joel Chandler Harris, argue that a pronunciation-spelling using the *r* as in *Marster* does not necessarily imply that /r/ is meant to be pronounced in the word. This is especially true, they note, if authors of the literary dialects that use this spelling speak or are in close contact with largely *r*-less varieties of American English, as are found in the South, including Chesnutt's North Carolina and Harris's Georgia. Rather, both Foster and Ives note, the *r* is used to represent the vowel substitution itself (Foster 25; Ives 160). All but one African American speaker interviewed in North Carolina for *LAMSAS* produced a lowered, back vowel for the stressed vowel in *master,* with only the seventy-seven-year-old Harnett County man consistently producing the /æ/ variant. Again, the problem of not having more recent Atlas data available makes it difficult to determine the status of the lowered, backed variant beyond the 1930s, but Chesnutt's literary data along with the Atlas data provide useful information regarding this sound change prior to that time.

Alternation of /e/ for /i/ before /r/ or /l/ seems also to be less common today, but Chesnutt's representation of Julius's pronunciation of *real* and *queer* as *rale* and *quare* indicates that alternation. None of the North Carolina Atlas interviewees produced either /ril/ or /kwir/. Rather, all of them used /e/ in pronunciations of *real* that were mainly variations on /reəl/, variants that would almost certainly be represented orthographically as *rale*. For *queer,* there is slightly more variability, with the Harnett County man producing /kwɛə/, the Sampson County woman producing /kwɛr/, and the Franklin County man producing /kwæə/ and /kwɑə/, with the latter pronunciation reported as "old" by the interviewee. Again, these variants jibe with Chesnutt's orthographic representation, *quare*. The question remains as to whether the variants documented by Chesnutt and by *LAMSAS* are evidence of a past language change, a change still in progress, or whether they simply constitute continuing variation among regionally and socially diverse

Table 5.2 Grammatical Features in Julius McAdoo's Speech

Feature	Example	Number of Occurrences
Auxiliary and copula deletion	he gwine ter shoot de fus' man he ketch	15
Done + verb	I s'pose yer all done hearn befo' now	5
Simple past done	dey done dey wuk better	3
Multiple negation	he couldn' tell no lie	33
But negative	dey wa'n't but th'ee er fo' poun's lef'	2
Negative inversion	Dey didn' nobody answer	1
Noninverted questions	w'at fer yer won' speak ter me?	1
Subject-verb nonconcord	I does	53
Unmarked past	he didn' tel Dilsey come on the plantation	34*
Regularized past	he seed dis gal a-cryin'	30
Relative pronoun deletion or alternation	a gemman over on Rockfish w'at died	20
Possessive they	dey wicked ways	5
Undifferentiated pronoun reflexives	hisse'f, deyselves	13
Object pronoun them for subject pronoun those	one er dem big waggins	3
A-prefixing	he seed dis gal a-cryin'	2
Existential it/they	Dey didn' nobody answer	1
For-to constructions	he'd be glad fer ter do w'at he could.	45

*There are an additional sixty-one instances of unmarked past, but Chesnutt indicates with apostrophes that they are the results of phonology (final consonant reduction or deletion, as in *smile'* for *smiled*) rather than grammatical variants.[1]

speakers. The answers to such questions are beyond the scope of the current discussion, but that they are raised at all by way of an examination of Chesnutt's phonological representations and supported by *LAMSAS* data demonstrates both Chesnutt's remarkable ear and the potential linguistic value of his literary dialect.

But despite the unquestionable rigor and evident dominance of Chesnutt's phonological representations, attributable both to their high level of visibility on the page as well as to the large number of different features and generally high frequencies of occurrence, grammatical features are also meticulously recorded in Julius's speech, as outlined in table 5.2, with seventeen features represented in "Dave's Neckliss" alone. The grammatical features Chesnutt distinguishes in the speech of Julius McAdoo will be familiar to readers and researchers acquainted with African American speech varieties

as well as to those acquainted with the body of scholarship documenting grammatical features of AAE. His exacting depiction of these features contributes substantially to an image of Chesnutt as a conscientious
and definitive recorder of late-nineteenth-century black speech in North
Carolina.

But Chesnutt's careful incorporation of an extensive array of grammatical
and phonological AAE features into the speech of Julius McAdoo is also
intriguing in terms of a contradiction it reveals about Chesnutt's relationship
to African American dialectal speech. As discussed above, what is known of
Chesnutt's biography and what he wrote in his journal entries contradict any
presumption that he was a member of the speech community that also included Julius McAdoo and other speakers of AAE. As Richard Brodhead,
editor of Chesnutt's journals, also observes, "the notion that black vernacular
culture was in any simple way *his* culture" is a "misapprehension" that a
reading of the journals clearly contradicts (Intro. to *Journals* 22, emphasis
in original). In other words, according to Brodhead, it is not his own set
of linguistic traditions that Chesnutt represents in his portrayal of Julius
McAdoo's speech. But despite his relative outsider status with respect to
most of the African American community in North Carolina, all the evidence points to the probability that Chesnutt, highly educated, upwardly
mobile, and light-skinned enough to be mistaken for white on a number of
occasions, felt profoundly that regardless of variations in skin tone, level of
education, or social position, the lot of all African Americans was commu-
nal and that therefore it was his personal responsibility to try to improve the
lives of all African Americans.

However, Chesnutt's "talented tenth"–style view of uplifting the race did
not extend to excluding the influence of African American folk culture, including linguistic culture, from his fiction, as it did for several of his contemporaries. Robert C. Nowatzki cites the fiction of Frances E. W. Harper
and Pauline Hopkins, who used standard English in the speech of their characters in order to "counter the stereotypes of blacks and mulattoes as being
ignorant and uncouth" (33n). Compared to the strategies of Harper and
Hopkins, then, Nowatzki continues, some might construe Chesnutt's use of
dialect in the conjure tales as his apparent confirmation of "the racial stereotypes of plantation fiction that Harper and Hopkins are trying to discredit"
(33n). Those writers and other African American writers well into the Harlem Renaissance in the 1920s were deeply concerned with what Eric J.
Sundquist describes as "the form that any black speech took in the white

mind" (306). The understandable desire for disassociation from the dialectal speech that white writers of the plantation genre represented their African American characters as speaking, dialect rightly perceived as being manipulated in the service of reestablishing pre–Civil War racial hierarchies, resulted in the wholesale rejection of dialect representations for black speakers in the work of many black writers. The decisions by Harper and Hopkins not to use dialect, and later the recommendations of James Weldon Johnson to black writers to avoid dialect (Johnson 880), make sense in the context of the white-authored plantation tradition, in which black speech was co-opted to help achieve racist political ends. But when viewed in the context of the twenty-first century, it seems counterintuitive that dialectal representations of African American English were supposed to be off-limits to African American writers, and accordingly, twentieth-century writers such as Zora Neale Hurston, Langston Hughes, Claude McKay, and Sterling Brown flouted tradition by using dialect in their writing in compelling and original ways. It is unlikely that Chesnutt's use of dialect reflects attempts like those of Hughes, Hurston, and Brown to reclaim black dialect speech from the stereotyped renderings of African American speech in the plantation fiction of writers such as Thomas Nelson Page, given the structural similarities between the works of Chesnutt and Page. Or, if Chesnutt's use of dialect is such an attempt, it is exceedingly subtle, even to the point of invisibility. As we have seen, Chesnutt makes it clear in his journals that as a young man, at least, he did not particularly value black vernacular speech. But while there is no question that Chesnutt used the plantation-tradition forms, including representations of dialectal speech, in order to market his fiction and philosophies, it is equally clear that Chesnutt disapproved of that tradition and also did not use dialect the way Page did, to reproduce and reinforce the social distance between black and white and to emphasize black inferiority and white supremacy.

Chesnutt's contemporary Paul Laurence Dunbar also wrote in dialect in order to get published and painfully admitted as much. According to Eric J. Sundquist, for Chesnutt, Dunbar, and other African American artists of their time, "the use of dialect was fraught with the tension between capitulation to stereotypes and the desire to find an audience for African American literature, whether one took that desire to be rank minstrelsy or a literary act of cultural consciousness" (304). In his extensive treatment of Chesnutt's dialect writing in *To Wake the Nation*, Sundquist argues that in addition to being problematical for Chesnutt, however, his dialectal writing could also mark his "shift into a mode of cultural discourse that deliberately signified upon stereotypes" (304). Sundquist offers an intriguing interpretation of Chesnutt's relationship with dialectal forms:

> Dialect . . . became the language of the folk trickster—both the protagonist and the author—transferred to literary narrative, and Chesnutt's use of dialect must therefore be taken in part as a subtle, self-conscious examination of his relation to both the white plantation tradition and to those black writers who may have pandered to the public taste for "darky" language. More than that, however, it was a means for him to explore the ways in which language is perspectival and coded with assumptions of hierarchy and power. (305)

Sundquist is not alone in interpreting Chesnutt's dialect writing as subversive "signifying" on a racist literary tradition. Lorne Fienberg notes that what some readers may interpret in Chesnutt as "the minstrel's mask of accommodating" also functions as "the mask of subversion" (162). Fienberg points to the structural similarities between Chesnutt's stories and works of the plantation tradition but calls the resemblance "superficial," arguing that "Chesnutt uses these similarities to subvert both the familiar conventions of those popular works and the unsuspecting white reader's acquiescence in the slave system and the racial inequality those works affirm" (163). Still, Fienberg concludes, the white narrator even in the work of Chesnutt is "firmly in control of the narrative situation. Put another way, the frame is a strategy of containment which returns the freed slave to a state of narrative bondage" (164).

Chesnutt's use of dialect, then, defies casual classification. When his story "The Goophered Grapevine" was published in the *Atlantic* in 1887, he had few if any black-authored literary models for the representation of authentic African American speech in literature. He established that an African American writer could use dialectal representations for African American characters, but his legacy to writers like Hurston and Hughes was his use of dialect more than his motives or methods for doing so. However, this is not to say that Chesnutt never developed an appreciation for African American folk traditions or folk speech. According to Richard Brodhead, Chesnutt did develop an interest in black folklife while in his twenties, once he had realized the potential commercial applications of black vernacular culture and speech, and at this point he began to study North Carolina folk culture, and his interest eventually moved beyond commercial motivation. This new avenue for study led the young teacher and potential author to what Brodhead calls "an appreciation of this local ethos" as he met, talked with, and listened to North Carolinians whose experiences were far different from his own (Intro. to *Journals* 25). It is during this period that Chesnutt's understanding of and appreciation for the art of conjure and the African American storytelling tradition developed. However, Brodhead claims, Chesnutt's appreciation "is inseparable from the process by which he strives to secure a life apart from that ethos—a life in the inevitably distant, different world of successful authors" (25).

In his journals, there is little if any evidence that Chesnutt recognized AAE as a powerful means of expression. Rather, the evidence indicates that he used it, at least initially, as a means of pleasing publishers and audiences and as a means of couching his probably unwelcome social critiques. However, in doing so, he managed to subvert a racist literary tradition as well as establish a new African American tradition of dialect writing. Also, and perhaps most importantly, his well-documented (youthful) distaste for dialectal varieties of African American speech cannot be said to extend to its speakers and is not to be mistaken for the racism of a light-skinned man for darker-skinned African Americans. Especially in the other story collection he published in 1899, *The Wife of His Youth and Other Stories of the Color Line,* Chesnutt repeatedly condemns intragroup racism. Chesnutt's problematical relationship with AAE, then, seems not to be the result of its association with blackness but rather is a consequence of its association in his mind with white oppression of blacks, especially including forced illiteracy, to which he apparently attributed dialectal black speech. The plantation tradition was in Chesnutt's time the major written source for literary representations of black speech, and after Reconstruction, minstrelsy was its only representative in the arena of public discourse. It is possible that Chesnutt had internalized the idea that AAE was an inferior form of expression because of its association in his experience with uneducated blacks, because it had been used negatively by many writers as well as in minstrelsy, and because it was widely considered one more example of black inferiority and used by writers as "proof" of the alleged inferiority. Chesnutt's earnest educational mission included the desire to eradicate black dialectal speech in order to stamp out what must have been in his mind just another excuse for marginalization of black Americans. Even though he uses AAE brilliantly and authentically as a device that subtly weaves together the dichotomy of Julius's dignity and continued subjugation, Chesnutt never openly acknowledged that AAE had this power. The realization must have sunk in on him the way he hoped his antiracist messages would slip into his readers' hearts and minds through his seemingly imitative plantation tales, but the extent of his own acceptance may never be known for certain.

6

Representations of Speech and Attitudes about Race in *The Sound and the Fury*

The subject of William Faulkner's attitudes about race has been widely debated, with Faulkner lauded by writers such as Ernest J. Gaines and Toni Morrison as "an excellent observer, who, despite the limitations of his vision, refuses to lie about the realities of the Southern past or present" (qtd. in Werner 40). Others criticize the representations of African American characters in his work, as in James Baldwin's charge that "Faulkner could see Negroes only as they related to him, not as they related to each other" (qtd. in Werner 40), with his fictional depictions echoing the complicated and occasionally contradictory public positions he took with respect to civil rights. Undoubtedly the debate is fueled by the inconsistencies in Faulkner's general attitudes as expressed in public declarations that reveal the complexity of his views. Noel Polk illustrates this complexity, citing Faulkner's juxtaposition, within a single interview, of statements declaring his strong opposition to racial injustice with a surprisingly violent and controversial expression of his support for states' rights.

> If I have to choose between the United States government and Mississippi, then I'll choose Mississippi. What I am trying to do now is not have to make that decision. As long as there's a middle road, all right, I'll be on it. But if it came to fighting I'd fight for Mississippi against the United States even if it meant going out into the street and shooting Negroes. (qtd. in Polk 136)

According to Polk, Faulkner later repudiated these comments, but he did not deny having made them, and Polk further argues that they stand in contradistinction to Faulkner's personal concern "with the individual" African American, a concern he frequently enacted, as seen in his establishment of scholarships for African American students, for example (136, 141). However, the comments continue to be troubling.

Given that a fleet of Faulkner's fellow novelists, such as Morrison, Gaines, Baldwin, Alice Walker, and Ralph Ellison, along with numerous critics, including Thadious M. Davis and Charles D. Peavy, have produced plentiful and substantial material on the subject of William Faulkner and race, this chapter does not seek to resolve the debate once and for all but rather attempts to focus the issue in a new way. This discussion of the portrayal of African American English in Faulkner's fiction explores the ways attitudes about race can be enacted and interpreted through representation of the linguistic behavior of (and by) individuals by means of analysis of linguistic characterization and narration strategies. While *The Sound and the Fury* (1929) is not the work most frequently cited with respect to a discussion of Faulkner's own position or of his exploration of the complexity of racial attitudes and their consequences in postbellum America, with many critics focusing rather on *Absalom, Absalom!, Go Down, Moses,* and *Light in August, The Sound and the Fury* has much to offer an inquiry into the literary representation of ethnic speech varieties, which can in turn offer new insights into the work itself, its characters, and its meanings. Specifically, this chapter addresses the relationship between attitudes about race and how black speech is represented in the text as well as the artistic functions of speech representation in *The Sound and the Fury.*

Computational analysis of the complete direct speech data of the six principal African American characters in the novel reveals that Faulkner was largely, but not entirely, accurate in his representation of particular features of dialectal African American speech. His representation of grammatical features of AAE includes both documented features and a few he appears to have incorporated by way of overgeneralization. For example, Faulkner uses legitimate morphological features such as third-person singular *s*-deletion (*he say he didn't do it*) and first-person *-s* (*I knows what I knows*), but he extends the analogy to second-person verb forms (*you goes* or, frequently, *you is*). The second-person *-s* constructions are rare in most varieties of English, including AAE, but as table 6.1 shows, Faulkner's AAE-speaking characters use them in all but one possible case throughout the novel.

However, another feature Faulkner incorporates is *was*-leveling—the use of *was* and *wasn't* to mark past tense even in second-person forms and in first- and third-person plural constructions, in contrast to Standard American English (SAE) *were* and *weren't*—common in AAE and other varieties

Table 6.1 Second-Person -s Use by Character

Speaker	Tokens/Types	Frequency
Dilsey	24/25	96%*
Luster	5/5	100%*
Deacon	2/2	100%*
Louis Hatcher	1/1	100%
Job	1/1	100%
Reverend Shegog	1/1	100%

*Significant at p<.05.

of American English. The distinctions between the legitimate features discussed here and Faulkner's creations are subtle, and it would be very difficult for an individual unfamiliar with scholarship on AAE, practically nonexistent in 1929 when the novel was published, to detect them unerringly. The similarities between the legitimate features and the less-common constructions Faulkner uses are probably sufficient to explain his use of the rarer forms. Therefore, my conclusion is that Faulkner's use of dialectal grammatical features probably indicates a sincere attempt to represent them realistically rather than stereotypically.

Such a position is also supported by an analysis of Faulkner's portrayal of phonological features of AAE. The phonological variants indicated by Faulkner's respellings can be documented by the scholarship, with only a few exceptions. Some of these exceptions constitute "eye dialect," respellings used to mark nonstandardness without attention to actual features and to mark speakers as lower class or uneducated or both. For example, in the speech of Job, Jason Compson's coworker at the hardware store, *what* is represented as *whut,* which for many American English speakers does not indicate an alternative pronunciation. On the other hand, the incidences of eye dialect as well as some other interesting phonological inconsistencies clear the way for further investigation, and it is here where the central question addressed in this chapter arises: the question of how racial attitudes are evidenced by way of speech representations with respect to the narrators of each of the four sections of the novel. The inconsistencies, or perhaps rather the complexities, in the variation of African American speech from one narrator's section of the novel to the next, even when the speaker is the same, provide interesting insights into the attitudes of each narrator, attitudes that seem to be closely tied to the way the speech of African American characters is represented in his section of the novel.

The most conspicuous and intriguing characteristic of the African American speech as it is portrayed across the four sections of the book is the varying degrees to which AAE features appear in the language of individual characters. It is clear from early in the Benjy section that African American speech is differentiated from white speech as well as from the narration, which in the sections narrated by Benjy, Quentin, and Jason amounts to internal monologue. In the final section, there is no internal monologue, but the third-person narrator still differentiates the speech of blacks from the language of the narration and of white characters. Most interesting about the black speech as it is represented across the sections is the significant increase in differentiation by race of speaker, at least with respect to phonological features articulated, after the Benjy section concludes. In fact, the increase is so great that some critics have been misled into thinking that no differentiation at all, or very little, occurs in the Benjy section. A closer look, however, reveals some interesting things.

Thadious M. Davis argues that "there is little difference between the colloquial speech of blacks and that of whites in the first section" (117), but there are in fact differences even according to the very examples Davis cites to support her argument. She compares two statements from the novel, one produced by Versh and one by Caddy, both addressed to Benjy. Versh says, "You better keep them hands in your pockets. . . . You get them froze onto that gate" (4), while Caddy's words are "Keep your hands in your pockets . . . or they'll get frozen. You don't want your hands froze on Christmas, do you" (4).[1] It is clear that the two statements are semantically similar, which is not surprising given that both address a little boy with cold hands, but there are also several linguistic differences between the two that Davis apparently overlooks, as she concludes from her comparison of the two statements that "a peculiarly 'Negro' dialect is not one of Faulkner's major intentions" in the Benjy section (117). Initially, Davis's observation seems accurate to a point. Because Faulkner clearly relies less on phonological distinctions in the Benjy section, it does in fact appear that the speech of the African Americans and that of the whites in this section is treated differentially to a far lesser degree than in the remaining three sections of the novel. However, even in the example Davis uses, there are important syntactic and morphological differences.

For example, Versh's lines contain two occurrences of auxiliary deletion, a well-documented feature of many varieties of AAE. Versh's "You better keep them hands in your pockets" corresponds to SAE "you *had* better" and his "You get them froze onto that gate" corresponds to SAE "you *will* get." Also, Versh merges or levels simple past and perfective in his use of *froze.* Caddy's version, on the other hand, contains no examples of auxiliary deletion. There is no opportunity for deletion in the first sentence of her sequence, but the second, "they'll get frozen," contrasts grammatically with Versh's "You get them froze" both in its lack of auxiliary deletion and in the use of perfective *frozen.* In the second part of Caddy's utterance, in which she adds, "You don't want your hands *froze*" (8, emphasis added), she produces a construction analogous to Versh's leveling to simple past, indicating some similarity between the individual varieties of Mississippi speech each character produces. Finally, Versh refers to "them hands," with *them* standing semantically for *your,* which Caddy uses, and otherwise corresponding to SAE *those.* Clearly, then, there are important grammatical differences between black and white speech even in the Benjy section.

And there are many additional examples of AAE features present in the speech of Dilsey and her family in Benjy's section. Focusing in particular on Dilsey and Luster, who produce the most talk of the African American characters in this section as well as in Jason's section and the final section, it is possible to observe that a number of grammatical features, and to a lesser extent several phonological features, of AAE are in fact present in their speech. Davis is partially correct in noting that the novel's African American speakers experience a noticeable shift in the number of features present in their speech, as well as in the frequencies with which those features occur, from the initial section through the remaining three sections, but this observation actually applies only to phonological features. It is true that for the number of phonological features represented and their frequencies, the increase between sections is considerable. But even in the Benjy section, the speech of Dilsey and Luster, along with the other members of the Gibson family, is to a great extent grammatically differentiated from that of the white characters, just as it is in the three remaining sections. In fact, in the Benjy section, both Dilsey and Luster produce grammatical features of AAE at frequencies comparable to or greater than those at which they are produced in the subsequent sections of the novel. For example, in Dilsey's speech in the Benjy section, auxiliary and copula deletion occur in sixty-four of the eighty-six possible opportunities for occurrence, or in 74 percent of the opportunities. Such deletion is realized in Luster's speech in twenty-six of thirty-five opportunities, again in 74 percent of the opportunities. The frequencies of occurrence for these features in the Jason section, the final

Table 6.2 Copula/Auxiliary Deletion Frequencies for Dilsey and
Luster[2]

Speaker		Tokens/Types	Frequency*
Dilsey			
	Benjy section	64/86	74%
	Jason section	18/31	58%
	Final section	78/105	74%
	All sections	160/222	72%
Luster			
	Benjy section	26/35	74%
	Jason section	5/5	100%
	Final section	31/38	82%
	All sections	62/78	79%

*Significant at p<.05.

section, and overall, as noted in table 6.2, show considerable levels of consistency in the representation of auxiliary and copula deletion across the sections of the novel for both speakers. The complete set of data shows that for other grammatical features under consideration here, frequencies of occurrence are also comparable across sections of the novel, as illustrated in the tables in appendix B.

But phonological features of AAE are not missing completely from the speech of the Gibsons in the Benjy section, even if the respellings that indicate variant pronunciations are considerably less common in this section than in the other three sections. In the Benjy section, Dilsey and Luster each produce five of the thirteen phonological features under consideration here. Both Dilsey and Luster exhibit unstressed initial syllable deletion, as in *bout* for *about,* vocalization of postvocalic /r/, as in *sho* for *sure,* loss of /r/ after consonants and in unstressed syllables, as in *liberry* for *library,* and merger of /ɛ/ and /ɪ/, as in *set* for *sit.* Dilsey also produces intervocalic /r/ loss with syllable loss, as in *Cahline* for *Caroline,* and Luster produces final consonant cluster reduction, as in *tole* for *told.* Elsewhere in the novel, Dilsey produces seven of the eight remaining features, and Luster produces all eight. (See appendix B for complete data.) The features and their frequencies are noted for Dilsey and Luster in the Benjy section and compared to their frequencies for the same features in the whole novel in tables 6.3 and 6.4.

These findings make it clear that in the Benjy section, phonological variation is not represented to the extent that it is in the subsequent sections as

Table 6.3 Phonological Data for Dilsey

Feature	Benjy Section	Overall
Vocalization of postvocalic /r/	3/111 (2.7%*)	79/259 (31%*)
Loss of /r/ after consonants	2/9 (22%*)	9/16 (56%*)
Intervocalic /r/ loss with syllable loss	2/6 (33%)	20/31 (65%*)
Consonant cluster reduction	0/153 (0)	65/337 (19%*)
Deletion of unstressed syllable	11/34 (32%*)	43/103 (42%*)
Merger of /ɛ/ and/I/	6/63 (9.5%*)	67/131 (51%)

*Significant at p<.05.

Table 6.4 Phonological Data for Luster

Feature	Benjy Section	Overall
Vocalization of postvocalic /r/	5/61 (8%*)	16/101 (16%*)
Loss of /r/ after consonants	1/5 (20%)	4/9 (44%*)
Intervocalic /r/ loss with syllable loss	0/0	8/11 (73%*)
Consonant cluster reduction	3/31 (9.6%*)	26/62 (42%*)
Deletion of unstressed syllable	2/9 (22%*)	8/19 (42%*)
Merger of /ɛ/ and /I/	1/15 (6.6%*)	17/36 (47%*)

*Significant at p<.05.

well as with the uniformity that grammatical features of AAE are generally represented throughout the novel, including in the Benjy section. The question is why grammatical markers of AAE are represented consistently in the speech of Dilsey and Luster throughout the novel while significantly fewer phonological features are represented in the Benjy section, and while those phonological features which are present appear with considerably lower frequencies.

In a rare features analysis of AAE as represented in *The Sound and the Fury*, Mark Lencho also notes the shift between the way the phonology of the Gibsons is portrayed in the Benjy section and the way it is portrayed in the subsequent sections of the novel. He offers two theories worth considering, one to try to explain why Faulkner's representation of phonological features of AAE increases in the later sections of the book, and the other to try to explain why the depiction of AAE varies between characters. While the latter question is not this chapter's central concern, it still has bearing on the discussion here and should be addressed.

First, Lencho looks at the composition history of the novel, arguing that the linguistic shifts occur "according to the chronology of composition [suggesting] that the author became increasingly concerned with verisimilitude in language as the story advanced" (410). Lencho further contends that Faulkner was disinclined to revise *The Sound and the Fury* once the manuscript was submitted for publication, claiming that this reluctance along with the speed with which Faulkner completed the novel—in approximately 160 days—"accounts for the persistence in the typescript, and each consecutive edition, of the obvious style shifts that might have been emended otherwise" (410–11). However, Lencho's "hypothesis of author-unconscious style shifting" (411) assumes that the variability in (phonological) dialectal representation between chapters is accidental rather than artistic, a conclusion that is at odds with the consistency with which grammatical features are represented throughout the novel.

Lencho's second theory appears incompatible with his first because it attributes dialectal variation to artistic strategies rather than to uncorrected accidents on Faulkner's part. In this sense, it is a more appealing theory than the first because it does not rely on the premise that Faulkner's dialectal representations are something other than carefully crafted attempts at depicting realistic speech, a possibility that the high level of linguistic accuracy and artistic believability simply does not support. In this hypothesis, Lencho differentiates between "functional" and "index" passages of the text, with the former "advancing the story line and establishing the theme" and the latter "simply [providing] a context in which the real concerns of the story may operate" (411). He contends that the speech of African American characters in "functional passages," that is, in utterances produced by central characters like Dilsey and Luster, contains both fewer AAE features and lower frequencies of occurrence for those features that are produced. But this stance is problematical precisely because it argues for extremely subtle linguistic distinctions between characters, which would be unlikely to occur in the hastily completed and unrevised text Lencho portrays, even taking into consideration his theory that Faulkner became increasingly concerned with his portrayal of AAE as he wrote. Lencho offers a brief comparison of the features produced by Dilsey and by Job in the Jason section by way of support for his contention that the intercharacter variation exists because of the functional-versus-index distinction. That is, he argues, Job's speech is more differentiated from that of white characters than is Dilsey's because of his character's function of "providing local color and . . . establishing a more complete setting for the principal action of the plot" (Lencho 411).

There are two problems with this analysis, in addition to the doubts it

Table 6.5 Phonological Features Shared by Dilsey and Job

Feature	Dilsey*	Job*
Vocalization of postvocalic /r/	12/23 (52%)	7/18 (39%)
Intervocalic /r/ loss with syllable loss	8/9 (89%)	4/4 (100%)
Stopping of syllable-initial fricatives	18/24 (75%)	33/33 (100%)
Stopping of voiceless interdental fricatives	4/5 (80%)	2/2 (100%)
Labialization of interdental fricatives	1/1 (100%†)	2/2 (100%)
Consonant cluster reduction	7/34 (21%)	2/5 (40%†)
Unstressed syllable deletion	6/18 (33%)	3/6 (50%)
Final unstressed /n/ for /ŋ/ in present participle	25/26 (96%)	7/7 (100%)
Other alternation of /n/ for /ŋ/	4/5 (80%)	2/2 (100%)
Alternation of /aɪ/ for /ɔɪ/	12/12 (100%)	1/1 (100%†)
Merger of /ɛ/ and /ɪ/	21/24 (88%)	5/9 (56%)

*Significant at p<.05, except where noted. †Not significant.

raises concerning Lencho's first theory. First, my analysis finds that in the Jason section, Dilsey and Job not only produce similar AAE features, but they do so at comparable frequencies, with each producing eleven of the thirteen phonological features under consideration here, and with Dilsey producing higher frequencies for two of the features, identical frequencies for two, and comparable frequencies (89 percent to Job's 100 percent, for instance) for five. Table 6.5 shows the phonological data produced by Dilsey and Job in the Jason section, comparing the frequencies with which each character articulates the eleven features shared by the two characters. And Lencho's own data actually reveals results that agree with my analysis. For example, in many cases, the discrepancies he cites in feature-production frequencies between the two speakers are slight and not statistically significant, as in the difference between the 100 percent frequency for Job's substitution of final unstressed /n/ for /ŋ/ in the present participle, as in *growin,* and Dilsey's 90 percent, especially considering that these percentages represent token-to-type ratios of, respectively, seven of seven and nine of ten opportunities for occurrence (Lencho 413). Additionally, again according to Lencho's data, Dilsey produces a higher frequency of postvocalic /r/ vocalization, 30 percent to Job's 26 percent, while producing frequencies identical to Job's for several features, including 100 percent occurrence on the parts of both speakers for multiple negation, which Lencho inexplicably interprets as indicative of Job's greater "[bias] toward nonstandard English, with respect to the given feature" (412). Therefore, Lencho's conclusion that "Job's speech is systematically more nonstandard than Dilsey's" (412) is simply not confirmed either by his own data or by the data collected and analyzed for my analysis.

The second problem with Lencho's analysis is lack of attention to a more plausible explanation for dialect variation between Dilsey and Job. No speaker of any variety of any language, including AAE, will incorporate every possible feature of that variety into his or her speech, will produce speech that contains no nondialectal features, and perhaps most important with respect to Lencho's analysis, will produce speech which contains the same features or frequencies as every or even any other speaker of the same or a similar variety. A conscientious attempt at representing dialect in literature usually involves representing variation among speakers as well as to some degree variation within the speech of a single speaker. Lencho allows for interspeaker and individual variation exclusively in the cases of Deacon and Reverend Shegog, for whom he makes only a geographic distinction from their Mississippi counterparts (415). But there are other linguistic and extralinguistic phenomena at work in the speech of both men. First, however, a return to the original question is in order.

If Lencho's explanation is not sufficient, the question of why there is significant phonological variation in the speech of individual characters from the Benjy section of the novel to the later sections remains unanswered. Still lacking is an explanation that takes Faulkner's artistry into consideration. Lencho's theory of the functional/index distinction between speakers attempts such consideration, but even if the hypothesis were supported by the data, still it would not explain the increase in representation of phonological features from the Benjy section to the rest of the novel. An alternative explanation is necessary, one which takes into consideration both artistic and linguistic aspects of the use of literary dialect.

In his "Theory of Literary Dialect," Sumner Ives argues that "lacking a uniform standard for spoken English, the author has no choice but to use the accepted criteria of his own region. This is perhaps the most important single axiom in the study of literary dialects" (158). In other words, knowledge of and attention to "the author's speech, or at least his speech type, is a necessary prelude to the interpretation of his dialect [representation]" (Ives 174). By considering Faulkner's biographical information along with a review of existing sound recordings of his actual speech,[3] it is possible to reconstruct a viable starting point for what Faulkner's speech sounded like and what phonological and grammatical features it may or may not have contained. The sound recordings and biographical information support a hypothesis that William Faulkner's speech was sufficiently similar to that of the Compsons as Faulkner represents them. Faulkner was born into a prominent Oxford family, spent most of his life in Mississippi, and was educated, if haphazardly, at the University of Mississippi. In these respects, he has much in common with his fictional Compsons, also lifelong Mississippians, described by John T. Matthews as enjoying for generations a position as "one of Jefferson's leading families" (37). Additionally, like Faulkner himself, Jason Compson III was educated at a Southern institution, the University of the South, in Sewanee, Tennessee (Faulkner 123). Therefore, it hardly seems a stretch to claim that Faulkner's own speech resembled that of the Compsons, or, rather, that theirs resembles his.

With this information, and considering Ives's axiom that literary dialect tends to be represented as it stands in relation to the speech of its author, it is not only likely but probable that Faulkner differentiated between his own speech—and therefore that of the Compsons—and AAE, and consequently represents only the latter as "other" with respect to the SAE most of the novel's white characters are portrayed as speaking. By itself, this offers no explanation for why the differential phonological representations of Gibson and Compson speech occur less frequently in the Benjy section. But it does explain why the speech of the Compsons, which would no doubt sound distinctive to non-Mississippians, is not differentiated from SAE, even though many of those non-Mississippians would undoubtedly argue that such speech, and Faulkner's, is not SAE at all. Ives argues that such nonrepresentation of even a highly salient variety is not at all unusual and is in fact to be expected:

> An author will fail to represent many features of his character's speech which may be regionally characteristic but which carry no implication of inferiority or "difference" within those regions where they are found. . . . As a matter of fact, the speech of educated persons is not ordinarily represented in "dialectal" spellings by authors who are portraying their own region. (163)

It is worth noting that on only two occasions in the novel is the speech of a white character differentiated conspicuously from that of the other white characters, and it is especially significant that one of the two characters is a member of the Snopes family, whom Faulkner uses in much of his fiction to typify lower-class whiteness in Yoknapatawpha County and who stand in stark contrast to the Compsons. In a conversation about financial ventures among speculators at the telegraph office, I. O. Snopes says to Jason, "Well, I've picked hit; I reckon taint no more than fair fer hit to pick me once in a while" (136). No Compson ever says *hit, taint,* or *fer.* The other white character whose speech is differentiated conspicuously is a farmer whom Jason assists at the hardware store, and to whom Jason refers tellingly as a "dam redneck" (122). Here, then, instead of race, speech differentiation is based on class.

In addition to the light Ives's claims shed on why Faulkner differentiates African American speech from white speech at all, they also turn out to be quite important to a discussion of the differential treatment of African American speech in the Benjy section compared to elsewhere in the novel. A plausible explanation is that Faulkner uses AAE features subtly in the Benjy section, hence his reliance on the less-obvious grammatical features. The grammatical features are just enough to mark the Gibsons as they appear in this section as "other" with respect to most of the Compsons, but not necessarily to Benjy. Among the Compsons, only Benjy forms a familial relationship with the Gibsons. Once Caddy leaves, and arguably before that, Dilsey is Benjy's primary caregiver, and her sons and grandson are consecutively dispatched as Benjy's constant companions. Therefore it makes sense that Benjy would not interpret the speech of the Gibsons as "other," which might explain why respellings of their speech to represent phonological variants are minimal in his section. Of course, there is no way to know whether Benjy is capable of interpreting dialectal differences in speech. Since he is unable to speak himself, there is also no way to know how Benjy would talk if he could. That is, there is no way to know whether Benjy's speech would sound more like that of a Gibson or a Compson. However, his experience of being raised mostly by Dilsey and her family could have resulted in his speech being strongly influenced by that of the Gibsons. Therefore, he would not necessarily reproduce their talk as being alien or unusual, and indeed he does not represent it as such to the degree that it is portrayed elsewhere in the novel. That it is represented differentially at all in the Benjy section could be an indication of the youngest Compson's awareness that even as he is in many ways of the Gibsons, the other Compsons are not, and even he is not completely. The attitudes of Quentin and Jason and their corresponding representations of black speech also support such an interpre-

Table 6.6 Phonological Feature Frequency Comparisons for Dilsey, Luster, and Job, by Section

	Speaker	Tokens/Types (All Phonological Features)	Frequency*
Benjy section			
	Dilsey	24/639	4%
	Luster	12/275	4%
Jason section			
	Dilsey	119/186	64%
	Luster	31/48	65%
	Job	68/97	70%

*Significant at p<.05.

tation and further reveal the skill and subtlety with which Faulkner implemented literary dialect.

Quentin and Jason simply do not share the kind of familial relationship with the Gibsons that their youngest brother enjoys. Therefore, since the elder Compson sons distance the Gibsons in relation to themselves far more than Benjy does, it is hardly surprising that the speech of the Gibsons and most other African Americans is represented as highly distinct from white speech in the sections narrated by Quentin and Jason. This distinction is evidenced by the considerable increases in the number and in the frequencies of occurrence of AAE phonological markers, a trend which continues in the final section of the novel. Because of the complexity of Quentin's perceptions about race and the clarity with which Jason's are portrayed in the novel, a brief discussion of the Jason section is in order before turning to Quentin.

In Jason's section, the speech of the Gibsons is made to stand out distinctly from the narration and from the speech of white characters, as is the speech of Job, Jason's coworker, the other significant African American character in the section. This is shown in table 6.6, which compares the frequencies for phonological features of AAE in the speech of Dilsey and Luster in the Benjy section to those present in their speech in the Jason section. The table also includes the frequencies of feature production in Job's speech in order to help illustrate the increase in differential representation of black speech between the two sections. As the table illustrates, the frequencies of occurrence for the phonological features are substantially higher in the Jason section than in the Benjy section in the speech of both Dilsey and Luster, with statistically significant differences of approximately sixty percentage points for both speakers. Similarly, the frequency of phonological features in the speech of Job, who appears only in the Jason section, is also high, at 70 percent.

Initially, Jason's attitudes about race appear to contrast sharply with those of his older brother, but ultimately the only real difference between the two is in the subtlety with which Quentin acts out his racial fantasies. There is nothing subtle about Jason, whose insulting treatment of Job and cruelty to Luster and also to Dilsey, whom he crudely dismisses as "an old half-dead n———" (116) after violently slamming a door in her face during an argument with his niece, leaves no doubts about his racial attitudes. Embittered by the loss of what he perceives as his birthright, white and male privilege, as both his family and the racial and sexual hierarchies of the Old South crumble before his eyes, he acts out his bitterness and rage through his virulent misogyny, racism, and anti-Semitism. Jason's misogyny is evidenced in his grudge against Caddy and her daughter Quentin, whom he holds responsible for his missed opportunities, and in his dismissive, sarcastic treatment of his mother and open contempt for Dilsey. Jason also treats Lorraine, his prostitute-lover, with his trademark viciousness: "That's the only way to manage [women]," he declares. "Always keep them guessing. If you cant think of any other way to surprise them, give them a bust in the jaw" (122).

The grossness of Jason's lashing out at practically everyone around him stands in unmistakable contrast to his brother Quentin's more ceremonious, cerebral, and ultimately self-destructive undertakings, but despite the very different strategies each employs in his attempts to deal with changes in the social organization, the basis for each brother's philosophy is revealed upon closer scrutiny to be the same: unwavering but frustrated belief in white entitlement and black subjugation. Certainly Jason's helpless fury is only one possible manifestation of the racial views the two brothers share.

In Quentin's section, there is very little Gibson speech at all. Dilsey and Versh appear only briefly and the other Gibsons not at all, in large part because of Quentin's absence from Mississippi during his year at Harvard, during which his section takes place. However, there are important African American characters in the section, and the ways their speech is represented are very telling with respect to Quentin's attitudes about race. The AAE in Quentin's section is for the most part very much differentiated from his own narration and from the speech of other white characters.

The most significant relationship Quentin has with an African American is with the Deacon, who has command of several varieties of English and is able to employ each as it suits his needs. When he greets the trains at the beginning of every new school year, unerringly picking out the new Southern students, he calculatingly affects the speech of a working-class Southern black in his phonological and grammatical linguistic features as well as in his deference to his white interlocutors, as in his offers to assist with their luggage: "Yes, suh. Right dis way, young marster, here we is. . . . hit'll be done got cold dar when you arrives" (62). However, once he has the student, as Quentin puts it, "completely subjugated," his speech "moves gradually northward" (62), meaning, ostensibly, closer to SAE. But there is no evidence in the text of the Deacon's speech shifting gradually; rather, he performs distinct code-switches from the SAE he is speaking when Quentin encounters him on June 2, 1910, to the AAE he uses to speak to the new arrivals, and then back to SAE for most of his conversation with Quentin.

It is interesting to consider the relationship between the two men, who by the time of Quentin's death seem to be more than simply acquaintances. Quentin has kind words for the Deacon: "You're a good fellow, Deacon. . . . I hope you'll always find as many friends as you've made" (64). However, it may be a stretch for Quentin to consider the older man his friend. Quentin inadvertently reveals this when he briefly confuses the Deacon with Roskus Gibson:

> He was looking at me now, the envelope white in his black hand, in the sun. His eyes were soft and irisless and brown, and suddenly I saw Roskus watching me from behind all his whitefolks' claptrap of uniforms and politics and Harvard manner, diffident, secret, inarticulate and sad. . . . [But] Roskus was gone. Once more he was the self he had long since taught himself to wear in the world's eye. (63–64)

It seems curious that the Deacon would remind Quentin of Roskus. Perhaps it is because both men are older, kind to Quentin, and, most importantly, African American. It is clear that Roskus Gibson is the model of mature African American maleness for Quentin. In other words, Quentin stereotypes the Deacon based on his experiences with Roskus, which are of course very different from his experiences with the Deacon. Quentin's tendency to stereotype African Americans in this way has already been revealed in the section he narrates by his reaction to an earlier encounter with a man on a mule, whom Quentin meets in Virginia on his way home from Harvard for the Christmas holiday. This man's blackness is to Quentin very different from the characteristics he observes in African American denizens of Cambridge. He attributes these differences to geography and to social change, embodied to Quentin's way of thinking by a prosperous-looking man he sees on the train with a "derby and shined shoes" (55). The man on the mule represents for Quentin what he idealizes as the "childlike and ready incompetence and paradoxical reliability" (56) of his idea of the authentic African American, also realized in Quentin's view by the Gibsons. Thus, the man on the mule reminds him of the Gibsons: "I didn't know that I had missed Roskus and Dilsey and them until that morning in Virginia" (55).

The well-dressed man Quentin sees on the train attracts his attention and triggers his ruminations on African Americans, during which some interesting attitudes surface, most notably his realization that "a n——— is not a person so much as a form of behavior, a sort of obverse reflection of the white people he lives among" (55). At once an indirect but scathing indictment of Southern whites and a stereotypical, dehumanizing view of African Americans, this statement exemplifies Quentin's attitudes toward African Americans.

The man on the train and the Deacon are juxtaposed in the Quentin section with another Southern speaker of AAE, Louis Hatcher, a friend of the Gibsons' with whom Quentin and Versh spent time as young boys. Interestingly and tellingly, Louis's speech contains many phonological features of AAE, of which Louis produces ten of the thirteen under investigation here, as noted in table 6.7. The table also shows high frequencies of occurrence, with Louis producing five of the phonological features 100 percent of the time and one 75 percent of the time. Louis's speech shows high frequencies for dialectal features, perhaps in order to distinguish it from Quentin's narration and from other white and Northern black speech, but the appearance here of questionable respellings, or eye dialect, could also indicate Faulkner's attempt simply to mark Louis socially and racially as an uneducated, rural African American without going to the trouble of a sensitive representation of AAE, or perhaps rather to mark Quentin's own insensitivity to the need to represent Louis's speech authentically.

The content of Louis's talk, largely consisting of an explanation for why he does not clean his lantern more frequently, gives Quentin a chance to patronize the much older man, who "wuz huntin possums in dis country when dey was still drowndin nits in [Quentin's or Versh's] pappy's head wid coal oil, boy" (73). The last time Louis cleaned his lantern, he reports, was

Table 6.7 Phonological Feature Frequencies for Louis Hatcher

Feature	Tokens/Types	Frequency*
Vocalization of postvocalic /r/	9/12	75%
Loss of /r/ after consonants	0/0	0
Intervocalic /r/ loss with syllable loss	1/2	50%†
Vocalization of unstressed syllabic /r/	0/8	0
Stopping of syllable-initial fricatives	31/31	100%
Stopping of voiceless interdental fricatives	2/2	100%
Labialization of interdental fricatives	0/0	0
Consonant cluster reduction	6/13	46%
Deletion of initial unstressed syllable	1/3	33%†
Final unstressed /n/ for /ŋ/ in present participle	6/6	100%
Other alternation of final unstressed /n/ for /ŋ/	0/0	0
Alternation of diphthongs /aɪ/ for /ɔɪ/	1/1	100%
Merger of /ɛ/ and /ɪ/	7/7	100%

*Nonzero frequencies are significant at p<.05, except where noted. †Not significant.

when he and his wife had received news of the possibility of a flood. Louis says he believes that cleaning the lamp that night saved the Hatchers from the flood, and so he claims he will not clean it again until another flood threatens: "Whut I want to clean hit when dey ain't no need?" (73) The scene, especially including Louis's exaggerated dialect and seemingly fallacious logic, is reminiscent of minstrel show routines, which frequently relied on such stereotypes. The dialect is exaggerated in that Faulkner peppers Louis's speech with eye dialect, using spellings such as *whut, wuz,* and *watter,* suspect representations of the type that some writers have traditionally used to indicate speaker inferiority or at least great social distance between speakers rather than any real dialectal feature, as is clear by their failure to differentiate a word's pronunciation from the standard. There are no instances of eye dialect in the Benjy section, and few elsewhere in the novel. The scene with Louis underscores for Quentin what he perceives as the man's inferiority to himself, demonstrated by his scornful rejoinder to Louis, that the flood "was way up in Pennsylvania. . . . It couldn't ever have got down this far" (72).

Where Benjy is encompassed in the Gibson family as much as he is with the Compsons, or perhaps more so, Quentin's attitude toward the Gibsons is more distant, patriarchal, and patronizing. He may perceive a sense of family with respect to the Gibsons, but only with himself in the role of patron and benefactor, a role he also enacts with the man on the mule. "Buy yourself some Santy Claus" (55), Quentin says, tossing a quarter to the man. The eldest Compson son is comfortable with African Americans only when he feels himself above them, such as in his conversation with Louis and in his final dealings with Deacon. Years earlier, Quentin's anger at Versh for helping Caddy to unbutton her dress, which Versh does unwillingly, only in response to Caddy's threat, and later his physical attack on T.P. when the younger Gibson son gets drunk—and gets Benjy drunk—during Caddy's wedding, indicate Quentin's patronizing attitude as well as the lengths to which he is willing to go to try to maintain his dominance. However, as is foreshadowed by T.P.'s laughter from the ground where he is lying as Quentin savagely and repeatedly kicks him, and as is seen later in Quentin's confrontation with Dalton Ames over the latter's affair with Caddy, Quentin is not dominant—and thus not a man—according to his own definitions. These definitions include loss of virginity in addition to possession of the physical wherewithal to convince Ames to leave town via a show of manly strength, neither of which can Quentin achieve. It is no coincidence that Quentin flashes back to his hunting trip with Louis and Versh and their conversation, in which he gets to feel like a man only through his naive underestimation of Louis's manhood and humanity, on the heels of remembering Caddy's confession to him of her pregnancy.

Caddy's ostensible violation of Quentin's self-awarded rights to her love and her body helps to cause what John T. Matthews calls his "overwhelming sense of displacement and impotence" (58). His sense of potency, then, no longer possible within a sexual hierarchy, remains an option only in a racial one, one which to his dismay is also shifting. His lifelong self-maintained emotional distance from African Americans has much to do with his desire for potency, and much to do with the portrayal of African American speech as radically different from his own.

Quentin's penultimate act is to get his personal affairs in order, an act consistent with his attempts to adhere to his code of manliness, and which includes an act of beneficence toward the Deacon when he leaves the older man a suit of clothes. Deacon is chosen partly because he has been kind to Quentin but mostly because he has played along with Quentin's game, playing the part of deferential servant to the young white "master." Quentin thus finds one last opportunity to act out the part of patron. Presumably, then, he gets to feel like his version of a man when he dies.

A question that arises with respect to the final section of *The Sound and the Fury* is why it is narrated in the third person. Each of the Compson sons gets to tell his version of the story, even one who presumably has no language of his own, but no woman gets to speak for herself, and no African American does, either. This means that characters of central significance to the narrative, especially Caddy, Dilsey, Luster, Mrs. Compson, and Miss Quentin, must remain silent as their stories materialize, despite the certainty that each could offer as compelling a point of view as the Compson boys. According to John T. Matthews, many critics interpret the final section as Dilsey's section, and he further notes that *The Portable Faulkner* actually uses the heading "Dilsey" for the April 8, 1928, section (77). But the last section differs conspicuously from the other three sections in its third-person narration, and more specifically in that no one is permitted to share Dilsey's thoughts or is privileged to overhear her internal monologue. Also contrary to such a designation is Faulkner's own claim with respect to the sections of the book: "I finished it the first time, and it wasn't right, so I wrote it again, and that was Quentin, that wasn't right. I wrote it again, that was Jason, that wasn't right, then I tried to let Faulkner do it, that still was wrong" (qtd. in Matthews 78).

A plausible explanation for the narrative shift in the final section, and one which has implications for the representation of dialect in this section, has to do with the way female characters, especially Dilsey and Caddy, are envisioned and constructed in the text. It is clear that Caddy and Dilsey are both idealized in this story, disallowing a glimpse into the complicated and contradictory facets of their humanity that a close look into their thoughts and feelings would reveal. Michael Millgate reports that Faulkner himself alluded to his own idealization of Caddy: "To me she was the beautiful one, she was my heart's darling" (qtd. in Millgate 165). Michael Gresset confirms the idealization, adding, "Caddy was his favorite child in more than one sense; in his gallery of characters, she is the first achievement of his vision of Eve before the Fall" (175).

It is not surprising that Faulkner infuses the Compson boys with the same passion for Caddy he feels himself. As Carvel Collins points out, "each of the brothers is obsessed by their sister" (125). Quentin's idealization of Caddy has much to do with his ultimate act of self-destruction, which Arthur F. Kinney calls "his incestuous, suicidal marriage with Caddy" (7). Similarly, it is Benjy's adoration and idealization of Caddy that leads to his hysterical response to her developing sexuality and later to his wordless, bellowing reaction to her absence. And while Jason pretends to idealize no one and nothing, his enraged fixation on Caddy as the cause of his own personal failure, and the revenge he takes on her through his mistreatment of her daughter, is much like that of an obsessed, thwarted lover. Clearly, then, all three brothers create an image of Caddy that no real person could possibly live up to, and when she inevitably fails to do so, her brothers respond with helpless, impotent emotion.

Conversely, only Quentin of the three brothers idealizes Dilsey (and also Roskus), but he apparently shares this idealization with Faulkner himself. Quentin's vision of Roskus during the Deacon's moment of vulnerability and his being reminded of Dilsey and Roskus by the man on the mule, who represents the social inferiority Quentin believes is the proper position for African Americans, are surely consequences of his idealization, or stereotyping, of the Gibsons, who exist for Quentin only in relation to himself. While Faulkner's views are perhaps more benign, his celebration of Dilsey, who according to Gresset represents "the living embodiment of so many of the virtues extolled by Faulkner at Stockholm" (179) in his Nobel prize speech, still places the responsibility for Compson souls squarely on Dilsey's shoulders. That the Compsons do not heed is irrelevant; Dilsey still functions as the moral and spiritual locus of the book and hence is representative of James Baldwin's charge, noted at the beginning of this chapter, that Faulkner portrays African Americans in relation to whites rather than in relation to one another. Faulkner's dedication of *Go Down, Moses* to Caroline Barr, argued by many critics to be the basis for Dilsey's character, shows further evidence of this idealization: "To Mammy Caroline Barr. . . . Who was born in slavery and gave to my family a fidelity without stint or calculation of recompense and to my childhood an immeasurable devotion and love" (qtd. in Gresset 180). On the other hand, the novel's juxtaposition of a strong, spiritually healthy African American family against a superficial and consequently declining white family is evidence that Faulkner does not share the negatively stereotypical views of either Quentin or Jason.

Faulkner's idealization of Dilsey has consequences for the representation of AAE in the final section. Where Benjy linguistically differentiates the Gibsons only subtly because of his close and even familial relationship with them, in contrast to both Quentin and Jason, who markedly differentiate the AAE produced in their sections because of attempts at maintaining social distance and racial hierarchy, Faulkner apparently represents the speech of African Americans in the final section to illustrate the moral and spiritual distance between the Gibsons, especially Dilsey, and the Compsons. As

Table 6.8 Phonological Frequency Comparisons for Dilsey and
Luster in the Benjy and Final Sections

	Speaker	Tokens/Type (All Phonological Features)	Frequency*
Benjy section			
	Dilsey	24/639	4%
	Luster	12/275	4%
Final section			
	Dilsey	461/707	65%
	Luster	171/236	72%

*Significant at p<.05.

shown in table 6.8, differences between the phonological frequencies in Dilsey and Luster's speech in the Benjy section and those in the final section are considerable and statistically significant.

Finally, no discussion of African American English as represented in *The Sound and the Fury* can be complete without attention to Reverend Shegog's speech, which occurs in its entirety in his Easter sermon in the final section. Like the Deacon, Reverend Shegog commands both SAE and AAE in his linguistic repertoire, and as his sermon demonstrates, he is skilled at selecting the most effective variety for particular speech situations. He begins his sermon in SAE, and then soon switches to AAE, a shift so subtle as to elude the congregation, who "did not mark just when his intonation, his pronunciation, became negroid, they just sat swaying a little in their seats as the voice took them into itself" (183). This is a telling line in the narration because it illustrates the power with which Reverend Shegog captivates his audience, which translates for Dilsey and other members of the congregation into power for spiritual healing. John J. Gumperz argues that performance style in sermons and especially as incorporated into African American preaching techniques "is not simply an adjunct to or accompaniment of speech content," but rather is "a major means of communicating content" (192). Among the systematically incorporated techniques Gumperz notes in African American preaching styles is dialect switching, which he argues "contributes to the illocutionary force" of sermons in which it occurs (195), and which Faulkner illustrates with Shegog's sermon. Faulkner's recognition of the power of African American preaching styles and strategies is evident both in the way the sermon is represented dialectally, with Shegog articulating phonological features of AAE in nearly 80 percent of possible occurrences, or in 181 of 227 opportunities, as well as in its effect on Dilsey after the sermon is over: "Dilsey sat bolt upright beside [Benjy], crying rigidly and quietly in the annealment and the blood of the remembered lamb. As they walked through the bright noon . . . she continued to weep, unmindful of the talk" (185). When Frony impatiently questions her mother about the tears, Dilsey replies, "I've seed de first and de last. . . . I seed de beginnin, and now I sees de endin" (185).

A textual reference to Shegog's "intonation [and] pronunciation" (183) also offers insight into the author's use of dialectal speech representations throughout the novel. It is in fact the only such reference in *The Sound and the Fury*. Stress patterns and intonation figure prominently in AAE just as in most varieties of language, but they do not figure much into Faulkner's representation of AAE. This is most likely because without complicated and potentially confusing italicization, which Faulkner already uses rather more effectively to mark time and reference shifts in the Benjy and Quentin sections, or use of confusing or distracting diacritics, it is nearly impossible for a writer of fiction to represent those patterns effectively. On the other hand, as Faulkner demonstrates, one of the most effective and hence most common strategies for dialectal representation in literature is reproduction of pronunciation variants produced by dialectal speakers. It is fairly uncomplicated for a writer with a good ear to use respellings to indicate alternative pronunciation, and Faulkner takes full advantage of this strategy in the Quentin, Jason, and final sections of the novel, as the phonological data shown in this chapter indicates.

Any critical study of a work of literature is necessarily incomplete. In the case of the current study, even a fairly exhaustive investigation into the strategies and successes of Faulkner as a literary dialectologist still leaves open many more areas for research into *The Sound and the Fury* and beyond, into Faulkner's other works. For further research into *The Sound and the Fury*, it would be interesting to analyze the narration styles of the novel to determine which socially, racially, or geographically idiosyncratic features occur either in the direct speech of white characters or in the narration. Specifically, Jason's narration and direct speech exhibit several interesting grammatical features usually attributed to nonstandard varieties of English, including the first person -s construction, as in "I says that's the last one anyhow" (135), and tense leveling, as in "She begun to eat" (161), which do not occur in the language of most of the novel's other white speakers. This could be Faulkner's way of distancing the other Compsons and especially himself, as narrator of the final section and perhaps even as author, from

Jason. Faulkner himself has said that Jason "to me represented complete evil. He's the most vicious character in my opinion I ever thought of" (qtd. in Millgate 158).

This preliminary evaluation of Faulkner's skill as a literary dialectologist and of his sensitivity to AAE and its speakers reveals that as a nonlinguist, and certainly very few linguists also possess the artistic genius of a William Faulkner, the author delivers a realistic and ultimately believable portrayal of African American speech. Perhaps more importantly, with the exception of a few lapses into eye dialect, especially in the speech of Louis Hatcher (and this is a lapse it may in fact be possible to attribute to Quentin), Faulkner's racial attitudes as expressed in his linguistic representations of African American characters may be more sensitive than some critics allow. On the other hand, what is known about Faulkner with respect to his personal and public views about race, certainly including his more infamous statements, will continue to insure that discussions about Faulkner and his art remain, like his works and like the man himself, complicated, contradictory, but always compelling.

7

Community in Conflict

Saying and Doing in *Their Eyes Were Watching God*

For all literary authors, it is axiomatic that their linguistic choices create plot, evoke setting, and define characters. In Zora Neale Hurston's *Their Eyes Were Watching God* (1937), the author's linguistic choices are particularly striking, especially in terms of the language and speech produced by the characters who people the text. Henry Louis Gates Jr. in his influential treatment of *Their Eyes Were Watching God* in his book *The Signifying Monkey*, aptly describes *Their Eyes* as a "speakerly text" because of the "privileging of oral speech and its inherent linguistic features" that distinguishes the novel (181). Dialectal features associated with African American English figure extensively in the speech of nearly every character in the novel as well as in a number of nonspeech segments of the narration, a unique application of, to use Gates's term, "dialect-informed" free indirect discourse. The remainder of the narration is represented in standard English, and at times the boundaries between exposition and dialogue are far from being as sharply defined as they are in most other works of fiction. The direct speech of the characters and the free indirect discourse that distinguishes the dialectally represented narration, which blends narrative omniscience with the personalized thought-language of characters, are as striking for their lyrical and poetic expressions as for their reliance on distinctly dialectal grammatical and phonological features. Gates argues that Hurston's reliance on dialectal features as key structural elements of her text indicates the importance not only of the story itself but also of the actual telling of the story, with her narrative design deliberately "imitating one of the numerous forms of oral narration to be found in classical Afro-American vernacular literature" (*Signifying* 181).

Gates's definition of *Their Eyes Were Watching God* as a "speakerly" text helps to point the way to a combined linguistic and literary approach to analyzing the novel and its linguistic and artistic components. The text is not only "speakerly" in the critical sense outlined by Gates, but it is quite literally speakerly in its high proportion of direct speech to exposition. In this approximately 60,000-word novel, nearly half of those words are represented as the direct speech of characters. For half of the entire novel to be related in direct speech, not even counting the substantial additional sections of dialect-enhanced narration, marks a highly unusual and innovative authorial strategy, and it makes a linguistic analysis of the speech instrumental to a broad understanding of the novel. Using computational methods as well as qualitative analysis, it is possible to mine the rich linguistic resources of the novel with the goals of using the linguistic data as a means for analyzing the literary text itself and for determining whether the data can provide answers to important linguistic questions that exist beyond the text. For *Their Eyes Were Watching God,* an analysis of the use of dialectal features yields interesting results with respect to the functions of the dialectal representations, but this complex "speakerly" text demands an approach including, but not limited to, a features analysis in an attempt to study the wider functions of spoken language as Hurston used it in her novel. Such functions include illustrating societal and novelistic political expectations, demonstrating the links between speech community and community itself, and exploring the power of speech to constitute, not simply to impersonate or generate, action. In addition to an exploration of the distribution and frequencies of features in the speech of various characters, then, this chapter also addresses the consequences of class, gender, and other intracommunity conflict as they impact linguistic behavior and help to forge the meanings and themes contained in the novel. Gates's notion of the "speakerly" text, even while his analysis focuses more specifically on Hurston's use of dialectal free indirect discourse, compared to this chapter's concern with direct speech, will continue to be a useful paradigm within which to examine the power spoken language has, and is represented as having in this novel, a text in which words quite often speak louder than actions.

An interesting and, in some ways, unexpected finding of the features analysis conducted on the direct speech in the novel is that there is relatively little interspeaker variation with respect both to the specific dialectal features of AAE present in the speech of a given character, and in the case of the phonological features, to the frequencies at which those features are produced. As shown in Table 7.1, the frequency differences among the major characters are for the most part slight. There are one or two anomalous features, such as the alternation of diphthong /aɪ/ for /ɔɪ/, which occurs exclu-

Table 7.1 Phonological Data for Major Characters*

Feature	Janie	Tea Cake	Nanny	Joe	Pheoby	Logan
Vocalization of postvocalic /r/	123/219 (56%)	124/212 (58%)	38/72 (53%)	39/80 (49%)	23/58 (40%)	25/30 (83%)
Loss of /r/ after consonants	6/25 (24%)	1/25 (4%†)	3/11 (27%)	6/10 (60%)	0/2†	0/0†
Vocalization of unstressed syllabic /r/	14/141 (10%)	5/134 (4%)	1/56 (2%†)	2/47 (4%†)	0/22†	0/8†
Stopping of syllable-initial fricatives	402/475 (85%)	341/374 (91%)	161/175 (92%)	91/99 (92%)	66/87 (76%)	26/26 (100%)
Voiceless interdental fricative stopping	61/68 (90%)	53/55 (96%)	18/22 (82%)	12/14 (86%)	9/9 (100%)	5/5 (100%)
Labialization of interdental fricatives	0/5†	0/0†	3/4 (75%)	2/2 (100%)	0/0†	0/0†
Consonant cluster reduction	50/524 (10%)	46/350 (13%)	17/205 (8%)	9/112 (8%)	5/85 (5%)	0/40†
Deletion of unstressed syllable	85/137 (62%)	77/123 (63%)	22/44 (50%)	17/31 (55%)	24/32 (75%)	6/11 (55%)
Final unstressed /n/ for /ŋ/ in present participle	184/202 (91%)	132/139 (95%)	69/70 (99%)	40/41 (98%)	27/29 (93%)	13/13 (100%)
Other alternation of /n/ for /ŋ/	43/56 (77%)	35/45 (78%)	14/17 (82%)	18/25 (72%)	11/14 (79%)	1/1 (100%)
Alternation of diphthongs /aɪ/ for /ɔɪ/	0/29†	0/25†	0/2†	0/3†	0/2†	2/3 (67%)
/ɛ/ and /ɪ/ merger	34/43 (79%)	64/68 (94%)	9/10 (90%)	9/15 (60%)	8/9 (89%)	3/5 (60%)
Glide reduction of /aɪ/ to /a/	406/416 (98%)	335/337 (99%)	180/184 (98%)	80/96 (83%)	37/39 (95%)	30/31 (97%)

*Significant at p<.05 except where noted. †Not significant.

sively in the speech of Logan Killicks, the first of protagonist Janie's three husbands. Logan uses *gwine* twice in three possible situations where other characters would use *going* or *goin,* and in fact Logan uses *goin* in the third instance. With only a few exceptions, then, nearly all the characters use mostly the same features, and they tend to use them at comparable frequencies. (Please see appendix C for complete phonological data for secondary characters.)

For the grammatical features under consideration, which were determined simply by observing which features Hurston's characters use and comparing them to examples found in the scholarly studies of African American English discussed in chapter 3, frequencies were not calculated because of problems, also discussed in chapter 3, inherent in trying to create a type-and-token breakdown for grammatical features. Rather, table 7.2, which shows

Table 7.2 Grammatical Features in Speech of Major Characters

Feature	Janie	Tea Cake	Nanny	Joe Starks	Pheoby	Mrs. Turner	Logan
Auxiliary and copula deletion	X	X	X	X	X	X	X
Be + done		X					X
Completive been	X	X			X		
Done + been	X		X				X
Done + verb	X	X	X	X	X	X	X
Simple past done		X	X	X	X	X	
Multiple negation	X	X	X	X	X	X	X
Negative inversion		X					
Noninverted questions	X						
Subject-verb nonconcord	X	X	X	X	X	X	X
Unmarked past	X	X	X	X	X	X	
Regularized past	X	X	X		X		
Relative pronoun deletion	X	X	X				
Possessive they	X	X	X				
Pronoun apposition	X						
Undifferentiated pronoun reflexives	X	X			X		
Object pronoun them for subject pronoun those	X	X	X		X	X	
Hypercorrect plural -s	X	X		X	X		X
Regularized plural	X		X				
Existential it/they	X	X	X	X	X	X	X
Tell + say					X		
Indignant come	X	X	X	X			
Counterfactual call	X						
Total grammatical features per speaker	19	17	14	9	13	8	8

the grammatical data for the major characters, simply indicates whether or not a feature occurs within a character's speech. Here too the findings are interesting, with an intriguing, albeit anecdotal, trend toward characters who produce more total speech also producing in most cases a greater number of total grammatical features used (not to be confused with greater incidence of occurrence for any particular feature). This observation is explored further below.

Linguistically, then, especially phonologically, at least at first glance, the question arises as to whether the dialect in the novel fails to represent realistic speech, if in fact realism is the goal. Hurston represents her characters as sharing phonological features and even frequencies, which might not be expected, given the diversity in the ages, levels of education, and social and geographical backgrounds of the characters—influences sociolinguists commonly point to as affecting language variation among speakers. Because the characters in *Their Eyes Were Watching God* vary widely with respect to these extralinguistic variables, we might expect some significant variation in their speech.

For example, Nanny, Janie's grandmother and a former slave, was probably born during the mid to late 1840s, and she tells her story to Janie around 1898 or 1899, when Janie is sixteen. We can assume these dates because of textual information that reveals that Leafy, Nanny's daughter and Janie's mother, was born, probably in 1865, just before the end of the Civil War. Leafy herself became pregnant after being raped by a schoolteacher when she was seventeen, putting Janie's probable birth date at 1882 or 1883. Prior to Emancipation, Nanny had been enslaved near Savannah, Georgia, and raised Janie in "West Florida," which probably refers to the Panhandle area. As a slave, Nanny was of course denied an education in her youth. Whether she acquired one post-Emancipation is unknown. It is known that Janie went to school as a child because as an adult, she tells her friend Pheoby about how "de chillun at school" teased her about her rapist father (9), but she does not go to school beyond age sixteen because of her sudden marriage, if in fact she is still attending up to that point.

Janie's first husband, Logan Killicks, whom she describes as looking like "some ole skull-head in de grave yard" (13), a view that may or may not allude to his age, is probably at least twenty or thirty years her senior, and little more is known about him apart from the hard-working image established by way of Nanny's remarks about his "house bought and paid for and sixty acres uh land" (23). Janie's second husband, Joe Starks, comes from "in and through Georgy" (28) and had worked at a bank in Atlanta before deciding at approximately age twenty-seven to move to Florida. He is approximately ten years Janie's senior, as revealed by an argument that occurs shortly before the onset of Joe's ultimately fatal illness, in which Joe announces Janie's age, "nearly forty," to all present at the store in an attempt to ridicule her over a mistake in measuring a plug of tobacco for a customer. "Yeah, Ah'm nearly forty and you'se already fifty," Janie retorts (79). Joe has presumably been to school, as evidenced by his former job at the bank and his abilities to invest money in real estate, start a successful business, and bring a post office to Eatonville. In fact, he is criticized behind his back by the citizens of Eatonville for talking "tuh unlettered folks wid books in his jaws" (49), an observation which, incidentally, Joe's speech data does not bear out in its lack of phonological or grammatical distinction from the speech of the other, many presumably less educated, characters in the novel. The public perception of Joe's speech is discussed further below.

Vergible "Tea Cake" Woods, Janie's third husband and the love of her life, is approximately twenty-seven years old and living in Orlando, near Eatonville in central Florida, when he and Janie meet, an event that probably occurs around 1920 or 1921, when Janie is in her late thirties and specifically notes the twelve-year difference in their ages during one of their evenings together. Little more is revealed of Tea Cake's past, but his considerable knowledge of people and cities in Florida, along with his colorful image as a traveling bluesman and gambler, clearly indicate that he has interacted with a wide variety of people and has traveled extensively around the state. His formal education, like that of many blacks in Florida around the turn of the twentieth century, is probably limited, but he writes a letter to Janie from Jacksonville, so it is likely that he has received at least some schooling.

The diverse backgrounds of the characters may lead to the impression that there will be substantial variation in the way their speech is represented, given that Hurston chose to represent it dialectally. Of course, if she had decided to represent the speech of her characters in standard English, there would be no such expectation of interspeaker variation, despite the realities both of regional standards—thus dispelling the notion of a single standard for all American English speakers—and of individual variation even among speakers of what may be more or less the "same" regional standard. But for dialect writers, many of whom use the device of dialect particularly to represent realism, the expectations are higher. And as we have seen, despite the diversity among the characters in terms of their ages, levels of education, and geographical histories, there is little linguistic variation, especially phonological, among Hurston's speakers.

But rather than being limited to skepticism concerning Hurston's success at representing African American speech, another way to view the data is in terms of Hurston's consistency in representing dialect throughout the novel. Hurston's use of the phonological features analyzed here is acutely perceptive and accurate when compared to linguistic data gathered for *LAGS* and *LAMSAS* from African American speakers. This includes data elicited from

Hurston's contemporaries in the 1930s, especially in *LAMSAS,* as well as from Floridians interviewed between 1968 and 1983 and documented in *LAGS,* interviewees whose backgrounds correspond geographically to the novel's Florida settings and who are generationally similar to many of the novel's characters. This position is supported by the findings of Betsy Barry, who maintains that Hurston's representations of spoken language "indicate important phonetic and phonological differences in pronunciation that reflect features typical of both southern American English and AAVE" and that "her use of 'non-standard' grammatical constructions reinforces the linguistic authenticity of her representation" (172). Further, Hurston's accurate and consistent incorporation of such a wide range and large quantity of grammatical and phonological features—there are thirty-eight such features considered in this analysis—is impressive in its own right. The sheer quantity and diversity of features that Hurston effectively and believably deploys in her text make it difficult to argue that her representation of the sounds and grammar of spoken language is anything but an artistic and linguistic tour de force.

As indicated above, there is a general trend in the speech data that the more speech a character produces, the greater the number of different grammatical features appear in their speech. Janie, who not surprisingly produces the most speech of any character in the novel with more than 7,000 words, produces nineteen of the twenty-three grammatical features considered here. Tea Cake produces nearly 6,000 words, a feat of production second only to Janie's and all the more remarkable because he appears for only ninety pages, or in just under half the novel. Leaving aside for now the discrepancy in the ratio of female speech compared to that of males, a discrepancy that is considerable as well as relevant to this discussion, Tea Cake's production of the second-greatest number of grammatical features, eighteen, also contributes to the impression that those who produce more speech also produce a greater number of grammatical features. With the exceptions of Pheoby and Joe, with Pheoby producing fewer words than Joe but a greater number of different features—in the case of each of the seven characters who figure individually both as characters important to the narrative and as significant speech-producers, characters who produce more words also produce more features. This trend is not particularly surprising, given that characters with more opportunities to speak are also shown in the text as experiencing more diverse types of linguistic demands to which to respond.

Table 7.3 Tense and Aspect Features Denoting Past Events in
Speech of Several Major Characters

Feature	Tea Cake	Eatonville Men	Nanny	Joe
Be + done	X			
Completive been	X	X		
Done + been			X	X
Done + verb	X	X	X	
Simple past done	X	X	X	X
Unmarked past	X	X	X	X
Regularized past	X	X	X	

For example, most of the speech of Nanny, who with nearly 3,000 words is the third leading individual speech-producer as well as grammatical-features-producer in the novel, occurs in her telling of a lengthy story of Janie's and her own family history. Not surprisingly, Nanny's speech contains a number of features that mark tense or aspect, especially those demarcating past events, as she shifts her narrative between the recent and distant past, describing completed actions, such as her escape with her newborn daughter from the plantation where she had been enslaved, and continuing actions, including her ongoing care for Janie and active determination that Janie would have a life better than her own. As shown in table 7.3, Nanny produces five of the seven verbal markers considered here that are connected to the expression of past events, including features such as simple-past *done* (*Ah done de best Ah could*), *done + been* (*Ah done been on mah knees*), and resultant *done + verb* (*Somebody done spoke to me 'bout you long time ago*), along with unmarked and regularized past tense formations (*Ah hide in dere day and night* and *next thing Ah knowed*). Similarly, storytelling is a major component of Tea Cake's speech as well, and as a result, dialectal tense and aspect features also figure strongly in his speech. As also shown in table 7.3, he produces six of the seven verbal markers indicating past events in his speech, the most of any character in the novel. Conversely, in the speech of Joe, who rarely discusses past events or participates in the community story-telling sessions, all but three of the verbal tense and aspect markers are absent.

The diversity of experience reported in the novel that might be expected to result in variation in feature production can also be seen in a collective analysis of the speech of the male citizens of Eatonville, exclusive of major characters such as Joe, as a group of speakers. The men seem largely to function as devices to keep textual attention on oral performance, a tradition to which critics such as Henry Louis Gates Jr. point as heavily informing the text of the novel. Many of the Eatonville men participate in verbal games, including acting out over-the-top flirtations with young single women of the town, "playing the dozens," and telling exaggerated stories about Matt Bonner's mule and mythical characters such as "Big John de Conquer." In his analysis of the novel, Gates emphasizes that "verbal rituals signify the sheer play of black language which *Their Eyes* seems to celebrate" (*Signifying* 194). In their capacity as oral performers, the men of Eatonville do not disappoint. They produce collectively nearly 5,000 words of dialogue, coming in third behind Janie and Tea Cake for total speech production as well as for grammatical features production, producing fifteen of the twenty-three features considered here, including, as shown in table 7.3, five of the seven verbal markers denoting past events, an apparent clue to their storytelling function. Little of the speech the Eatonville men produce has any narrative function beyond oral performance for its own sake, yet it constitutes a large component of the text and is generally without any obvious functions of character development or plot advancement.

The trends revealed in the grammatical analysis, viewed alongside the phonological data, might lead to the conclusion that Hurston's representation of speech with respect to individual linguistic features is generally not a factor in the individuation of characters in the sense that Sylvia W. Holton describes in her discussion of "the fusion of dialect speech and characterization." Holton raises this issue with regard to the linguistic characterization of Jim in *Huckleberry Finn* in which, she demonstrates, dialectal features are part of the strategy Twain uses in his portrayal of Jim (Holton 88–89). At first this seems a surprising discovery, given Hurston's artistic feats in creating the vivid characters and settings of *Their Eyes,* and also given that so much of the novel is related by way of spoken language and especially through the telling of stories, exemplified by but not limited to the conversation between Janie and Pheoby that frames the novel. But the kind of character individuation Holton describes is not necessarily limited to dialectal features. In *Huckleberry Finn,* as Holton notes, the features in Jim's speech are themselves part of distinguishing him, for better or for worse, depending on which critics are consulted (see chapter 4), as the only major African American character in the novel.

In *Their Eyes Were Watching God,* Hurston's artistic and thematic strategies are very different from those of Twain in *Huckleberry Finn,* and her methods of characterization via speech features are complex. Character functions have to be considered alongside the features themselves, and it is clear that such functions have a major impact on what is contained in the speech of each character. We have already noted the examples of the concentration of tense and aspect features in Nanny's speech, which is right in line with her function as Janie's link to the past and her family's history, as well as in the speech of the Eatonville men, who function as bearers and exemplifiers of the vernacular tradition. It seems likely that those functions largely dictate at least the grammatical patterns found in a character's speech. Individuating characters, then, is not left to differential feature-production in the speech of the characters of *Their Eyes Were Watching God;* to decontextualize the linguistic data from character function could result in the conclusion that, as Mark Twain jokingly put it in his preface to *Huckleberry Finn,* "all these characters were trying to talk alike and not succeeding," only in this case, without further exploration into the characters themselves and their functions, they seem to succeed.

The functionality theory considered here, to explain the similarity among linguistic features of all the speaking characters in the novel, is not intended to be conclusive. Rather, it is posited as a potential means for approaching an analysis of the spoken language in *Their Eyes Were Watching God.* But there is at least one other compelling explanation for the lack of linguistic variability. It may be that one of the major functions of the dialect Hurston uses in the novel is to illustrate a community of the African American characters, with shared membership in the community resulting from their shared experiences. In other words, despite the diversity in the characters' ages, geographical and social histories, and levels of education, important factors usually associated with variation, Hurston may be indicating that the shared experiences of being African American transcend the individual dissimilarities and interpersonal and intergroup conflicts resulting from imbalances in gender, class, and other relations. Further, Hurston might have used dialect deliberately both to reclaim it from the stereotypical and minstrelized representations that so repulsed James Weldon Johnson and many of the Harlem Renaissance writers and to establish dialect as a method of communicating black meanings to black audiences, a kind of community-reinforcing and collective cultural celebration. Gayl Jones confirms that the minstrel tradition "contributed to the ambivalent attitudes of the early Afro-American writers toward 'the dialect'" and poses a question that writers such as Hurston must have asked themselves: "[H]ow does one use in literature a dialect that has already been codified into burlesque?" (141–43). In *Their Eyes Were Watching God,* Jones maintains, Hurston "fulfills the possibility of what dialect might do when moved beyond the literary conventions and allowed more of the image and flexibility of authentic folk creation" (152).

In fact, according to a position articulated by a number of critics, including in Henry Louis Gates's definition of *Their Eyes* as a speakerly text, the celebration of a shared culture, and perhaps more importantly, one that is a uniquely oral culture, is a major component of Hurston's use of dialect in her fiction, including in *Their Eyes Were Watching God.* Elizabeth Meese contends that Hurston's "brilliant use of dialect, specifying pride and ownership, lends credibility to the novel's claim as a work for the black community" (61). Karla F. C. Holloway, in her important treatment of Hurston's use of dialect across texts, observes that "readers who share the dialect, or the heritage of the dialect, recognize that the speech act itself is a way of framing a community, acknowledging a membership and sharing a culture" (8). She asserts that "Within the dialect, in its sound, its structures, and its meanings, the culture of a people is preserved and protected. Within the artistry of Hurston, this oral culture is rendered literate" (114). Hurston, concludes Holloway, "celebrated and flaunted her community—daring the world to contradict what was her reality" (117). Additionally, Gates observes that the individual speaker in the novel may be perceived as speaking from and for a collective culture, with the textual voice "extending far beyond the merely individual" (*Signifying* 183). This voice, contends Gates, transcends the individual by means of the "impersonality, anonymity, and authority of the black vernacular tradition, a nameless, selfless tradition, at once collective and compelling, true somehow to the unwritten text of a common blackness" (*Signifying* 183).

As elucidated by Meese, Holloway, Gates, and others, the critical position that *Their Eyes Were Watching God* is largely a document of the voice of a collective society is an important and appealing one. The representation of the speech of diverse characters as strikingly similar in terms of linguistic features used, which are throughout the text represented as heavily dialectal, makes it also a convincing position. The unstated argument seems to be that the chasms resulting from individual as well as gender and class differences, for example, which are clearly evident in *Their Eyes,* fully humanize any community. In this sense, Hurston humanizes rather than idealizes, showing that the community still exists as a strong entity, with intracommunity conflict simply a defining distinction of any thriving community.

But such conflicts as occur in the novel also create problems for the popular critical perception of *Their Eyes Were Watching God* as primarily a celebration of community by way of a celebration of oral culture. The novel makes clear the serious damage that results from sexism, classism, and intragroup racism, the last personified in the character of Mrs. Turner, and such conflicts and their damaging results are far too consequential to an understanding of the text to be interpreted merely as supporting players to a top-billed oral culture. Focusing for a moment on one of the conflicts, intragroup racism, it is possible to assess not only the textual and social significance of such conflicts but also the critical role spoken language plays in them, both within and outside the text. In the novel, Mrs. Turner is a light-skinned African American woman, although her skin is not as light as Janie's. For this reason, Mrs. Turner idolizes Janie yet can't "forgive her for marrying a man as dark as Tea Cake" (140) nor for the couple's friendship with other dark-skinned people in Belle Glade. Mrs. Turner openly exhibits her racist attitudes to Janie: "Ah never dreamt so many different kins uh black folks could colleck in one place. Did Ah never woulda come. . . . Ah don't blame de white folks from hatin' 'em because Ah can't stand 'em mahself" (140–41).

Janie reacts only mildly to Mrs. Turner's undisguised and unapologetic hatred, perhaps out of naiveté, although Mary Helen Washington is understandably more critical of Janie's reaction. Washington observes that despite the racist attitudes and very personal ground upon which Mrs. Turner treads in her insults of Tea Cake and criticism of Janie's love for him, "Janie is nearly silent" ("Emergent" 104), an important point addressed in greater detail below. Janie finally does respond to Mrs. Turner's skepticism regarding Tea Cake's worth as a husband and as a man by articulating her love for him: "He kin take most any lil thing and make summertime out of it when times is dull. Then we lives offa dat happiness he made till some mo' happiness come along" (141). Mrs. Turner is not convinced and continues to argue that lighter-skinned people like herself and Janie should "class off" in the hope that "De white folks would take us in wid dem" (141).

Looking at Mrs. Turner's racial views through a linguistic lens yields interesting results. Mrs. Turner produces only about 750 words of direct speech in the novel, but even within this relatively small sample, her frequencies for eight phonological features are statistically significant, with high frequencies for seven of them, as shown in table 7.4. Mrs. Turner produces eight of the grammatical features considered in this chapter and all but three of the phonological features addressed, with similar frequencies of occurrence to

Table 7.4 Phonological Data for Mrs. Turner

Feature	Tokens/Types	Frequency*
Vocalization of postvocalic /r/	12/17	71%
Stopping of syllable-initial fricatives	40/43	93%
Stopping of voiceless interdental fricatives	8/8	100%
Consonant cluster reduction	9/39	23%
Deletion of initial or medial unstressed syllables	10/15	67%
Alternation of final unstressed /n/ for /ŋ/	30/30	100%
Merger of /ɛ/ and /ɪ/	4/4	100%
Glide reduction of /aɪ/ to /a/	41/42	98%

*Significant at p<.05.

those of other characters, regardless of skin tone. (Please refer to appendix C for her complete data.) Mrs. Turner would no doubt find it surprising, if not ironic, to learn that her speech characteristics link her closely to the community of people she despises, a community which, incidentally, finally rejects her for her racism.

For Mrs. Turner, class is closely associated, or perhaps confused, with subtle shadings of skin, but for the citizens of Eatonville, there is no such confusion. For them, the symbols of class inequality are Joe and Janie Starks, apparently because of Joe's money and influence rather than because of his skin tone, which is never explicitly addressed. Joe deliberately perpetuates the image of himself and Janie as separate from and of higher social rank than the rest of the town, in part by actively preventing Janie from socializing with citizens of the town and in part by way of his own patronizing demeanor toward them. "Ain't got no Mayor!" Joe exclaims upon arriving in Eatonville. "Well, who tells y'all what to do?" (35). Part of Joe's program of self-promotion includes his deliberate and successful establishment of a public perception of his wife as elevated and aloof from the rest of the town. Janie quickly and sadly realizes "the impact of awe and envy against her sensibilities" on the part of the rest of Eatonville, and she clearly understands that as a result, "she couldn't get but so close to most of them in spirit" (46).

But an elevated image of Janie has already persisted for some time even prior to her arrival with Joe in Eatonville. The image might well result from stereotypical views of her based on, as Mary Helen Washington observes, "her extraordinary, anglicized beauty" ("Emergent" 99). It is that beauty that probably attracts her first husband, Logan Killicks, while her anglicized features and light skin later attract Mrs. Turner. Ironically, Logan is the only character who challenges her on the misperception, one which is of course no fault of her own, pointing out that Janie's background is far from aristocratic: "Ah just as good as take you out de white folks' kitchen," he finally exclaims shortly before Janie leaves him (31). By the time Janie falls in love with Tea Cake following Joe's death, it is her money and property that perpetuate the view of Janie as "classed off." The majority opinion in Eatonville is that because Tea Cake "ain't got doodly-squat," in the words of Janie's teenage employee, Hezekiah, "He ain't got no business makin' hissef familiar" with Janie, a woman of means (103). Janie repeatedly rebels against the false image of her refinement, first in a conversation with Pheoby. "You always did class off," says Pheoby, articulating the prevailing view held by her fellow Eatonville citizens. "Joe classed me off," responds Janie. "Ah didn't" (112). Later, even Tea Cake falls for the stereotypical view of Janie, mistaking her possessions for her true self. He excludes her from his party in Jacksonville because he fears she would be offended by his railroad-worker friends, only telling her about the party after it is over. "Well, how come yuh didn't come git me?" demands Janie. Tea Cake replies, "You ain't usetuh folks lak dat and Ah wuz skeered you might git all mad and quit me for takin' you 'mongst 'em." Janie quickly sets him straight: "Looka heah, Tea Cake, if you ever go off from me and have a good time lak dat and then come back heah tellin' me how nice Ah is, Ah specks tuh kill yuh dead. You heah me?" (124).

Linguistically, Joe Starks's public image raises several interesting issues. Like Janie, Joe is perceived by the other residents of Eatonville as separate from the rest of the town. In the narration, Hurston declares that "There was something about Joe Starks that cowed the town," but it is neither "physical fear" nor that "he was more literate than the rest" (47). Even though it may not be the source of his neighbors' deference to him, Joe's greater literacy is the subject of Eatonville conversation. Behind his back, Joe is criticized specifically for his literate linguistic style and content. Amos Hicks observes, "Whut Ah don't lak 'bout de man is, he talks tuh unlettered folks wid books in his jaws. Showin' off his learnin'" (49). Interestingly, Joe's speech data is not consistent with this observation. As shown in table 7.5, for the nine phonological features whose frequencies are statistically significant in the data of both Joe and the Eatonville men (analyzed in aggregate), the differences between their frequencies are in all but one case so slight as to be statistically insignificant.

One interesting phonological anomaly that emerges from the analysis

Table 7.5 Phonological Feature Frequency Comparison for Joe and Eatonville Men*

Feature	Joe	E'ville Men	Difference
Vocalization of postvocalic /r/	39/80 (49%)	93/167 (56%)	Not significant
Stopping of syllable-initial fricatives	91/99 (92%)	293/328 (89%)	Not significant
Stopping of voiceless interdental fricatives	12/14 (86%)	26/28 (93%)	Not significant
Consonant cluster reduction	9/112 (8%)	23/328 (7%)	Not significant
Deletion of unstressed syllable	17/31 (55%)	71/123 (58%)	Not significant
Final unstressed /n/ for /ŋ/ in present participle	40/41 (98%)	101/104 (97%)	Not significant
Other final unstressed /n/ for /ŋ/	18/25 (72%)	34/44 (77%)	Not significant
Merger of /ɛ/ and /ɪ/	9/15 (60%)	36/40 (90%)	Significant†
Glide reduction of /aɪ/ to /a/	80/96 (83%)	179/187 (96%)	Not significant

*Frequencies are significant at p<.05. †Difference is significant at p<.05.

of Joe's speech is his occasional articulation of the first-person pronoun *I*. In nearly every instance in the novel, the characters, including Joe, are represented as pronouncing this word as *Ah,* a form that Joe produces 43 times. However, Joe also pronounces the pronoun as *I* on 14 occasions. Only Nanny also produces an original (rather than imitative) occurrence of *I,* and she produces it only once, compared to 110 occurrences in her speech of *Ah.* The only other occurrences of *I* rather than *Ah* are produced by Hezekiah, "the best imitation of Joe that his seventeen years could make," after Joe's death, when the teen begins to imagine himself Joe's successor because of his position as clerk at the store. In this capacity, Hezekiah produces three occurrences of Joe's favorite expression, "I god" (92). Of Joe's fourteen occurrences of *I* rather than *Ah,* all fourteen are collocative with *god,* to form the phrase Hezekiah later so enjoys using, *I god.* Barbara Johnson and Henry Louis Gates Jr. assert that Joe uses the expression to name himself as godlike. He "fondly and unconsciously refers to himself as I-God," Johnson and Gates note, seeing himself and "wish[ing] to be seen as the God-figure of his community" (73). Leaving aside for a moment the important implications and consequences of this self-perception, especially as they affect Janie, the linguistic question of why Joe uses *I* instead of *Ah* only in the *I god* construction is worth considering. One possibility is that Joe, able to choose either variant from his phonological repertoire, deliberately chooses *I* for the *I god* utterances and *Ah* the rest of the time in order to emphasize his view of himself as godlike. Or it may be less semantically conscious on his part and more a consequence of his intonation. Joe is usually annoyed or otherwise emotional when he uses the expression, as in his frequent rebukes of Janie: "I god, Janie, why don't you go on and see whut Mrs. Bogle want?" (70). The level of emotion or tension in his voice may cause him to exert approximately equal levels of stress on both *I* and *god,* as a speaker might when expressing a similar expression, although it is more common for most speakers who use such expressions to articulate *my* in place of *I*. Hurston herself provides a clue in her 1934 article "Characteristics of Negro Expression." In the article, she notes that she is more likely to represent an unstressed pronoun dialectally than a subject pronoun, as in the sentence "*You* better not let me ketch *yuh*" (93, emphasis added). Of course *Ah/I* is by definition always in subject position, but the question of stress may still be the key here. Of course, it is impossible to know for certain whether the representation results from semantic or intonational constraints or whether Joe's anomalous *I* pronunciation is merely the result of orthographic concern over whether *Ah god* would be understood by readers with the same impact as *I god.*

Producing fifteen of the grammatical features under consideration here, the men of Eatonville apart from Joe produce rather more grammatical features than Joe does himself, with Joe producing only nine of the features, but they also produce nearly three times as much speech, uttering nearly 5,000 words to Joe's 1700 words. Joe's average sentence length of nine words per sentence and average word length of four letters per word also closely correspond to those of the other Eatonville men, whose average sentence length of ten words per sentence is actually a bit longer than Joe's, and whose average word length of four letters per word is the same. Along with similarities in sentence length and vocabulary, there is also no evidence that Joe's sentences are more complex than those of the other men. But because of Joe's stature in the community, and because of what is known of his background, Amos Hicks's observation regarding Joe's literacy is plausible. Further, there is no evidence in the text that Hicks's statement is expected to be questioned, despite the lack of linguistic evidence, which should surely indicate major differences between Joe's speech and that of nearly every other character in the novel. Rather, what Hicks observes is simply to be accepted because it is consistent with Joe's public image as well as with one of the most significant speech-related characteristics of this "speakerly" text: the authorial strategy of telling rather than showing. With respect to Hurston's dialectal representation, one of my initial operating assumptions, that authors tend to use literary dialect as a function of characterization, seems, at least on the surface, not to apply. At first glance, it might appear that Hurston fails to use dialect effectively to construct a realistic speech community, if indeed that was her intention. But at the same time, her representations of speech do make important statements about the people and the community she represents.

A striking characteristic of *Their Eyes Were Watching God* is that substantial portions of the novel consist not of narration or presentation of the actual events but in fact are related second-hand in conversation. In this speakerly text, saying seems quite literally to make it so. Much of the action in the story is told rather than shown, or as Otis Ferguson pointed out in his 1937 *New Republic* review of the novel, "everything is more heard than seen" (22). This observation, that there is more *talking about* what happens than there is representation of what happens, has a number of applications throughout the novel and is interesting in light of Hurston's own writings on the subject of language, especially as articulated in "Characteristics of Negro Expression." In the article, Hurston argues that the African American's "very words are action words. His interpretation of the English language is in terms of pictures. One act described in terms of another. . . . Everything is acted out" (79). In one sense, this may be interpreted as antithetical to her reliance in *Their Eyes* of talk at the expense of action and drama. On the other hand, the story of Tea Cake's adventures during the time of his twenty-four-hour disappearance, during which time he organizes a public chicken and macaroni dinner using money he pilfers from Janie, is vividly and entertainingly told by Tea Cake himself, by way of a dialectally represented free indirect discourse that closely resembles direct speech, only without the quotation marks. In this instance, Hurston's view of African American language as visual drama is borne out by way of Tea Cake's skillful telling, complete with represented dialogue within his own monologue. In fact, Tea Cake is said to have "talked and *acted out* the story" (122, emphasis added). The telling may be thus interpreted as being almost as good as being there. But in learning of the episode second-hand, the audience is not permitted to "partake wid everything" (124), in much the same way that Janie is excluded from Tea Cake's party, an exclusion she clearly resents. This leads

Table 7.6 Comparison of Amounts of Speech Production, by Sex of
Speaker (Male Speaker Data Shaded)

Speaker	Total Number of Words Spoken	Percentage of Total Speech Produced*
Janie	7130	27%
Tea Cake	5770	21%
Eatonville men	4810	18%
Nanny	2760	10%
Joe	1700	6%
Everglades men	1470	5%
Pheoby	1260	5%
Mrs. Turner	740	3%
Eatonville women	650	2%
Logan	510	2%
Total female	12,540	47%
Total male	14,260	53%

*Significant at p<.05. Because of rounding, percentages do not add up to 100%.

to other problems that arise from a text in which so much is told rather than shown.

Gender conflicts may be the most salient type of conflict in *Their Eyes*, but they are difficult to evaluate in terms of linguistic features analysis. Using the phonological data, for which it is possible to make reliable comparisons between speakers, only minor frequency differences between female and male speakers are evident. Grammatical feature-production data is no more conclusive. There is other compelling data, however, that helps to illustrate the linguistic consequences of the gender conflicts depicted in the novel. An analysis of amounts of speech produced indicates the unequal distribution of air time, as it were, for the utterance of female speech as compared to that of male. As shown in table 7.6, despite the novel's primary function as a woman's story of her journey toward self-realization, and despite the considerable contribution the protagonist, Janie, makes to the total amount of speech produced, male voices still dominate the text by 6 percentage points, which represents nearly 2,000 words. The gap widens when the data of the top female and top male speech producers are separated from the rest: Female speakers other than Janie produce only 20 percent of the total speech while males other than Tea Cake produce 32 percent. Interestingly, Janie's first two husbands, Logan and Joe, together produce only 8 percent of the total speech. Joe's control over Janie, linguistic and otherwise, then, does not result in his producing great quantities of speech, despite his proclaimed goal of becoming a "big voice" in Eatonville (46). Here then is a relatively rare case in which actions take precedence over talk: certainly few if any citizens of Eatonville would argue that Joe does not succeed in his goal.

Tea Cake produces a great deal of talk in the half of the novel in which he is present. He is a highly verbal individual and a skilled storyteller, and in fact Janie is attracted early on to his humor and ease with language, along with the freedom she feels in his presence to express her own verbal capacity. She is energized by their first encounter. "Look how she had been able to talk with him right off!" the narration announces, sharing Janie's thoughts (99). Interestingly, though, Janie produces only slightly more speech in conversation with Tea Cake, approximately 2,370 words, than she does in conversation with Pheoby, approximately 2,270 words, who has only a few scenes with Janie. While Tea Cake does not silence Janie, then, the community of the novel still exerts power over and thus limits female speech. The men of Eatonville, whose function is largely to represent the centrality of oral performance to the African American community in the novel and outside it, also represent a major influence on the limiting of female speech in the novel. In their narrative capacity as entertaining scene-stealers, then, the men of Eatonville also perform a normative function for the women in the text, which may correspond to similar male prescriptive functions outside it. Ironically, despite their role as representatives of a close-knit community, the sheer quantity of their talk, nearly 5,000 words, helps to reinforce the notion that the oral tradition is primarily a male one, a view elucidated by Mary Helen Washington. "When the voice of the black oral tradition is summoned in *Their Eyes*," Washington argues, "it is not used to represent the collective black community, but to invoke and valorize the voice of the black *male* community" ("Emergent" 99, emphasis in original).

Moreover, the controlling function the male verbal tradition enacts in *Their Eyes* presents a serious challenge to the popular image of the novel as a celebration of community cohesion in other ways as well. For example, Hurston skillfully illustrates the proscription against female participation in the public oral culture in what seems to be an episode of minor significance but is in fact a very enlightening event. That this event is performed and not merely reported or commented on in the narrative is paradoxical to the novel's recurrent reliance on telling rather than showing and as such represents a subtle but revealing approach to the exclusion of women from public-sphere verbal games. In the episode, Janie watches while Joe teases Mrs. Robbins "as he always did when she came to the store" (72). Mrs. Robbins, the narration informs us, is clearly playing along, as she "struck her pity-pose and assumed the voice" (73). She and Joe banter and joke, with Mrs. Robbins pretending that she and her children are starving because her husband "don't fee-eed me!" (73). At first, the response from the men on the porch is positive. But as the display continues, rather than enjoying the show, some of the men become incensed at Mrs. Robbins's performance. She apparently does not act in accordance with the male limitations on female participation in public performance, perhaps especially by way of her joking critique of Mr. Robbins's skills as a provider. "If dat wuz mah wife, Ah'd kill her cemetery dead," declares one, after Mrs. Robbins has left. "Ah'd break her or kill her," announces another. "Makin' uh fool outa me in front of everybody." "Ah'd kill uh baby just born dis mawnin' fuh uh thing lak dat" adds a third. "'Tain't nothin' but low-down spitefulness 'ginst her husband make her do it" (74–75). Janie is angered by the violent reactions of the men, and in a rare moment of public verbal expression, she tells the men off and displays her own considerable verbal skills:

> Sometimes God gits familiar wid us womenfolks too and talks His inside business. He told me how surprised He was 'bout y'all turning out so smart after Him makin' yuh different; and how surprised y'all is goin' tuh be if you ever find out you don't know half as much 'bout us as you think you do. It's so easy to make yo'self out God Almighty when you ain't got nothin' tuh strain against but women and chickens. (75)

Not surprisingly, Joe's response to Janie is to tell her, "You gettin' too moufy, Janie," and he then sends her off on an errand to end the exchange (75). But in this instance, Janie has successfully performed a verbal action, incorporating the same kind of quick-witted orality the men had previously claimed exclusively for themselves.

Later, Janie flexes her linguistic muscles again, this time using the power of her speech against Joe in response to his deliberate public humiliation of her over a mistake she has made in the store. In response to his insults regarding her age and physical appearance, Janie responds forcefully: "Talkin' 'bout me lookin' old! When you pull down yo' britches, you look lak de change uh life" (79). In this episode, Janie's "very words are action," to paraphrase Hurston, an achievement that results in Joe's downfall in the eyes of the male community and eventually in his death, ostensibly from kidney failure but certainly hastened by the humiliation he suffers. Sam Watson, husband of Janie's friend Pheoby, overtly acknowledges Janie's verbal-performative skill. "Great God from Zion! Y'all really playin' de dozens tuhnight" Sam exclaims, and this is the only incident in the novel in which a female speaker is acknowledged by a male to be an equal participant in the male-dominated and male-controlled verbal games (79). These rare instances support an interpretation that Janie's final triumph involves claiming her voice. But as we have seen elsewhere in this novel, the reality is more complicated.

The problem with the textual privileging of telling over showing intersects with the intracommunity conflicts about which this chapter has been concerned. The narrative reliance on the notion that saying makes it so presents a compelling challenge to the view of some critics that the novel represents the ultimate triumph of a woman finding her voice after decades of enforced silence. The triumph Janie experiences at the end of the novel, when she has experienced the richness of life for which she had previously longed and finds peace and joy in her memories, is often seen to be associated with her transcendence of the community's male silencing of women, a logical position given her survival of the twenty-year enforced silence she endures during her marriage to Joe. Upon her return to Eatonville after Tea Cake's death, Janie has ostensibly gained her voice, as evidenced by the frame story in which she is portrayed as telling her story to Pheoby. But critics such as Robert B. Stepto and Mary Helen Washington challenge the position that celebrates Janie's newly empowered voice. Stepto observes that the structure of the novel, the frame story that generates the impression that Janie is the first-person narrator of her story, "creates the essential illusion that Janie has achieved her voice (along with everything else), and that she has even wrested from menfolk some control of the tribal posture of the storyteller" (7). Stepto calls it an illusion because, he maintains, "the tale undercuts much of this, not because of its content," which he agrees does support the view of Janie's final achievement of personal autonomy, "but because of its narration," which for most of the book is related in the third person, despite the framing device that purports that the text is related in Janie's words. She does begin the tale herself, but narrative control is taken from her only a few paragraphs into the story and never returned to her, not even in the closing chapter of the novel when the frame is ostensibly resumed, but in which Janie still speaks only within a third-person narrative frame. Stepto argues that this narrative structure means that Janie does not ultimately speak for herself, that it "implies that Janie has not really won her voice and self after all" (7).

Building on Stepto's provocative treatment of *Their Eyes,* Mary Helen Washington points to significant parts of the novel in which Janie should be represented as speaking but instead remains silent. Washington also demonstrates that significant events in Janie's life are related from the points of view of male observers rather than from her own. For example, she notes that when Janie and Joe arrive in Eatonville, Janie's experience is "described through the eyes and speech of the men on the front porch." While Joe remains on the porch with the men, Washington observes, "Janie is seen 'through the window getting settled'" ("Emergent" 100). Years later, when Tea Cake beats Janie in order to discourage another man from trying to attract her, it is only through a conversation among males that the incident is considered at all, a conversation that clearly conveys that Janie's experience of the beating is irrelevant. Tea Cake tells his male friends, "Ah didn't whup Janie 'cause *she* done nothin'. Ah beat her to show dem Turners who is boss" (148, emphasis in original). The men affirm Tea Cake's action and express their envy that Tea Cake is entitled to beat a "tender woman lak Janie" (148), and with that, the subject is closed. Washington rightly remarks, then, that the incident "is seen entirely through the eyes of the male community, while Janie's reaction is never given" ("Emergent" 102). Janie's lack of (public) reaction in response to the beating leads at least one critic to conclude that she accepts it (Kubitschek 24, 28), an interpretation that strikes me as a dangerous fallacy, with silence automatically constituting acceptance. Washington returns to Stepto's early observations in response to the scene of Janie's trial, in which Janie certainly must have spoken for herself, but her words are not recorded. This seems an odd turn of events in a text that otherwise relies so heavily on direct speech to act out its drama. Further, Washington reminds us, in response to Mrs. Turner's racist tirades, which as cited above include insults of Tea Cake as well as of Janie's own judgment for loving him, "Janie is nearly silent" ("Emergent" 104).

Washington argues convincingly not that the novel is flawed in its seemingly contradictory messages of Janie's personal emancipation and at the same time continuing silence but that it succeeds as a "critique of patriarchal norms" ("Emergent" 106) while it also realistically "represents women's exclusion from power, particularly from the power of oral speech" ("Emergent" 98). Comparing the experience of Janie to that of John Pearson, protagonist of Hurston's 1934 novel *Jonah's Gourd Vine*, Washington observes that John benefits from public-sphere linguistic performance and is encouraged to use his voice in a way Janie never is. Washington shows how John's "relationships with women . . . [lead] him to literacy and to speech while Janie's relationships with men deprive her of community and of her voice" ("Emergent" 98). Janie's only friendship with a woman is with Pheoby, of course, and this is a relationship which, Washington observes, exists "apart from the community" ("Emergent" 99).

The observations of Stepto and Washington are consistent with a view of the text as one in which saying makes it so, in which words are so often designed to speak louder than actions. The friendship between Janie and Pheoby is another interesting example. The friendship seems to be primarily a narrative device for the structural frame of the novel, to provide Janie an opportunity to tell what happened, to make it seem as though she has in fact, as Stepto terms it, "achieved her voice." The device functions to tell rather than show that part of her personal journey involved the cultivation of deep relationships with other women, because what is shown is that female friendships are not necessarily an important component of Janie's life and narrative. Janie actually fails to develop any other female friendships, and even during the happiest period of her life, the time in Belle Glade with Tea Cake, the friendships that surround her are Tea Cake's and not hers, as is painfully revealed when these male friends turn viciously against her at her trial. The friendship between Janie and Pheoby is barely developed in the story, as Washington notes, and it is hard to imagine given Janie's isolation in Eatonville how it ever could have become so close. Joe rigidly restricts Janie's opportunities for socializing, so the friendship only could have occurred within the context of Janie's work at the store. No doubt Joe would not have tolerated much non-business-related talk while Janie was on the job, and in fact there is much evidence of this, as he silences her every time she speaks in public. But again we are expected to take the novel at its word that it was a significant friendship, when the evidence is that it functions mostly as a structural device to enable the frame and a thematic device to enable the "essential illusion," in Stepto's words, of Janie's empowered voice, which at as late a point in the novel as her trial is still not entirely empowered. And when Janie arrives back in Eatonville at the end of the novel, she is not welcomed by the community. Rather, as she walks by, the community gossips about her behind her back. She is still effectively an outsider in Eatonville, just as she had been in Belle Glade, else she might have stayed in the town where she had lived joyfully with Tea Cake.

The issue of community as a dominant theme in the novel and as attendant to Janie's journey is not without merit but neither is it without contradictions and complexity. The joy Janie takes from the community, and its continued exclusion of her from participating fully in it, whether because of her perceived class or because she is a woman, may in fact mirror Zora Neale Hurston's own possible ambivalence, especially as an African American woman who was also an artist. The linguistic and social consequences of gender inequality may be among the most important themes of *Their Eyes Were Watching God,* and this theme reaches beyond the text itself to the critical response to it. Richard Wright's famously scathing review, which appeared in October 1937, shortly after the publication of the novel, attacks Hurston for what the reviewer perceived as her betrayal of African America "to a white audience whose chauvinistic tastes she knows how to satisfy." Hurston's portrayals of African Americans, Wright added, "[evoke] a piteous smile on the lips" of what he perceived to be her mostly or exclusively white readership. The dialect spoken in the novel is dismissed with no attention beyond Wright's elitist-sounding claim that Hurston's "dialogue manages to catch the psychological movements of the Negro folk-mind in their pure simplicity, but that's as far as it goes" (17). Wright's frustration with what he interpreted as Hurston's continuing failure to "move in the direction of serious fiction" (16) seems to have resulted from a limited view of what the motives and strategies of African American artists should be. In other words, Wright judged *Their Eyes Were Watching God* as a political failure, at least according to his priorities, shared by a number of his male contemporaries. In her foreword to a recent edition of the novel, Mary Helen Washington interprets Wright's reaction as reflective of his view that social protest was the appropriate motivation and theme for a black artist. Unfortunately for Hurston, Washington adds, because of the influence of Wright, along with Hurston's other male contemporaries, "the quieter voice of a woman searching for self-realization could not, or would not, be heard" ("Foreword" x). Thus Wright's condemnation of *Their Eyes* is severely limited in two major ways. First, it ignores the artistic achievement of the novel, a fallacy that Hurston herself emphasized in her retort to Wright's review, pointing out, according to Henry Louis Gates Jr., that she was in the business of creating fiction "and not treatises on sociology" (qtd. in Gates, *Signifying* 184). Secondly, even allowing for the importance of creative expression of African American political thought during the 1930s, Wright's critique falls short in its extremely limited view of what constitutes a political issue.

Barbara Johnson articulates the short-sightedness of Wright's view, along with that of many of Hurston's other African American male predecessors and contemporaries, such as W. E. B. DuBois and James Weldon Johnson, in her contention that "Hurston's work is often called non-political simply because readers of Afro-American literature tend to look for confrontational *racial* politics, not sexual politics" (53, emphasis in original). Hurston got into trouble with her male African American critics, suggests Johnson, because of an unspoken but prevalent rule: "If the black woman voices opposition to male domination, she is often seen as a traitor to the cause of racial justice" (53). Johnson asserts that Janie's story, in which she struggles within a patriarchal system that silences her for much of her life, has no political relation to the view of Hurston's male critics that "without question . . . the black subject is male" (52). For these critics, Janie's experiences are not seen as in any way representing black life in America because "The black woman is totally invisible in [their] descriptions of the black dilemma" (52–53).

The African American woman, Nanny tells her teenaged granddaughter early in the novel, is "de mule uh de world" (14). Nanny's strategy for saving Janie from this fate is to marry her off to Logan against her will. Janie rebels with anger against Nanny, even believing years later, after Joe's death, that "[s]he hated her grandmother" (89). But Janie's angry if delayed rebellion against her grandmother is in actuality rebellion against the truth Nanny told her about black women's lives. Janie's ultimate failure in her attempt at rebellion, as evidenced linguistically by her continuing silence at the end of the novel, is neither a shortcoming of the novel nor of Janie. Rather, it reflects the reality of Nanny's experience as symbolic even for subsequent generations of African American women: enslaved, silenced, and controlled by males for their own purposes, as in the sexual entitlement to Nanny's body enacted by her slave master and Joe's enforced control over Janie during their marriage. Ironically, for Zora Neale Hurston, her death in solitary destitution in 1960, following denunciation by the contemporary African American male critical establishment and false sexual accusations made against her in the 1940s, demonstrates that even her great talent and initial success were not enough to transcend the hardships faced by African American women of her time, not the least of which was exclusion from the benefits of community. *Their Eyes Were Watching God* succeeds as a political statement in its treatment of a woman struggling for her own voice, making advances for herself and for those she inspires, both within the text and outside it, without denying the reality of the difficulty for an African American woman in the 1930s at once to be free, to be part of a community, and to thrive as an artist and human being.

8

Conclusions

From the humorist traditions to local color to twentieth-century realistic fiction, representations of dialect in American literature have evolved into a complex array of meanings, both linguistic and artistic, and those meanings have only rarely been without political and social underpinnings. This is especially true in the case of representations of African American speech. Its complicated history includes use by white authors for artistic reasons, as in Mark Twain's professed attempts to recreate realistic speech and William Faulkner's subtle interpretations of the racial attitudes of his characters and first-person narrators, but it has also been engaged more controversially in the service of trying to differentiate African Americans culturally from a white norm, including in the work of both Faulkner and Twain. The question of whether their representations are designed deliberately to try to enforce racial and social norms, even as they seem, paradoxically, to be trying to promote progressive thinking about race issues, is subject to debate, as seen in the previous chapters. For African American authors who use dialect in portraying the speech of their characters, the decision to do so is no less charged with conflict. As we have seen, authors such as Charles W. Chesnutt and Zora Neale Hurston have faced agonizing dilemmas within which the desire to represent black experiences authentically competes both with the demands of the market and with trends within the political and literary movements of African American thinkers and artists. When John R. Rickford and Russell J. Rickford ask in *Spoken Soul* whether "dialect literature limit[s] or liberate[s]," they must have exactly these kinds of contradictions in mind (38).

One important point I hope to make in this book is that in trying to understand how authors have reconciled for themselves the dichotomies inherent in representing dialect, in considering how to respond to dialectal representations of African American speech, and in trying to determine whether literary dialect limits or liberates, the representations have to be approached using interdisciplinary methods that look thoroughly at the texts themselves as well as at the actual spoken language beyond that which is represented in the literature. The logic behind this is simply that in order to give a thorough evaluation of an artist's work with respect to literary dialect, neither exclusively linguistic nor exclusively literary approaches can do justice to literature that incorporates imaginative recreations of the sounds of language along with the social themes surrounding the places in time that are recreated. All four of the authors whose work is analyzed herein deserve to have their work taken far more seriously than an impressionistic evaluation of their dialectal representations allows, especially if that evaluation isolates the dialect from its artistic and historical contexts, and especially if it ignores the linguistic realities that may be contained within representations that may be orthographically unappealing. At the same time, a linguistic analysis of the dialect in isolation from those same artistic and historical contexts risks dismissing credible literary interpretations of how dialect functions in a given work of literature by arguing that a linguistically accurate representation of speech negates the possibility that other social and racial dynamics may be at work also.

For Mark Twain, whose personal attitudes about race were far from uncomplicated but whose work also clearly shows that his artistic and political aims cannot be reduced to perpetuation of racial hierarchy, the characterization of Jim and his language are among his most important contributions to the continuing American dialogue on race. That *Huckleberry Finn* continues to be a touchstone for that dialogue even more than a century after its first publication is a tribute to its enduring significance. As Toni Morrison, whose conflicted views toward the novel are eloquently elucidated in her afterword to the 1996 Oxford University Press edition, has noted, "The brilliance of *Huckleberry Finn* is that it *is* the arguments it raises" (386, emphasis in original).

The dichotomy between limitation and liberation when applied to *Huckleberry Finn* leads to at least two possibilities to consider: with respect to Twain and with respect to Jim. Twain was probably liberated as he incorporated what he determined to be realistic forms of dialectal speech, including the African American variety he represents Jim as speaking. This liberation occurred within the context of the changing literary trends in postbellum letters, which made literature accessible to a wider audience, no longer simply the upper-class elite of Victorian times, and which portrayed a wider variety of characters from increasingly diverse walks of life. These changes must have been pleasing to Twain. *Adventures of Huckleberry Finn,* and not incidentally its portrayal of Jim as fully human and mostly sympathetic, the views of several dissenting critics notwithstanding, must have been liberating for Twain, whose youthful adventures as a river boat pilot's apprentice and as a miner in the western United States exemplify his own Huck Finn–like rebellion against Victorian conformity. The novel provided him with an avenue for his nontraditional explorations of social and racial questions, and the result is both an enduring artistic masterpiece and an important historical document.

For Jim, the question is more complicated. While he is quite literally "liberated" in the novel by a provision in Miss Watson's will, his status as an African American man in the United States in the nineteenth century leaves him with limited opportunities. By the time the novel was published in 1884, Jim would have been contending with the pressures and burdens of the post-Reconstruction period, when definitions of freedom continued to be extraordinarily complicated for African Americans. Functioning within the novel itself, Jim is far from emancipated, limited as he is by his capacity as subordinate and adjunctive to Huck, who is of course portrayed as the focus of the novel that bears his name, as well as by Twain's use of Jim as occasional comic relief. These are precisely the limitations in his characterization to which critics of Twain's portrayal point.

As an African American writer at work during the time that Jim was faced with the tribulations of Jim Crow and who was faced with open discrimination and contempt himself, Charles W. Chesnutt tried to use his literature as a tool for social change. His portrayal of Julius McAdoo as a dialect-speaking former slave offered the young writer entry into the white-controlled publishing world. Chesnutt, then, was commercially liberated to a degree by his use of dialect, but like his contemporary Paul Laurence Dunbar, he clearly had mixed feelings about using the device in order to sell stories and books. Later in his career, he wrote more openly antiracist fiction that did not rely on dialect in the characterization of African Americans, and his nondialect writing suffered a fate similar to that of Dunbar's nondialect writing in that it failed to attract public or positive critical attention. For Chesnutt, the paradox is of course that he might not have been published at all had he not used his dialect writing to gain entry into the elite community of published writers in his attempts both to make a living as a writer, which he did successfully for some years, and to change attitudes about race through his fiction. But at the same time, he was seriously limited by the critical and public tastes of his day, which devoured literature belonging to the plantation tradition to which Chesnutt seemingly acquiesced but also subverted, and in his apparent acquiescence, he became trapped by his own reputation as a writer of that tradition.

The question of true emancipation for Julius is equally complicated. He appears to adhere to the stereotype of the diffident, nostalgic former slave, but his subtly antislavery stories and the economic goals he accomplishes by way of their telling are an interesting case of his use of dialect as a tool for survival, if not liberation. For Julius, while he may be able to bring about gradual change in understanding on the parts of his in-text audience, John and Annie, and perhaps this effect might have extended to readers of Chesnutt's day, he still ends up at the end of *The Conjure Woman* as economically and socially subservient to whites. For Julius, like Chesnutt, the use of dialect is a major part of what made his subversive ideas palatable to a mostly white reading audience of which John and Annie are themselves representatives.

William Faulkner's representations of dialectal African American speech in *The Sound and the Fury* are rendered skillfully and even subtly with respect to the intricate variations between sections as they reflect the racial perceptions of each section's narrator. But at the same time, the assumptions underlying the story of the Gibsons' triumph in the face of the decline of the Compsons risk a stereotypical idealization of Dilsey Gibson and her family, even though the stereotype may be positive. Additionally, the novel seems to show that in spite of the perceived social inferiority of the Gibsons, as illustrated in part by way of their dialectal speech, they manage to transcend this "inferiority," social and linguistic, and prevail, a view which might be based in part on an unspoken assumption that black dialectal speech truly is inferior. Certainly Quentin and Jason perceive it to be so, and the question of whether Faulkner agreed with that assessment is legitimate in light of his contradictory public statements regarding racial issues.

That the socially and, according to the prevailing views of their culture, racially superior but morally corrupt Compsons still have the power to control and practically enslave the Gibsons leaves Dilsey and her family in a contradictory junction between moral and spiritual superiority and corporal servitude, in which the former does little to relieve the latter. While the dialect is used to differentiate the honorable Gibsons from the decadent Compsons, whether this linguistic "othering" should be interpreted as ironic is left ambiguous. This is not necessarily to be perceived as a flaw in the text; rather, it helps to illustrate the intricacies of racial attitudes and their manifestations in language as well as in perceptions about language variation. In *The Sound and the Fury*, then, limitation and liberation are inextricable from one another.

The same might be said for *Their Eyes Were Watching God*, in which Zora Neale Hurston creates a linguistic world in which African American dialectal speech is not only the norm, but in its poetry of sound and meaning, it effectively liberates the dialect from its negative literary reputation as an inferior linguistic form incapable of complex expression. This reclamation is one of Hurston's most enduring artistic legacies, and it also represents a significant turning point in American literature, which she achieved along with other writers of her generation such as Sterling Brown, Claude McKay, and Langston Hughes. The irony is that many of Hurston's contemporaries read the dialect not for what it contains but rather interpreted it as functioning within the stereotypical tradition. In that respect, those critics and thinkers who chose to disassociate themselves from dialect were limited far more so than the dialectal speakers in the novel who are free to speak dialectally without fear of ridicule or stereotype.

Mostly because of the black-dominated world portrayed in *Their Eyes Were Watching God*, the characters are for the most part linguistically liberated, as their impressive verbal skill indicates. Janie's situation is more complicated, but not necessarily with respect to her dialectal speech, as she is usually portrayed as verbally skilled when she does speak up, and her dialect functions only to enhance the power of her skill. However, her continued struggle for her voice takes place outside the conflict over the value of dialectal speech and is a function of her existence as a woman in a male-dominated oral culture, a struggle that in some ways mirrors that of Hurston herself.

For each of the four authors discussed here, then, the decision to incorporate African American dialectal speech was one that clearly involved controversy and contradiction as well as both limitation and liberation. I hope that the discussion contained in the previous chapters can contribute to the continuing conversation surrounding these authors and their work by offering a combination of literary and linguistic methods that can result in new kinds of access to literary texts and their representations of speech. I hope also that the preceding chapters have shown that using interdisciplinary methods to access literary texts helps to offer fresh insight not only into the texts themselves but also into issues of language variation and attitudes surrounding it. Finally, I hope the methods described here can help to illustrate the importance of attention to the historical contexts that are inextricable from views about language and about literary trends, including how those views function within the text as well as in the attitudes surrounding it.

Appendix A

Phonological Data for Jim in *Huckleberry Finn*

Table A.1 Vocalization of Postvocalic /r/

Examples from Jim's Speech (Number)	Nonoccurrence of Feature (Number)
asho' (1), bo'd'nhouse (1), coase (1), fo' (0), heah (13), mo' (22), sho (4), sholy (2), skasely (3)	ashore (0), boardinghouse (0), coarse (0), course (2), for (28), fer (4), f'r (3), hear (8), here (8), more (2), shore (1), sure (0), surely (0), scarcely (0)
Total=47 (46%*)	Total=56 (54%*)

*Not significant.

Table A.2 Loss of /r/ after Consonants

Examples from Jim's Speech (Number)	Nonoccurrence of Feature (Number)
fum (1), hund'd (4), pooty (7), thoo (1)	from (0), hundred (0), pretty (0), through (0)
Total=13 (100%*)	Total=0

*Significant at p<.05.

Table A.3 Intervocalic /r/ Loss with Syllable Loss

Examples from Jim's Speech (Number)	Nonoccurrence of Feature (Number)
considable (5), diffunt (1), tolable (1)	considerable (0), different (0), tolerble (1; Twain's spelling)
Total=7 (87.5%*)	Total=1 (12.5%*)

*Significant at p<.05.

Table A.4 Stopping of Syllable-Initial Fricatives

Examples from Jim's Speech (Number)	Nonoccurrence of Feature (Number)
dah (16), dan (1), dat (87), de (238), dem (7), den (26), dese (4), dey (64), dis (14)	there (0), than (0), that (2), the (1), them (0), then (0), these (0), they (0), this (0)
Total=457 (99%*)	Total=3 (1%*)

*Significant at p<.05.

Table A.5 Labialization of Interdental Fricatives

Examples from Jim's Speech (Number)	Nonoccurrence of Feature (Number)
bofe (1), breff (1), mouf (2), nuffn/nuff'n (7)	both (0), breath (0), mouth (0), nothing (1)
Total=11 (92%*)	Total=1 (8%*)

*Significant at p<.05.

Table A.6 Consonant Cluster Reduction, Especially Word-Final

Examples from Jim's Speech (Number)	Nonoccurrence of Feature (Number)
ain' (15), an' (1), en (222), behine (4), bes' (2), chile (19), coss (1), doan' (33), kep' (3), raf/raff[s] (13)	ain't (15), and (6), behind (0), best (0), child (0), costs (0), don't (12), kept (0), raft[s] (0)
Total=313 (90%*)	Total=33 (10%*)

*Significant at p<.05.

Table A.7 Deletion of Initial or Medial Unstressed Syllable

Examples from Jim's Speech (Number)	Nonoccurrence of Feature (Number)
'bout (28), 'bove (1), 'dout (3), 'kase/'kaze (9), 'nough (1)	about (1), above (0), without (0), because/bekase (5), enough (0)
Total=42 (87.5%*)	Total=6 (12.5%*)

*Significant at p<.05.

Table A.8 Final Unstressed /n/ for /ŋ/ in Present Participle

Examples from Jim's Speech (Number)	Nonoccurrence of Feature (Number)
bein' (1), bilin' (1), blim-blammin' (1), buyin' (1), callin' (1), comin' (6), cryin' (1), doin' (3), drinkin' (3), flyin' (1), gitt'n/gittn (2), goin' (2), havin' (2), hoverin' (1), hummin' (1), jawin' (1), killin' (1), listenin' (1), lookin' (2), makin' (1), mournin' (1), movin' (1), patchin' (1), risin' (1), runnin' (2), sayin' (1), smilin' (2), sprawlin' (1), stannin' (4), startin' (1), stirrin' (0), talkin' (2), tellin' (1), thinkin' (1), tremblin' (1), tryin' (3), willin' (1)	being (0), biling (0), boiling (0), blim-blamming (0), buying (0), calling (0), coming (0), crying (0), doing (0), drinking (0), flying (0), getting (0), going (1), having (0), hovering (0), humming (0), jawing (0), killing (0), listening (0), looking (0), making (0), mourning (0), moving (0), patching (0), rising (0), running (0), saying (0), smiling (0), sprawling (0), standing (0), starting (0), stirring (1), talking (0), telling (0), thinking (0), trembling (0), trying (0), willing (0)
Total=57 (97%*)	Total=2 (3%*)

*Significant at p<.05.

Table A.9 Other Alteration of Unstressed /n/ for /ŋ/

Examples from Jim's Speech (Number)	Nonoccurrence of Feature (Number)
anythin' (0), evenin' (1), mawnin' (3), nuffn/nuff'n (7), shavin's (1)	anything (1), evening (0), morning (0), nothing (1), shavings (0)
Total=11 (85%*)	Total=2 (15%*)

*Significant at p<.05

Table A.10 /t/ in Final Position

Examples from Jim's Speech (Number)	Nonoccurrence of Feature (Number)
across (3), chanst (2), twyste (1), wunst (3)	across (0), chance (1), twice (1), once (0)
Total=9 (82%*)	Total=2 (18%*)

*Significant at p<.05.

Table A.11 /j/ after Velar Stops /k/ and /g/ before Vowels Followed by /r/

Examples from Jim's Speech (Number)	Nonoccurrence of Feature (Number)
g'yarter (1), k'yards (1), k'yer (2), sk'yarlet (1), sk'yerd (1)	other /gar/ constructions or pronunciations (0), other /kar/ constructions or pronunciations (0), other /ker/ constructions or pronunciations (0), scarlet and similar constructions (0), scared (0), scarcely, spelled skasely (3)
Total=6 (86%*)	Total=1 (14%*)

*Significant at p<.05.

Table A.12 Alternation of Diphthongs /aɪ/ for /ɔɪ/

Examples from Jim's Speech (Number)	Nonoccurrence of Feature (Number)
biler (1), bilin' (1), agwyne/a-gwyne/gwyne/ gwineter (42), pint[s]/p'int (4)	boiler (0), boiling (0), [a]goin[g] (3), point[s] (0)
Total=48 (94%*)	Total=3 (6%*)

*Significant at p<.05.

Table A.13 Alternation of /e/ for /ɔ/

Examples from Jim's Speech (Number)	Nonoccurrence of Feature (Number)
bekase/'kase/'kaze (14)(100%*)	because (0)

*Significant at p<.05.

Table A.14 Merger of /ɛ/ and /ɪ/

Examples from Jim's Speech (Number)	Nonoccurrence of Feature (Number)
agin (19), resk (2), git [-s]/[-ing] (31)	again (1), risk (0), get [-s]/[-ing] (1)
Total=52 (96%*)	Total=2 (4%*)

*Significant at p<.05.

Appendix B

Speaker Data from *The Sound and the Fury,* by Character and Section of the Novel

Grammatical Data

Table B.1 Grammatical Data for Dilsey, by Section

Feature	Benjy Section	Jason Section	Final Section	Overall
Auxiliary and copula deletion	64/86 (74%*)	18/31 (58%*)	78/105 (74%*)	160/222 (72%*)
Done + verb	1	1	2	4
Multiple negation	14	5	14	33
Negative inversion	1	0	2	3
Noninverted questions	2	1	4	7
3rd person singular s̲-deletion	15/17 (88%*)	3/4 (75%*)	9/11 (82%*)	27/32 (84%*)
1st person singular/plural -s̲	5/5 (100%*)	5/5 (100%*)	14/18 (78%*)	24/28 (86%*)
2nd person -s̲	7/8 (88%*)	7/7 (100%*)	10/10 (100%*)	24/25 (96%*)
Unmarked past	4	1	3	8
Regularized past	1	1	8	10

*Significant at p<.05.

Table B.2 Grammatical Data for Luster, by Section

Feature	Benjy Section	Jason Section	Final Section	Overall
Auxiliary and copula deletion	26/35 (74%*)	5/5 (100%*)	31/38 (82%*)	62/78 (79%*)
Done + verb	2	0	0	2
Multiple negation	13	4	10	27
Negative inversion	0	0	0	0
Noninverted questions	2	0	0	2
3rd person singular s-deletion	8/9 (89%*)	2/2 (100%*)	12/13 (92%*)	22/24 (92%*)
1st person singular/plural -s	2/2 (100%*)	0/0	9/9 (100%*)	11/11 (100%*)
2nd person -s	2/2 (100%*)	0/0	3/3 (100%*)	5/5 (100%*)
Unmarked past	3	1	9	13
Regularized past	0	0	2	2

*Significant at p<.05.

Table B.3 Grammatical Data for Deacon (Quentin Section)

Feature	Frequency	Feature	Frequency
Auxiliary and copula deletion	1/13 (8%)	3rd person singular s-deletion	0/2
Done + verb	1	1st person singular/plural -s	4/11 (36%*)
Multiple negation	1	2nd person -s	2/2 (100%*)
Negative inversion	0	Unmarked past	0
Noninverted questions	0	Regularized past	0

*Significant at p<.05.

Table B.4 Grammatical Data for Louis (Quentin Section)

Feature	Frequency	Feature	Frequency
Auxiliary and copula deletion	6/11 (55%*)	3rd person singular s-deletion	2/2 (100%*)
Done + verb	0	1st person singular/plural -s	4/4 (100%*)
Multiple negation	2	2nd person -s	1/1 (100%)
Negative inversion	0	Unmarked past	7
Noninverted questions	0	Regularized past	1

*Significant at p<.05.

Table B.5 Grammatical Data for Job (Jason Section)

Feature	Frequency	Feature	Frequency
Auxiliary and copula deletion	8/16 (50%*)	3rd person singular s- deletion	1/3 (33%)
Done + verb	0	1st person singular/ plural -s	5/5 (100%*)
Multiple negation	4	2nd person -s	1/1 (100%)
Negative inversion	1	Unmarked past	0
Noninverted questions	0	Regularized past	0

*Significant at p<.05.

Table B.6 Grammatical Data for Rev. Shegog (Final Section)

Feature	Frequency	Feature	Frequency
Auxiliary and copula deletion	12/13 (92%*)	3rd person singular s- deletion	2/2 (100%*)
Done + verb	2	1st person singular/ plural -s	27/30 (90%*)
Multiple negation	0	2nd person -s	1/1 (100%)
Negative inversion	0	Unmarked past	2
Noninverted questions	0	Regularized past	0

*Significant at p<.05.

Phonological Data

Table B.7 Phonological Data for Dilsey (Benjy Section)

Feature	Tokens	Types	Frequency
Vocalization of postvocalic /r/	3	111	2.7%
Loss of /r/ after consonants and in unstressed syllables	2	9	22%
Intervocalic /r/ loss with syllable loss	2	6	33%
Vocalization of unstressed syllabic /r/	0	40	0
Stopping of syllable-initial fricatives	0	93	0
Stopping of voiceless interdental fricatives	0	15	0
Labialization of interdental fricatives	0	22	0
Consonant cluster reduction	0	153	0
Deletion of initial unstressed syllable	11	34	32%*
Final unstressed /n/ for /ŋ/ in present participle	0	67	0
Other alternation of final unstressed /n/ for /ŋ/	0	6	0
Alternation of diphthongs /aɪ/ for /ɔɪ/	0	20	0
Merger of /ɛ/ and /ɪ/	6	63	9.5%*

*Significant at p<.05.

Table B.8 Phonological Data for Dilsey (Jason Section)

Feature	Tokens	Types	Frequency
Vocalization of postvocalic /r/	12	23	52%*
Loss of /r/ after consonants and in unstressed syllables	1	1	100%
Intervocalic /r/ loss with syllable loss	8	9	89%*
Vocalization of unstressed syllabic /r/	0	4	0
Stopping of syllable-initial fricatives	18	24	75%*
Stopping of voiceless interdental fricatives	4	5	80%*
Labialization of interdental fricatives	1	1	100%
Consonant cluster reduction	7	34	21%*
Deletion of initial unstressed syllable	6	18	33%*
Final unstressed /n/ for /ŋ/ in present participle	25	26	96%*
Other alternation of final unstressed /n/ for /ŋ/	4	5	80%*
Alternation of diphthongs /aɪ/ for /ɔɪ/	12	12	100%*
Merger of /ɛ/ and /ɪ/	21	24	88%*

*Significant at p<.05.

Table B.9 Phonological Data for Dilsey (Final Section)

Feature	Tokens	Types	Frequency
Vocalization of postvocalic /r/	64	125	51%*
Loss of /r/ after consonants and in unstressed syllables	6	6	100%*
Intervocalic /r/ loss with syllable loss	10	16	63%*
Vocalization of unstressed syllabic /r/	0	43	0
Stopping of syllable-initial fricatives	165	167	99%*
Stopping of voiceless interdental fricatives	9	9	100%*
Labialization of interdental fricatives	4	11	36%*
Consonant cluster reduction	58	150	39%*
Deletion of initial unstressed syllable	26	51	51%*
Final unstressed /n/ for /ŋ/ in present participle	55	56	98%*
Other alternation of final unstressed /n/ for /ŋ/	7	11	64%*
Alternation of diphthongs /aɪ/ for /ɔɪ/	17	18	94%*
Merger of /ɛ/ and /ɪ/	40	44	91%*

*Significant at p<.05.

Table B.10 Phonological Data for Dilsey (All Sections)

Feature	Tokens	Types	Overall Frequency
Vocalization of postvocalic /r/	79	259	31%*
Loss of /r/ after consonants and in unstressed syllables	9	16	56%*
Intervocalic /r/ loss with syllable loss	20	31	65%*
Vocalization of unstressed syllabic /r/	0	87	0
Stopping of syllable-initial fricatives	183	184	99%*
Stopping of voiceless interdental fricatives	13	20	65%*
Labialization of interdental fricatives	5	34	15%*
Consonant cluster reduction	65	337	19%*
Deletion of initial unstressed syllable	43	103	42%*
Final unstressed /n/ for /ŋ/ in present participle	80	149	54%*
Other alternation of final unstressed /n/ for /ŋ/	11	22	50%*
Alternation of diphthongs /aɪ/ for /ɔɪ/	29	50	58%*
Merger of /ɛ/ and /ɪ/	67	131	51%*

*Significant at p<.05.

Table B.11 Phonological Data for Luster (Benjy Section)

Feature	Tokens	Types	Frequency
Vocalization of postvocalic /r/	5	61	8%*
Loss of /r/ after consonants and in unstressed syllables	1	5	20%
Intervocalic /r/ loss with syllable loss	0	0	0
Vocalization of unstressed syllabic /r/	0	15	0
Stopping of syllable-initial fricatives	0	78	0
Stopping of voiceless interdental fricatives	0	10	0
Labialization of interdental fricatives	0	12	0
Consonant cluster reduction	3	31	9.6%
Deletion of initial unstressed syllable	2	9	22%
Final unstressed /n/ for /ŋ/ in present participle	0	16	0
Other alternation of final unstressed /n/ for /ŋ/	0	10	0
Alternation of diphthongs /aɪ/ for /ɔɪ/	0	13	0
Merger of /ɛ/ and /ɪ/	1	15	6.6%

*Significant at p<.05.

Table B.12 Phonological Data for Luster (Jason Section)

Feature	Tokens	Types	Frequency
Vocalization of postvocalic /r/	1	4	25%
Loss of /r/ after consonants and in unstressed syllables	1	1	100%
Intervocalic /r/ loss with syllable loss	2	2	100%*
Vocalization of unstressed syllabic /r/	0	10	0
Stopping of syllable-initial fricatives	8	9	89%*
Stopping of voiceless interdental fricatives	2	2	100%*
Labialization of interdental fricatives	1	1	100%
Consonant cluster reduction	4	6	67%*
Deletion of initial unstressed syllable	0	0	0
Final unstressed /n/ for /ŋ/ in present participle	6	6	100%*
Other alternation of final unstressed /n/ for /ŋ/	1	1	100%
Alternation of diphthongs /aɪ/ for /ɔɪ/	1	2	50%
Merger of /ɛ/ and /ɪ/	4	4	100%*

*Significant at p<.05.

Table B.13 Phonological Data for Luster (Final Section)

Feature	Tokens	Types	Frequency
Vocalization of postvocalic /r/	10	36	28%*
Loss of /r/ after consonants and in unstressed syllables	2	3	67%*
Intervocalic /r/ loss with syllable loss	6	9	67%*
Vocalization of unstressed syllabic /r/	8	22	36%*
Stopping of syllable-initial fricatives	47	47	100%*
Stopping of voiceless interdental fricatives	5	5	100%*
Labialization of interdental fricatives	1	7	14%
Consonant cluster reduction	19	25	76%*
Deletion of initial unstressed syllable	6	10	60%*
Final unstressed /n/ for /ŋ/ in present participle	32	32	100%*
Other alternation of final unstressed /n/ for /ŋ/	9	9	100%*
Alternation of diphthongs /aɪ/ for /ɔɪ/	14	14	100%*
Merger of /ɛ/ and /ɪ/	12	17	71%*

*Significant at p<.05.

Table B.14 Phonological Data for Luster (All Sections)

Feature	Tokens	Types	Overall Frequency
Vocalization of postvocalic /r/	16	101	16%*
Loss of /r/ after consonants and in unstressed syllables	4	9	44%*
Intervocalic /r/ loss with syllable loss	8	11	73%*
Vocalization of unstressed syllabic /r/	8	47	17%*
Stopping of syllable-initial fricatives	55	134	41%*
Stopping of voiceless interdental fricatives	7	17	41%*
Labialization of interdental fricatives	2	20	10%
Consonant cluster reduction	26	62	42%*
Deletion of initial unstressed syllable	8	19	42%*
Final unstressed /n/ for /ŋ/ in present participle	38	64	59%*
Other alternation of final unstressed /n/ for /ŋ/	10	20	50%*
Alternation of diphthongs /aɪ/ for /ɔɪ/	15	29	52%*
Merger of /ɛ/ and /ɪ/	17	36	47%*

*Significant at p<.05.

Table B.15 Phonological Data for Deacon (Quentin Section)

Feature	Tokens	Types	Frequency
Vocalization of postvocalic /r/	3	23	13%
Loss of /r/ after consonants and in unstressed syllables	0	3	0
Intervocalic /r/ loss with syllable loss	0	0	0
Vocalization of unstressed syllabic /r/	0	10	0
Stopping of syllable-initial fricatives	5	27	19%*
Stopping of voiceless interdental fricatives	0	4	0
Labialization of interdental fricatives	0	3	0
Consonant cluster reduction	1	18	6%
Deletion of initial unstressed syllable	0	4	0
Final unstressed /n/ for /ŋ/ in present participle	0	7	0
Other alternation of final unstressed /n/ for /ŋ/	0	3	0
Alternation of diphthongs /aɪ/ for /ɔɪ/	0	0	0
Merger of /ɛ/ and /ɪ/	1	5	20%

*Significant at p<.05.

Table B.16 Phonological Data for Louis (Quentin Section)

Feature	Tokens	Types	Frequency
Vocalization of postvocalic /r/	9	12	75%*
Loss of /r/ after consonants and in unstressed syllables	0	0	0
Intervocalic /r/ loss with syllable loss	1	2	50%
Vocalization of unstressed syllabic /r/	0	8	0
Stopping of syllable-initial fricatives	31	31	100%*
Stopping of voiceless interdental fricatives	2	2	100%*
Labialization of interdental fricatives	0	0	0
Consonant cluster reduction	6	13	46%*
Deletion of initial unstressed syllable	1	3	33%
Final unstressed /n/ for /ŋ/ in present participle	6	6	100%*
Other alternation of final unstressed /n/ for /ŋ/	0	0	0
Alternation of diphthongs /aɪ/ for /ɔɪ/	1	1	100%
Merger of /ɛ/ and /ɪ/	7	7	100%*

*Significant at p<.05.

Table B.17 Phonological Data for Job (Jason Section)

Feature	Tokens	Types	Frequency
Vocalization of postvocalic /r/	7	18	39%*
Loss of /r/ after consonants and in unstressed syllables	0	1	0
Intervocalic /r/ loss with syllable loss	4	4	100%*
Vocalization of unstressed syllabic /r/	0	7	0
Stopping of syllable-initial fricatives	33	33	100%*
Stopping of voiceless interdental fricatives	2	2	100%*
Labialization of interdental fricatives	2	2	100%*
Consonant cluster reduction	2	5	40%
Deletion of initial unstressed syllable	3	6	50%*
Final unstressed /n/ for /ŋ/ in present participle	7	7	100%*
Other alternation of final unstressed /n/ for /ŋ/	2	2	100%*
Alternation of diphthongs /aɪ/ for /ɔɪ/	1	1	100%
Merger of /ɛ/ and /ɪ/	5	9	56%*

*Significant at p<.05.

Table B.18 Phonological Data for Rev. Shegog (Final Section)

Feature	Tokens	Types	Frequency
Vocalization of postvocalic /r/	12	28	43%*
Loss of /r/ after consonants and in unstressed syllables	2	3	67%*
Intervocalic /r/ loss with syllable loss	6	10	60%*
Vocalization of unstressed syllabic /r/	0	7	0
Stopping of syllable-initial fricatives	81	84	96%*
Stopping of voiceless interdental fricatives	17	20	85%*
Labialization of interdental fricatives	0	0	0
Consonant cluster reduction	25	33	76%*
Deletion of initial unstressed syllable	1	3	33%
Final unstressed /n/ for /ŋ/ in present participle	26	26	100%*
Other alternation of final unstressed /n/ for /ŋ/	1	1	100%
Alternation of diphthongs /aɪ/ for /ɔɪ/	6	6	100%*
Merger of /ɛ/ and /ɪ/	4	6	67%*

*Significant at p<.05.

Appendix C

Speaker Data from *Their Eyes Were Watching God*

Phonological Data for Secondary Characters

Table C.1 Phonological Data for Eatonville Men

Feature	Tokens	Types	Frequency
Vocalization of postvocalic /r/	93	167	56%
Loss of /r/ after consonants and in unstressed syllables	2	17	12%*
Intervocalic /r/ loss with syllable loss	1	4	25%
Vocalization of unstressed syllabic /r/	3	83	4%*
Stopping of syllable-initial fricatives	293	328	89%*
Stopping of voiceless interdental fricatives	26	28	93%*
Labialization of interdental fricatives	0	2	0
Consonant cluster reduction	23	328	7%*
Deletion of initial unstressed syllable	71	123	58%
Final unstressed /n/ for /ŋ/ in present participle	101	104	97%*
Other alternation of final unstressed /n/ for /ŋ/	34	44	77%*
Alternation of diphthongs /aɪ/ for /ɔɪ/	0	16	0
Merger of /ɛ/ and /ɪ/	36	40	90%*
Glide reduction /aɪ/ to /a/	179	187	96%*

*Significant at p<.05.

Table C.2 Phonological Data for Mrs. Turner

Feature	Tokens	Types	Frequency
Vocalization of postvocalic /r/	12	17	71%
Loss of /r/ after consonants and in unstressed syllables	1	3	33%
Intervocalic /r/ loss with syllable loss	0	2	0
Vocalization of unstressed syllabic /r/	0	27	0
Stopping of syllable-initial fricatives	40	43	93%*
Stopping of voiceless interdental fricatives	8	8	100%*
Labialization of interdental fricatives	0	0	0
Consonant cluster reduction	9	39	23%*
Deletion of initial unstressed syllable	10	15	67%
Final unstressed /n/ for /ŋ/ in present participle	30	30	100%
Other alternation of final unstressed /n/ for /ŋ/	1	2	50%
Alternation of diphthongs /aɪ/ for /ɔɪ/	0	3	0
Merger of /ɛ/ and /ɪ/	4	4	100%
Glide reduction /aɪ/ to /a/	41	42	98%*

*Significant at p<.05.

Table C.3 Phonological Data for Everglades Men

Feature	Tokens	Types	Frequency
Vocalization of postvocalic /r/	25	37	68%*
Loss of /r/ after consonants and in unstressed syllables	3	7	43%
Intervocalic /r/ loss with syllable loss	0	1	0
Vocalization of unstressed syllabic /r/	3	29	10%*
Stopping of syllable-initial fricatives	78	80	78%*
Stopping of voiceless interdental fricatives	6	6	100%*
Labialization of interdental fricatives	1	1	100%
Consonant cluster reduction	11	83	13%*
Deletion of initial unstressed syllable	13	22	59%
Final unstressed /n/ for /ŋ/ in present participle	36	37	97%*
Other alternation of final unstressed /n/ for /ŋ/	7	8	88%*
Alternation of diphthongs /aɪ/ for /ɔɪ/	0	13	0
Merger of /ɛ/ and /ɪ/	12	12	100%*
Glide reduction /aɪ/ to /a/	74	74	100%*

*Significant at p<.05.

Table C.4 Phonological Data for Eatonville Women

Feature	Tokens	Types	Frequency
Vocalization of postvocalic /r/	12	27	44%
Loss of /r/ after consonants and in unstressed syllables	8	8	100%*
Intervocalic /r/ loss with syllable loss	0	0	0
Vocalization of unstressed syllabic /r/	8	16	50%
Stopping of syllable-initial fricatives	26	31	84%*
Stopping of voiceless interdental fricatives	7	8	88%*
Labialization of interdental fricatives	1	1	100%
Consonant cluster reduction	12	58	21%*
Deletion of initial unstressed syllable	8	12	67%
Final unstressed /n/ for /ŋ/ in present participle	17	19	89%*
Other alternation of final unstressed /n/ for /ŋ/	1	3	33%
Alternation of diphthongs /aɪ/ for /ɔɪ/	0	3	0
Merger of /ɛ/ and /ɪ/	1	2	50%
Glide reduction /aɪ/ to /a/	24	27	89%*

*Significant at p<.05.

Grammatical Data

Table C.5 Grammatical data for minor characters, collectively.

Feature	Eatonville Men	Glades Men	Eatonville Women
Auxiliary and copula deletion	X	X	X
Be + done			
Completive been	X		
Done + been			
Done + verb	X	X	X
Simple past done	X		X
Multiple negation	X	X	X
Negative inversion			
Noninverted questions		X	X
Subject-verb nonconcord	X	X	X
Unmarked past	X	X	X
Regularized past	X		
Relative pronoun deletion	X		
Possessive they	X		X
Pronoun apposition	X		
Undifferentiated pronoun reflexives	X		
Object pronoun them for subject those	X	X	X
Hypercorrect plural -s	X	X	
Regularized plural			
Existential it/they	X	X	X
Tell + say			
Indignant come		X	
Counterfactual call			
Total features present	15	10	10

Notes

Chapter 3

1. A few points about what constitutes a feature of African American English in my analysis: As indicated in much of the leading scholarship, some features considered here are not unique to African American English and are in fact shared with other varieties of American English. I identify the features with AAE after consulting the scholarship cited in chapter 3, which notes the association between particular linguistic features and some African American speakers. It is not my intent to try to determine what might constitute a unique or distinctly "African American" feature. That question is of course open to debate within the linguistic community. Attempts to characterize exactly what distinguishes African American English are probably better left to researchers working on descriptive grammars and other documentation of African American English, including the researchers and other sources discussed in chapter 3, whose work I encourage curious readers to consult for more information about AAE and features associated with it. My goal is to apply the methods outlined here to literary texts in order to see what new insights they might yield in terms of the individual texts and characters, along with what new options they make possible for further inquiry into areas such as language variation, language attitudes, and older varieties of AAE.

Chapter 4

1. According to a letter by South Carolina community activist David Nolan in the March 11, 1971, *New York Review of Books,* Dr. Gatch was also subjected to public criticism from South Carolina Governor Robert McNair and Senator Ernest Hollings, who believed his testimony would negatively affect tourism in South Carolina. According to Nolan's letter, Dr. Gatch was also the subject of an FBI investigation at the behest of Mississippi Congressman Jamie Whitten and was indicted in late 1969 for alleged violations of state drug laws in his medical practice. According to Nolan, Dr. Gatch was told that all charges against him would be dropped if he left South Carolina. Most of the charges were dismissed at the August 1970 trial and

Dr. Gatch was assessed a fine for not keeping adequate records. Today a community medical center in Hardeeville, South Carolina, bears his name.

Chapter 5

1. The question of whether the apostrophe-less instances of unmarked past could be the result of sound reduction or deletion is far from settled, but because Chesnutt apparently differentiates them from those spelled with apostrophes, they have been interpreted in this analysis as functions of grammar. Of course, this raises the eternal question for several grammatical features as to whether they might more accurately be interpreted as the result of pronunciation. For example, might possessive *they* be an *r*-less articulation of *their*?

Chapter 6

1. Davis cites the 1929 Cape and Smith edition of *The Sound and the Fury*, page 3, which corresponds to page 4 of the Norton Critical Edition, used in the preparation of this analysis.

2. Tallies from the Quentin section are not included here because Dilsey appears only briefly in this section and produces a negligible amount of speech, and because Luster, not yet born in 1910, does not appear at all.

3. Fortunately, several sound recordings of William Faulkner's voice are available, including a recording of his Nobel prize speech as well as readings by the author of several of his works, including *The Sound and the Fury*.

Works Cited

Bailey, Guy, and Erik Thomas. "Some Aspects of African-American Vernacular English Phonology." Mufwene, Rickford, Bailey, and Baugh 85–109.

Baker, Houston A., Jr. *Modernism and the Harlem Renaissance.* Chicago: U of Chicago P, 1987.

Barry, Betsy. "It's Hard fuh Me to Understand What You Mean, de Way You Tell It: Representing Language in Zora Neale Hurston's *Their Eyes Were Watching God.*" *Language and Literature* 10.2 (2001): 171–86.

Bernstein, Cynthia Goldin. "The Contextualization of Linguistic Criticism." Bernstein, *The Text and Beyond* 3–14.

———. "Misrepresenting the American South." *American Speech* 75.4 (2000): 339–42.

———, ed. *The Text and Beyond: Essays in Literary Linguistics.* Tuscaloosa, AL: UP of Alabama, 1994.

———. "Text and Context." Bernstein, *The Text and Beyond* 1–2.

Bernstein, Cynthia, Thomas Nunnally, and Robin Sabino, eds. *Language Variety in the South Revisited.* Tuscaloosa, AL: UP of Alabama, 1997.

Bigart, Homer. "Hunger in America: Stark Deprivation Haunts a Land of Plenty." *New York Times* 17 Feb. 1969: 1+.

Birnbaum, Michele. "Dark Dialects: Scientific and Literary Realism in Joel Chandler Harris's Uncle Remus Series." *New Orleans Review* 18.1 (1991): 36–45.

Blair, Walter. Introduction. Blair and McDavid ix–xxvii.

Blair, Walter, and Raven I. McDavid, Jr., eds. *The Mirth of a Nation: America's Great Dialect Humor.* Minneapolis: UP of Minnesota, 1983.

Blank, Paula. *Broken English: Dialects and the Politics of Language in Renaissance Writings.* New York: Routledge, 1996.

Bloom, Harold, ed. *Modern Critical Interpretations: Zora Neale Hurston's Their Eyes Were Watching God.* New York: Chelsea House, 1987.

Brasch, Walter M. *Black English and the Mass Media.* Boston: U of Massachusetts P, 1981. New York: Authors Guild, 2000.

———. *Brer Rabbit, Uncle Remus, and the 'Cornfield Journalist.'* Macon, GA: Mercer UP, 2000.

Braxton, Joanne M. Introduction. *The Collected Poetry of Paul Laurence Dunbar.* By Paul Laurence Dunbar. Ed. Braxton. Charlottesville: UP of Virginia, ix–xxxvi.

Brodhead, Richard H. Introduction. Chesnutt *Conjure* 1–21.

———. Introduction. Chesnutt *Journals* 1–28.

Brown, Sterling. Review of *Their Eyes Were Watching God,* by Zora Neale Hurston. *The Nation.* October 16, 1937. Gates and Appiah 20–21.

Carkeet, David. "The Dialects in *Huckleberry Finn.*" *American Literature* 51 (1979): 315–32.

Carton, Evan. "Speech Acts and Social Action: Mark Twain and the Politics of Literary Performance." Robinson 153–74.

Cassidy, Frederic, and Joan H. Hall, eds. *Dictionary of American Regional English.* Vol. 3. Cambridge: Belknap-Harvard UP, 1996.

Chesnutt, Charles W. *The Conjure Woman and Other Conjure Tales.* 1899. Ed. Richard H. Brodhead. Durham, NC: Duke UP, 1993.

———. "Dave's Neckliss." 1889. Chesnutt *Conjure* 123–35.

———. "Dave's Neckliss." 1889. University of North Carolina Libraries: Documenting the American South. 2001. <http://docsouth.unc.edu/southlit/southlit.html>.

———. "The Goophered Grapevine." Chesnutt *Conjure* 31–43.

———. *The Journals of Charles W. Chesnutt.* Ed. Richard H. Brodhead. Durham, NC: Duke UP, 1993.

———. "Po' Sandy." Chesnutt *Conjure* 44–54.

———. "Sis' Becky's Pickaninny." Chesnutt *Conjure* 82–93.

———. *The Wife of His Youth and Other Stories of the Color Line.* 1899. Ridgewood, NJ: Gregg, 1967.

Cohen, Hennig, and William B. Dillingham, eds. *Humor of the Old Southwest.* 3rd ed. Athens, GA: UP of Georgia, 1994.

Cole, Roger W. "Literary Representation of Dialect: A Theoretical Approach to the Artistic Problem." *The Language Quarterly* 24.3–4 (1986): 3–8, 48.

Collins, Carvel. " *The Sound and the Fury:* The Tragedy of the Lack of Love." Kinney 124–26.

Cooley, Marianne. "An Early Representation of African-American English." Bernstein, Nunnally, and Sabino 51–58.

Davis, Thadious M. *Faulkner's "Negro": Art and the Southern Context.* Baton Rouge, LA: Louisiana State UP, 1983.

Dillard, J. L. "The Relative Value of Ex-Slave Narratives: A Discussion of Schneider's Paper." Mufwene and Condon 222–231.

Duncan, Charles. *The Absent Man: The Narrative Craft of Charles W. Chesnutt.* Athens, OH: Ohio UP, 1998.

Ellis, Michael. "Literary Dialect as Linguistic Evidence: Subject-Verb Concord in Nineteenth-Century Southern Literature." *American Speech* 69.2 (1994): 128–44.

Esau, Helmut, Norma Bagnall, and Cheryl Ware. "Faulkner, Literary Criticism, and Linguistics." *Language and Literature* 7.1–3 (1982): 7–62.

Evans, William. "French-English Literary Dialect in *The Grandissimes.*" *American Speech* 46:3–4 (1971), 210–22.

Fasold, Ralph. *Tense-Marking in Black English: A Linguistic and Social Analysis*. Arlington, VA: Ctr. for Applied Linguistics, 1972.

Faulkner, William. "Nobel Prize Speech, December 10, 1950." *Great American Speeches*, Vol. 4. LP. New York: Caedmon, 1969.

———. *The Sound and the Fury*. 1929. Ed. David Minter. 2nd ed. New York: Norton, 1994.

———. "William Faulkner Reads Selections from *The Sound and the Fury* and *Light in August*." LP. Old Greenwich, CT: Listening Library, no date.

Fennell, B. A. "Literary Data and Linguistic Analysis: The Example of Modern German Immigrant Worker Literature." Bernstein, *The Text and Beyond* 241–62.

Fennell, Barbara A. and John Bennett. "Sociolinguistic Concepts and Literary Analysis." *American Speech* 66:4 (1991): 371–79.

Ferguson, Otis. Review of *Their Eyes Were Watching God*. *The New Republic*. October 13, 1937. Gates and Appiah 22–23.

Fienberg, Lorne. "Charles W. Chesnutt and Uncle Julius: Black Storytellers at the Crossroads." *Studies in American Fiction* 15.2 (1987): 161–73.

Fishkin, Shelley Fisher. *Was Huck Black? Mark Twain and African American Voices*. New York: Oxford UP, 1993.

Foster, Charles W. *The Phonology of the Conjure Tales of Charles W. Chesnutt*. Publication of the American Dialect Society 55. Tuscaloosa: UP of Alabama, 1971.

Foster, Frances Smith, and Richard Yarborough. Introduction to Charles W. Chesnutt. Gates and McKay 522–23.

Fowler, Doreen, and Ann J. Abadie, eds. *Faulkner and Race: Faulkner and Yoknapatawpha*. Jackson: UP of Mississippi, 1986.

Gates, Henry Louis, Jr. "Zora Neale Hurston: 'A Negro Way of Saying.'" Afterword. Hurston, *Their Eyes Were Watching God* 195–205.

———. *The Signifying Monkey: A Theory of African-American Literary Criticism*. New York: Oxford UP, 1988.

Gates, Henry Louis, Jr., and K. A. Appiah, eds. *Zora Neale Hurston: Critical Perspectives Past and Present*. New York: Amistad, 1993.

Gates, Henry Louis, Jr., and Nellie Y. McKay, eds. *The Norton Anthology of African American Literature*. New York: Norton, 1997.

Green, Lisa. *African American English: A Linguistic Introduction*. Cambridge: Cambridge UP, 2002.

———. "Aspect and Predicate Phrase in African-American Vernacular English." Mufwene, Rickford, Bailey, and Baugh 37–68.

Gresset, Michael. "The Ordeal of Consciousness: Psychological Aspects of Evil in *The Sound and the Fury*." Kinney 173–181.

Gumperz, John J. *Discourse Strategies*. Cambridge: Cambridge UP, 1982.

Holloway, Karla F. C. *The Character of the Word: The Texts of Zora Neale Hurston*. New York: Greenwood, 1987.

Holton, Sylvia W. *Down Home and Uptown: The Representation of Black Speech in American Fiction.* Rutherford, NJ: Associated UP, 1984.

Hughes, Langston. "Feet Live Their Own Life." Gates and McKay 1297–99.

Hurston, Zora Neale. "Characteristics of Negro Expression." 1934. *Within the Circle: An Anthology of African American Literary Criticism.* Ed. Angelyn Mitchell. Durham, NC: Duke UP, 1994. 79–94.

———. *Their Eyes Were Watching God.* 1937. New York: Perennial, 1999.

Ives, Sumner. "A Theory of Literary Dialect." 1950. Williamson and Burke 145–77.

Johnson, Barbara. "Metaphor, Metonymy and Voice in *Their Eyes Were Watching God.*" Bloom 41–57.

Johnson, Barbara, and Henry Louis Gates Jr. "A Black and Idiomatic Free Indirect Discourse." Bloom 73–85.

Johnson, James Weldon. Preface. *The Book of American Negro Poetry.* 1922. Gates and McKay 861–84.

Jones, Gavin. *Strange Talk: The Politics of Dialect Literature in Gilded Age America.* Berkeley, CA: UP of California, 1999.

Jones, Gayl. "Breaking Out of the Conventions of Dialect." Gates and Appiah 141–53.

Keeling, John. "Paul Dunbar and the Mask of Dialect." *Southern Literary Journal* 25.2 (1993): 24–38.

Kessler, Carolyn. "Noun Plural Absence." Fasold 223–37.

Kinney, Arthur F., ed. *Critical Essays on William Faulkner: The Compson Family.* Boston: G. K. Hall, 1982.

Krapp, George Philip. *The English Language in America.* New York: Century, 1925.

Kretzschmar, William A., Jr., ed. *The Linguistic Atlas of the Middle and South Atlantic States.* 2001. The University of Georgia. <http://us.english.uga.edu>.

Kretzschmar, William A., Jr., Virginia G. McDavid, Theodore K. Lerud, and Ellen Johnson, eds. *Handbook of the Linguistic Atlas of the Middle and South Atlantic States.* Chicago: U of Chicago P, 1993.

Kubitschek, Missy Dehn. "'Tuh de Horizon and Back': The Female Quest in *Their Eyes Were Watching God.*" Bloom 19–33.

Labov, William. "Co-existent Systems in African-American Vernacular English." Mufwene, Rickford, Bailey, and Baugh 110–53.

Lencho, Mark. "Dialect Variation in *The Sound and the Fury:* A Study of Faulkner's Use of Black English." *Mississippi Quarterly* 41.3 (1988): 403–19.

Lenz, William E. "Confidence and Convention in *Huckleberry Finn.*" Sattelmeyer and Crowley 186–200.

Leonard, James S. and Thomas A. Tenney. Introduction. Leonard, Tenney, and Davis 1–11.

Leonard, James S., Thomas A. Tenney, and Thadious M. Davis, eds. *Satire or Evasion? Black Perspectives on* Huckleberry Finn. Durham: Duke UP, 1992.

Locke, Alain. Review of *Their Eyes Were Watching God.* By Zora Neale Hurston. *Opportunity.* June 1, 1938. Gates and Appiah 18.

Lott, Eric. "Mr. Clemens and Jim Crow: Twain, Race, and Blackface." Robinson 129–52.

Martin, Stefan, and Walt Wolfram. "The Sentence in African-American Vernacular English." Mufwene, Rickford, Bailey and Baugh 11–36.

Matthews, John T. The Sound and the Fury: Faulkner and the Lost Cause. Boston: Twayne, 1991.

McDavid, Raven I., Jr. "Design, Data-gathering, and Interpretation." The Second and Third Lincolnland Conference on Dialectology. Eds. Jerry Griffith and L. E. Miner. Tuscaloosa, AL: UP of Alabama, 1972. 1–19.

———. "The Dialects of American English." The Structure of American English. Ed. Nelson Francis. New York: Ronald, 1958. 480–543.

———. "Linguistic Note." Blair and McDavid 279–183.

Meese, Elizabeth. "Orality and Textuality in Their Eyes Were Watching God." Bloom 59–71.

Mille, Katherine Wyly. "Ambrose Gonzales's Gullah: What It May Tell Us about Variation." Bernstein, Nunnally, and Sabino 98–112.

Millgate, Michael. "The Composition of The Sound and the Fury." Kinney 155–72.

Morrison, Toni. "This Amazing, Troubling Book." Twain, Huckleberry Finn 385–92.

Mufwene, Salikoko S., John R. Rickford, Guy Bailey, and John Baugh, eds. African-American English: Structure, History and Use. New York: Routledge, 1998.

Mufwene, Salikoko S., and Nancy Condon, eds. Africanisms in Afro-American Language Varieties. Athens: UP of Georgia, 1994.

Mufwene, Salikoko S. "The Structure of the Noun Phrase in African-American Vernacular English." Mufwene, Rickford, Bailey, and Baugh 69–83.

Nagel, James. "The Literary Context." Introduction. The Portable American Realism Reader. Eds. Nagel and Tom Quirk. New York: Penguin, 1997. xx–xxxii.

Nolan, David. "The Hunger Doctor." Letter. The New York Review of Books 16.4, 11 March 1971. <http://www.nybooks.com/articles/10639>.

North, Michael. The Dialect of Modernism: Race, Language, and Twentieth-Century Literature. New York: Oxford UP, 1994.

Nowatzki, Robert C. " 'Passing' in a White Genre: Charles W. Chesnutt's Negotiations of the Plantation Tradition in The Conjure Woman." American Literary Realism 27.2 (1995): 20–36.

Page, Norman. Speech in the English Novel. 2nd ed. Houndmills, Eng: Macmillan, 1988.

Peavy, Charles D. Go Slow Now: Faulkner and the Race Question. Eugene: UP of Oregon, 1971.

Pederson, Lee. "Language in the Uncle Remus Tales." Modern Philology 82 (1985): 292–98.

———. "Mark Twain's Missouri Dialects: Marion County Phonemics." American Speech 42 (1967): 261–278.

———. "Negro Speech in Adventures of Huckleberry Finn." Mark Twain Journal 13 (1965): 1–4.

———. "Rewriting Dialect Literature: 'The Wonderful Tar-Baby Story.'" *Atlanta Historical Journal* 30 (1986–1987): 57–70.

Pederson, Lee A., Susan L. McDaniel, Carol M. Adams, and Caisheng Liao, eds. *The Linguistic Atlas of the Gulf States: Technical Index for the Linguistic Atlas of the Gulf States.* Athens: UP of Georgia, 1989.

Petrie, Paul R. "Charles W. Chesnutt, *The Conjure Woman,* and the Racial Limits of Literary Meditation." *Studies in American Fiction* 27.2 (1999): 183–204.

Polk, Noel. "Man in the Middle: Faulkner and the Southern White Moderate." Fowler and Abadie 130–51.

Preston, Dennis R. "Folk Dialectology." *American Dialect Research.* Ed. Preston. Amsterdam: Benjamins, 1993. 333–78.

———. "The Li'l Abner Syndrome: Written Representations of Speech." *American Speech* 60.4 (1985): 328–36.

Rampersad, Arnold. "*Adventures of Huckleberry Finn* and Afro-American Literature." *Mark Twain: A Collection of Critical Essays.* Ed. Eric J. Sundquist. Englewood Cliffs, NJ: Prentice Hall. 103–12.

———. Introduction to the Harlem Renaissance. Gates and McKay 929–36.

Rickford, John Russell and Russell John Rickford. *Spoken Soul: The Story of Black English.* New York: Wiley, 2000.

Robinson, Forrest G., ed. *The Cambridge Companion to Mark Twain.* Cambridge: Cambridge UP, 1995.

Rulon, Curt. "Geographical Delimitation of the Dialect Areas in *Adventures of Huckleberry Finn.*" Williamson and Burke 215–21.

Sattelmeyer, R. and J. D. Crowley, eds. *One Hundred Years of Huckleberry Finn: The Boy, His Book, and American Culture.* Columbia: UP of Missouri, 1985.

Schneider, Edgar. "Africanisms in the Grammar of Afro-American English: Weighing the Evidence." Mufwene and Condon 209–21.

———. "Earlier Black English Revisited." Bernstein, Nunnally, and Sabino 35–50.

Sewell, David. "We Ain't All Trying to Talk Alike: Varieties of Language in *Huckleberry Finn.*" Sattelmeyer and Crowley 201–15.

Smith, David L. "Black Critics and Mark Twain." Robinson 116–128.

Smitherman, Geneva. *Talkin and Testifyin: The Language of Black America.* Detroit: Wayne State UP, 1977.

Spears, Arthur. "The Semi-Auxiliary *Come* in Black English Vernacular." *Language* 58 (1982):850–72.

Stepto, Robert B. "Ascent, Immersion, Narration." Bloom 5–8.

Sundquist, Eric J. *To Wake the Nation: Race in the Making of American Literature.* Cambridge: Belknap-Harvard UP, 1993.

Taliaferro, Hardin E. "Ham Rachel, of Alabama." 1859. Cohen and Dillingham 136–143.

Tamasi, Susan. "Huck Doesn't Sound Like Himself: Consistency in the Literary Dialect of Mark Twain." *Language and Literature* 10.2 (2001): 129–44.

Thompson, William Tappan. "Major Jones at the Opera." 1843. Cohen and Dillingham 168–72.

Thorpe, Thomas Bangs. "The Big Bear of Arkansas." 1854. Cohen and Dillingham 336–47.

Twain, Mark. *Adventures of Huckleberry Finn.* 1884. Ed. Thomas Cooley. New York: Norton, 1998.

———. *Adventures of Huckleberry Finn.* 1884. University of Virginia Electronic Text Center. <http://etext.lib.virginia.edu>.

Walker, Alice. "In Search of Zora Neale Hurston." *Ms.* Mar. 1975: 74+.

Washington, Mary Helen. Foreword. *Their Eyes Were Watching God* by Zora Neale Huston, Hurston, x–xvii.

———. "'I Love the Way Janie Crawford Left Her Husbands': Zora Neale Hurston's Emergent Female Hero." Gates and Appiah 98–109.

Werner, Craig. "Minstrel Nightmares: Black Dreams of Faulkner's Dreams." Fowler and Abadie 35–57.

Williamson, Juanita V. and Virginia M. Burke, eds. *A Various Language.* New York: Free Press, 1971.

Winford, Donald. "On the Origins of African American Vernacular English—A Creolist Perspective" *Diachronica* XV.1 (1998): 99–154.

Wolfram, Walt. "The Southern Context(s) of Earlier AAVE." Plenary address. Southeastern Conference on Linguistics LX. Norfolk, Virginia, 1999.

Wonham, Henry B. "'The Curious Psychological Spectacle of a Mind Enslaved': Charles W. Chesnutt and Dialect Fiction." *Mississippi Quarterly* 51.1 (1997–1998): 55–69.

Woodward, Frederick, and Donnarae MacCann. "Minstrel Shackles and Nineteenth-century 'Liberality.'" Leonard, Tenney, and Davis 141–53.

Wright, Richard. "Between Laughter and Tears." *New Masses.* Review of *Their Eyes Were Watching God.* October 1937. Gates and Appiah 16–17.

Index

The letter *t* following a page number denotes a table.

accuracy of literary dialectal representations. *See* literary dialect: accuracy of; *and specific authors and literary titles*

Adventures of Huckleberry Finn (Twain), xix, 14, 31, 39, 41, 46–50, 52, 90, 131, 149–50; accuracy of dialect in, 62–64, 67–68; artistic value of, 59, 76, 149–50; as antiracist text, 60–61, 75; critical responses to, 59–64, 67–76, 130; historical value of, 76, 150; literary dialect in, 149; linguistic value of, 76; and minstrelsy, influence of, 73–75; and race, 59–61, 75; revisions of, 73; and slavery, 72, 75; Tom Sawyer in, 72, 74; Tom's speech in, 70. *See also* Finn, Huckleberry (character); Jim; and Twain, Mark

African American English: attitudes about, xx–xxi, 16, 18, 40, 50–51, 53, 68, 75, 78–81, 83–84, 86, 94–97, 137–38, 151–52, 173n1 (chap. 3); documentation of, 43–44, 50, 51–53, 55–58t, 63–67, 87–89, 94, 100–101, 124, 173n1 (chap. 3); earlier varieties of, 28, 45, 52–53, 63, 89, 92–94, 173n1 (chap. 3) (*see also* literary dialect: and historical reconstruction); features of, 43, 55–58t, 88, 94, 173n1 (chap. 3) (*see also*

specific features). *See also* literary dialect: African American speech as

alternation: of /ɑ/ for /æ/, 56t, 87t, 92; of /a/ for /ɛ/ before /r/, 56t, 87t; of /ɑɪ/ for /ɔɪ/, 55t, 66t, 87t, 107t, 115t, 123–24; of /b/ or /b/ for /v/, 55t, 87t; of /e/ for /i/ before /r/ and /l/, 56t, 87t, 92–93; of /e/ for /ɔ/, 56t, 64–65, 66t, 87t, 89–92; of /n/ for /ŋ/, 55t, 66t, 87t, 70–71, 107, 115t, 124t, 134t, 136t; of unaspirated /w/ for /hw/, word-initial, 55t

American English, 3, 9–10

American literature: trends in, 3–16, 19–21, 22–25, 27, 148–49, 153. *See also* Harlem Renaissance; humor tradition; local color; modernism; naturalism; Old Southwestern tradition; plantation tradition; and Realism

analysis of literary dialect. *See* literary dialect analysis

a-prefixing, 58t, 67t, 93t

Archive of Folk Songs, 52

artistic value of literary dialect. *See* literary dialect: artistic value of

Atlanta Constitution, 36

Atlanta, Georgia, 126

Atlantic Monthly, the, 14–15, 79, 86, 96

attitudes: about African American En-